Essential
Office 365

Third Edition

Kevin Wilson

D1335844

Elluminet Press
www.elluminetpress.com

Essential Office 365: Third Edition

Publisher: Elluminet Press
Director: Kevin Wilson
Lead Editor: Steven Ashmore
Technical Reviewer: Mike Taylor, Robert Ashcroft
Copy Editors: Joanne Taylor, James Marsh
Proof Reader: Mike Taylor
Indexer: James Marsh
Cover Designer: Kevin Wilson

eBook versions and licenses are also available for most titles. Any source code or other supplementary materials referenced by the author in this text is available to readers at

www.elluminetpress.com/resources

For detailed information about how to locate your book's resources, go to

www.elluminetpress.com/resources

Table of Contents

About the Author

With over 15 years' experience in the computer industry, Kevin Wilson has made a career out of technology and showing others how to use it. After earning a master's degree in computer science, software engineering, and multimedia systems, Kevin has held various positions in the IT industry including graphic & web design, building & managing corporate networks, training, and IT support.

He currently serves as Elluminet Press Ltd's senior writer and director, he periodically teaches computer science at college in South Africa and serves as an IT trainer in England. His books have become a valuable resource among the students in England, South Africa and our partners in the United States.

Kevin's motto is clear: "If you can't explain something simply, then you haven't understood it well enough." To that end, he has created the Exploring Technology Series, in which he breaks down complex technological subjects into smaller, easy-to-follow steps that students and ordinary computer users can put into practice.

Acknowledgements

Thanks to all the staff at Luminescent Media & Elluminet Press for their passion, dedication and hard work in the preparation and production of this book.

To all my friends and family for their continued support and encouragement in all my writing projects.

To all my colleagues, students and testers who took the time to test procedures and offer feedback on the book

Finally thanks to you the reader for choosing this book. I hope it helps you to use your computer with greater ease.

Getting Started with Office

Office 365 is a subscription-based version of Microsoft Office. This means you pay a monthly or annual subscription that allows you download and use the Office applications.

An Office 365 subscription guarantees that you'll always have the latest version of Microsoft Office Suite available to you, and is usually updated once per quarter.

Office 365 offers access to cloud-hosted storage called OneDrive where you can store your documents, as well as share and collaborate with others. You can also access your documents from all your devices - phone, tablet, laptop and, computer.

As well as the full Office Suite, you can download to your computer or laptop, Office 365 includes Office Web Apps suite with lightweight versions of Word, Excel, OneNote, and PowerPoint, that can be used online within a web browser

Office Packages

There are various different options and packages available depending on what your needs are.

Office 365 Home - can be used by up to 6 different users either on a PC or Mac, each with their own Microsoft Account. The package includes Word, Excel, PowerPoint, Outlook, OneNote, Access and Publisher. Also comes with 1TB of OneDrive space for each user. Ideal for families.

Office 365 Personal - Has pretty much the same as Office 365 Home, except it can only be used by one user (one Microsoft Account). You can install Office on all your devices and sign in to up to 5 at the same time.

Office Home & Student - can be installed on one PC or Mac only and includes Word, Excel, and PowerPoint. This is a one off payment rather than a subscription. Note there is no subscription to OneDrive or access to Skype. Also you won't get any updates to new versions of Office.

Have a look at the following website. Select the 'for home' option.

`products.office.com/compare-all-microsoft-office-products`

Here is a comparison summary according to Microsoft's website.

To help you decide, take some time to think about the features that are most important to you and how they fit into your budget.

Below are some questions you may want to ask yourself:

- If you just need Word, Excel, and PowerPoint - the core Office applications, it may be best to buy Office Home & Student, since it's the cheapest option over the long term. This one is a one off payment, so it is unlikely you would get any of the updates in the future, but can only be installed on one machine.

- If you need the more advanced applications such as Access, Publisher, Outlook Email, or OneDrive storage, then Office 365 Personal is a good option. Also comes with 1TB of space on OneDrive.

- If you need to install Office for more than one user or for your household, Office 365 Home subscription is a good option. You can install the Office Suite for up to 6 different users and have them all sign in with their own Microsoft Accounts. Also comes with 1TB of space on OneDrive.

- Will you do a lot of editing on the go? If you use public computers at libraries or business centres, at your office, home, or on your tablet while travelling on the train for example, Office 365 Personal may be your best option, since it includes the Office Apps for mobile devices, and web based versions of the Office applications. If you do this and also have a family, then use Office 365 Home, as each family member can have their own Microsoft Account.

Business users have different services available to them. Have a look at

products.office.com/compare-all-microsoft-office-products

Select the 'for business' option.

Students & teachers can get discounts and free versions for either themselves with Microsoft Education.

www.microsoft.com/education

What is the Cloud?

Cloud computing is about running applications over the Internet and being able to access your files from wherever you may be - at your desk, on a train, in a coffee shop, airport and so on, using a variety of different devices. These could be laptops, desktops, macs, mobile phones, or tablets.

Microsoft Office 365 is an example of a cloud service and utilises cloud computing for storage, allowing you can run applications such as Word, Excel, PowerPoint, and OneNote over the internet.

Some other major examples are Google Drive and Apple iCloud.

When you run programs from the hard drive on your computer, it's called local storage. Everything is stored on your computer.

With cloud computing, you access your data and run your applications over the Internet.

Chapter 1: Getting Started with Office

These applications, services and data are stored on large server farms and are managed by the cloud service.

Your OneDrive files are stored on a server in this server farm rather than locally on your computer.

In the photograph above, there can be about 20 or more servers stacked up in each cabinet and hundreds of cabinets filling entire rooms serving millions of people who subscribe to the service.

The advantage is, you can log in and access your files anywhere on the internet and your files are backed up by the cloud service, so should your computer fail, your files will still be on your OneDrive.

Purchasing Office Online

First open your web browser and go to Microsoft Office website

`products.office.com`

In this example we are purchasing the home version. If you want to download a different version change it by clicking 'products' on the red bar at the top and select the version from the drop down box. The procedure is the same.

From the home page select 'For Home'.

You can either pay a monthly subscription or pay an annual cost. Choose depending on your budget. If you want to pay monthly, click 'or buy for £$ a month'. In this example I'm going to pay the annual fee, so click 'buy now' in the Office 365 Home column.

Paying monthly will spread the cost over the year rather than paying one lump sum.

Chapter 1: Getting Started with Office

Check the amount then click 'next'.

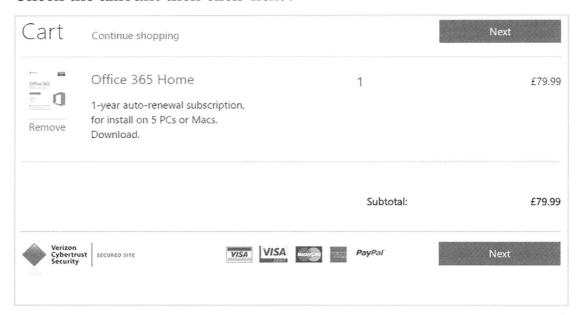

Once you have done that you will be prompted to sign in with your Microsoft account.

If you are using Windows 8 or 10 you will probably already have a Microsoft account that you created when you set up your machine. This is usually the username/email and password you used to sign into Windows.

If so enter these details into the screen below.

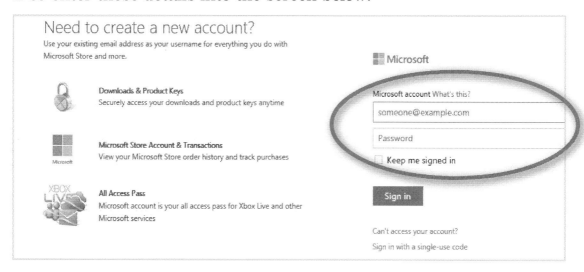

If this is not the case then you can quickly create one. See 'create a microsoft account' on page 27

You will be prompted to enter your payment details. If you have purchased from the Microsoft store before, then you can choose to pay with an existing card or you can add a different card number.

Enter your information in all the fields, then click 'next' at the bottom of the screen.

Click 'buy now' to confirm your order.

Downloading Office Suite

You can download Microsoft Office from the Microsoft's website. Open your web browser on the machine you want to install Office and navigate to...

office.com

Click 'Sign in' on the top right of your screen and enter your Microsoft Account email address and password.

Click 'install office' on the top right of the screen.

Scroll down to 'install office on all your computers'. Click 'install office'.

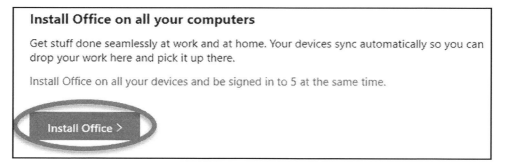

Click 'other options' and select the 64bit version.

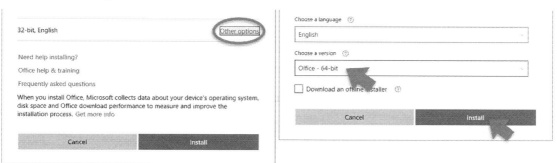

Click 'run' when prompted by your browser.

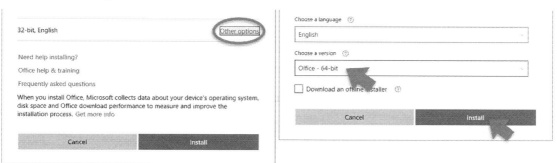

The Office installer will run and begin downloading the necessary files to install Office on your computer.

This can take a while to complete depending on the speed of your computer and your internet connection.

The Installer will run once it has finished downloading. You may need to enter your computer's password you used to log into Windows.

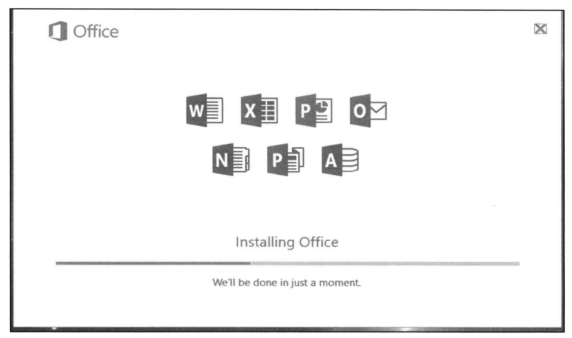

Once Office is installed, click 'close'

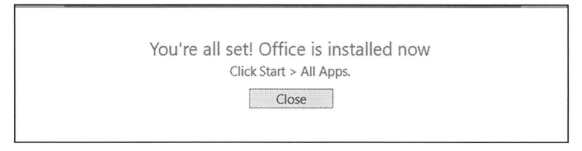

You will be able to find your Office Apps installed on your start menu. You may have to scroll down the list of apps on the left hand side, if you don't see the tiles or shortcuts on your start menu.

If this is your own computer then you can skip the next step.

If this is not your computer and belongs to someone else in the family, open up an office application such as Microsoft Word.

From the screen that appears, select 'account' from the bottom left..

In the main window, Click on 'sign out'. This will sign out of your account.

Now you can allow another person to sign in using their own Microsoft Account, rather than using yours.

Now the other person can sign in with their Microsoft Account.

Create a Microsoft Account

To set up a Microsoft Account you need to open a new web browser. To do this, click your web browser icon on the start menu. Go to the following website

```
signup.live.com
```

You can use your current email address if you have one, or you can create a new one.

In this example I'm going to use an existing email address. *To create a new email address, just click 'get a new email address' instead.*

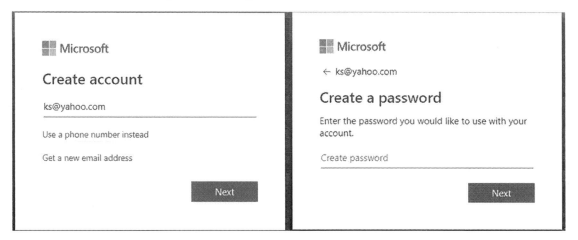

Enter your name, country and date of birth.

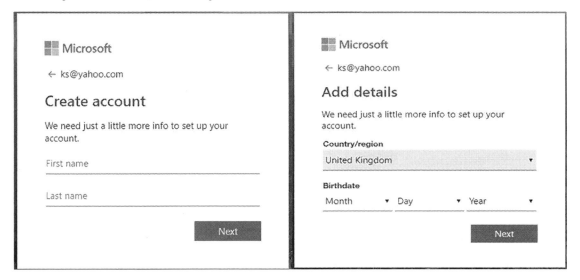

Click 'next' to continue.

Now go check your email. You'll receive a message from Microsoft with a code. Enter the code into the 'verify email' dialog box then click 'next'.

Enter the CAPTCHA code. If you have trouble reading the code, click 'new' to generate another code, or click 'audio' to hear the code read aloud. Click 'next'.

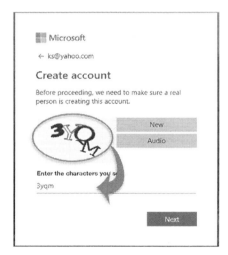

Confirm your account details. Click 'looks good'.

Once you've signed up, you'll land on your Microsoft Account dashboard.

Outlook Email on your iPhone

Open your settings app, tap 'passwords & accounts', then 'add account'.

Tap 'outlook.com' from the account type list.

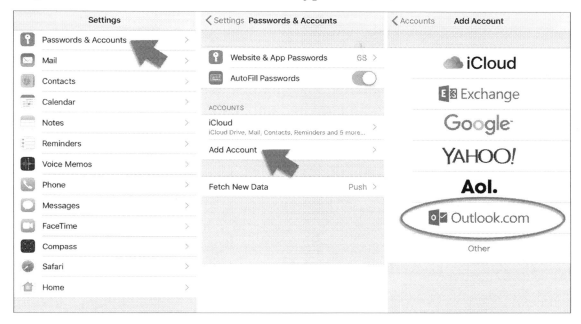

Enter your Microsoft Account email and password. Tap 'next' on the upper-right corner of the screen.

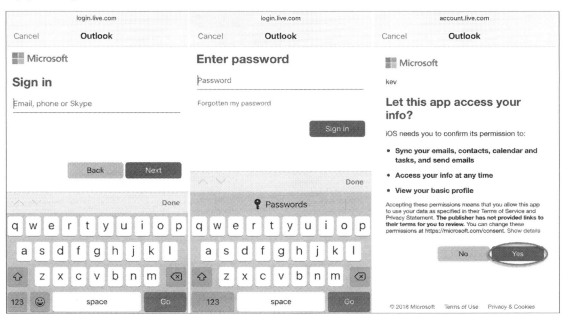

The mail app will automatically detect settings for server names etc.

If your iPhone doesn't automatically detect the settings you can enter them manually. Use:

> Server name for IMAP is **imap-mail.outlook.com**
> **Port 993** with **SSL/TLS** encryption

> Server name for POP is **pop-mail.outlook.com**
> **Port 995** with **SSL/TLS** encryption

> Server name for SMTP is **smtp-mail.outlook.com**.
> **Port 587** with **STARTTLS** encryption

These settings can be used if you are using the latest version of Office 365.

Select what information you want to synchronize or copy between your phone and your Office 365 account, eg, Mail, Contacts, and Calendar information.

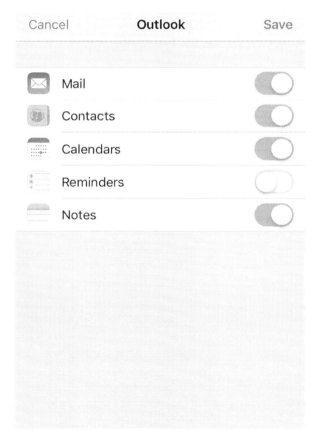

If you're prompted to create a passcode, tap Continue and type in a numeric passcode. If you don't set up a passcode, you can't view your email account on your iPhone.

Outlook Email on Android

To add your Microsoft Account Outlook email to your android phone, first open the Gmail App.

Tap the icon on the top right of the mail window. From the slideout, tap your account at the top, then select 'add account'.

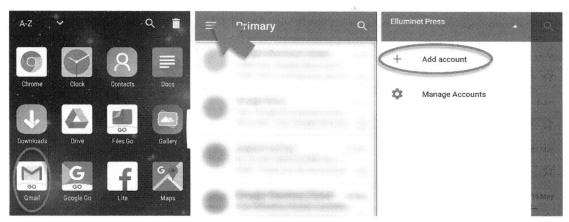

Select 'outlook, hotmail and live' from the account types, then sign in with your Microsoft Account email address and password.

You'll find your accounts on the slideout window. Just click the icon on the top left of the screen, then tap the account name at the top. You'll see your Microsoft Account listed. Tap on it to view your email.

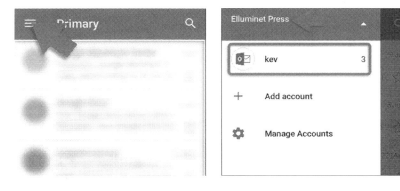

Setting up Outlook Desktop App

When you start Outlook for the first time, you will be asked to enter your Microsoft Account email address and password.

In the 'Windows Security' dialog box, enter your Microsoft Account password. Tick 'remember my credentials', then click 'ok'.

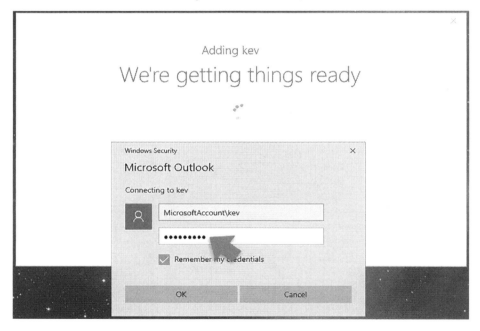

Click 'Next'. Microsoft Outlook will scan the email address you have entered and enter all the server and mail settings for you. Click 'ok' when the account setup is complete.

Office Apps for iOS

Microsoft has released its office apps for the iPad & iPhone. You can find the apps on Microsoft's web site using the following link

```
products.office.com/mobile
```

Or search for 'microsoft office' in the App Store on your iPad/iPhone

Tap 'Get' to download the apps you want to use. You may be prompted to enter your Apple ID email address and password - this is different from your Microsoft Account.

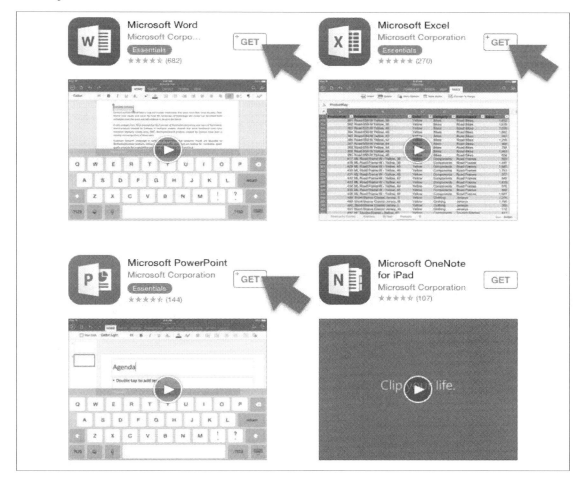

You'll find the apps on the home screen on your iPhone/iPad.

Setting up OneDrive on iOS

You can access your files on your iPhone or iPad. To do this, you'll need to download OneDrive from the App Store. Open the App Store on your iPhone/iPad.

Type OneDrive into the search field on the top right of the App Store.

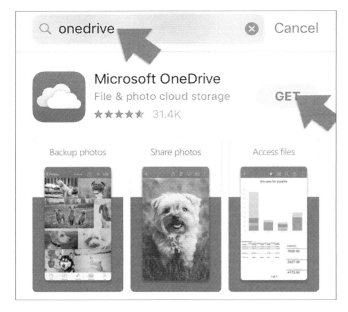

You will need an Apple ID to download the apps from the App store. Remember, your Apple ID is different from your Microsoft Account. Your Apple ID is just to access your iPhone/iPad's App Store.

Open the OneDrive app on your iPhone/iPad and sign in with your Microsoft Account email address and password.

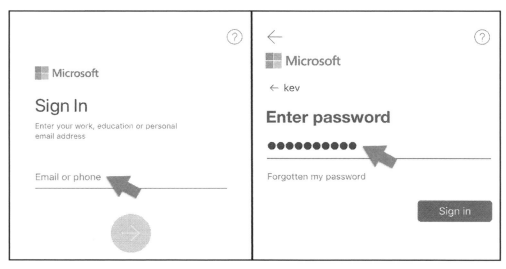

Office Apps for Android

Microsoft has released its office apps for your android device. You can find the apps on Microsoft's web site using the following link

`products.office.com/mobile`

Or search for 'microsoft office' in the Play Store on your android device.

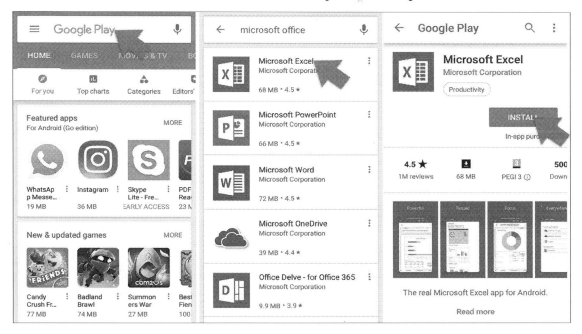

Tap on each of the apps you want to use, then on the screen that appears, tap 'install'. You may be prompted to enter your GMail email address and password - this is different from your Microsoft Account.

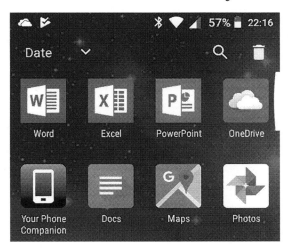

You'll find the apps on the home screen on your device.

Chapter 2

Using Office on the Web

Office 365 has a wealth of online applications. You can access office through your web browser using web apps, you can synchronise all your files and keep them in the cloud using OneDrive, so your files are available wherever you go.

For example, if you have Office installed on your machine at work or college, you can synchronise all your files with your computer at home, or a tablet/ phone when you're out and about.

Lets begin by taking a look at Microsoft Office web apps.

Web Apps

With your Office 365 subscription, you can access your favourite Office applications such as Word, Excel, PowerPoint or Outlook through your web browser. This can be useful if you need to edit a document or perhaps give a PowerPoint presentation on a computer that doesn't have Office installed, or the same version of Office.

Open your web browser and navigate to

www.office.com

Click 'sign in' on the top right corner and enter your Microsoft account details.

From here you can open Word, Outlook Email, OneNote, PowerPoint, see your Outlook Calendar, open Excel or your OneDrive. You can use these applications in the same way you would your ordinary Office applications.

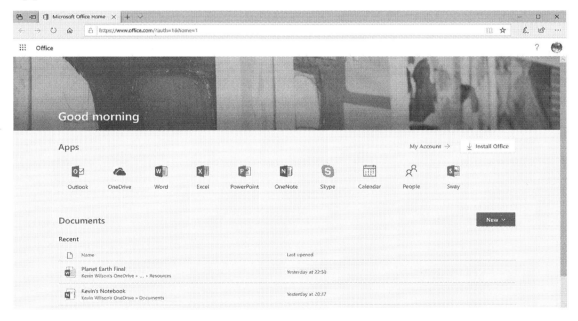

Your recently opened documents are listed down the bottom half of the screen.

The web apps are integrated into OneDrive and open automatically when you select documents, Excel spreadsheets, or PowerPoint presentations.

Word

You can access Word through a web browser. If you are already signed into your account click on the icon for Word. Or go to **word.office.com**

Here you can select a recently opened document, create a new blank document or use a template.

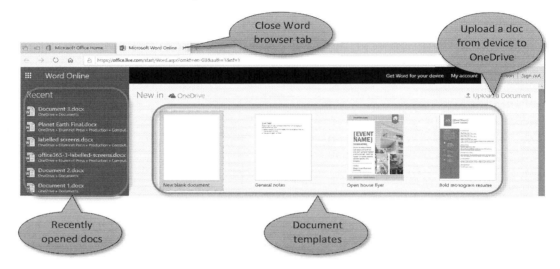

Select a document to open or select a template. You'll be able to use Word as normal, see page 66.

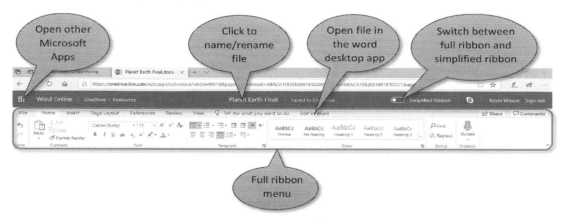

You can choose between a simplified ribbon and the full ribbon. The simplified ribbon is good for small devices, such as tablets or phones, but if you are using a PC or laptop, change this to full ribbon using the 'simplified ribbon' slider on the top right.

Excel

You can access Excel through a web browser. If you are already signed into your account click on the icon for Excel. Or go to **excel.office.com**

Here you can select a recently opened workbook, create a new blank workbook or use a template.

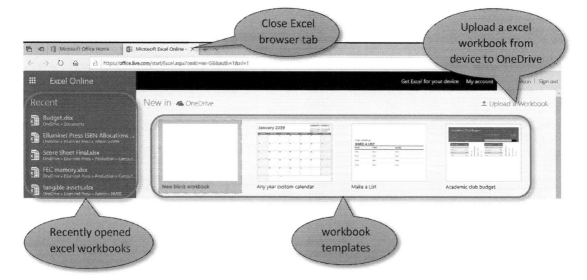

Select a workbook to open or select a template. You'll be able to use Excel as normal, see page 186.

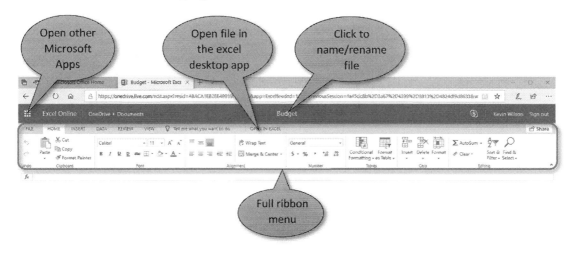

PowerPoint

You can access PowerPoint through a web browser. If you are already signed into your account click on the icon for PowerPoint. Or go to **powerpoint.office.com**

Here you can select a recently opened presentation, create a new blank presentation or use a template.

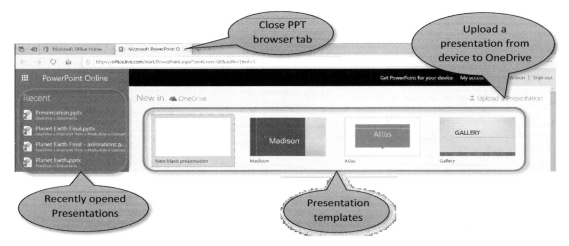

Select a presentation to open or select a template. You'll be able to use PowerPoint as normal, see page 302.

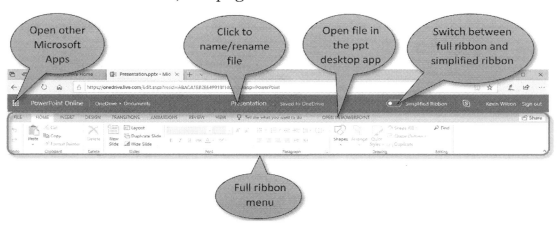

You can choose between a simplified ribbon and the full ribbon. The simplified ribbon is good for small devices, such as tablets or phones, but if you are using a PC or laptop, change this to full ribbon using the 'simplified ribbon' slider on the top right.

Mail

You can access your mail through a web browser. If you are already signed into your account click on the icon for mail

If not open your web browser and navigate to

```
outlook.com
```

Sign in with your Microsoft Account email address and password. Once you've signed in, you'll see your main screen.

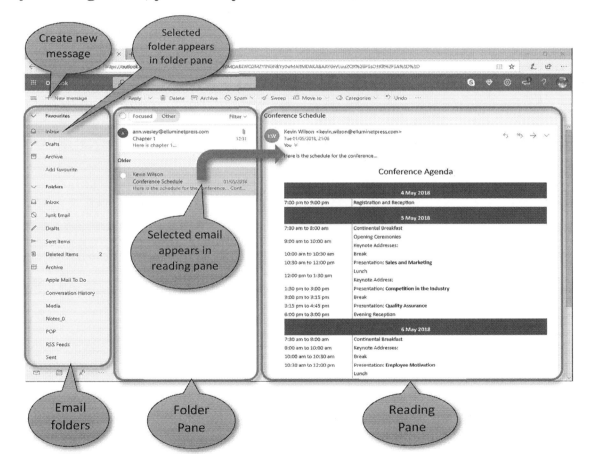

The screen is divided into three panes. The first pane on the left lists all the folders in your email account. The middle pane displays the contents of the folder you've selected in the first pane. The pane on the right is the reading pane, and displays the contents of the email message you've selected in the middle pane.

Calendar

You can access your calendar through a web browser. If you are already signed into your account click on the icon for calendar. Or open your web browser and navigate to **calendar.live.com**

Once you've signed in, you'll see your main screen.

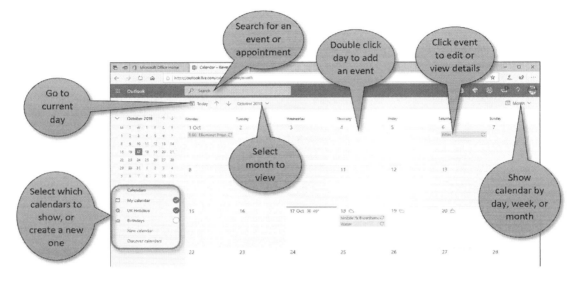

Double click on a day to add an event. Fill in the fields with the appointment/event details.

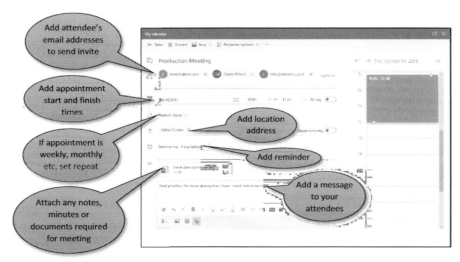

Click 'send' or 'save' from the top left when you're finished.

People

Click the people icon on your homepage or navigate to **people.live.com**

The people App is equivalent to your contacts list or address book. Click on a name in your contact list down the left hand side of the screen. That person's details will appear in the pane on the right.

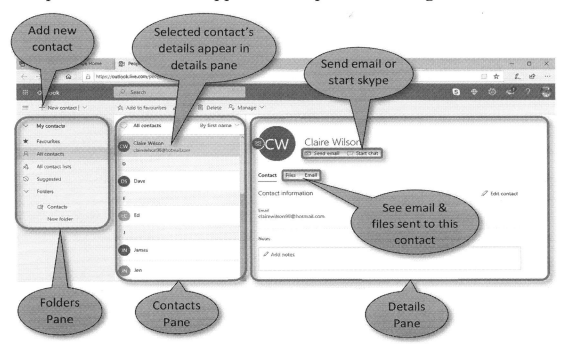

Click 'send email' to send a new message, or click the phone number to call the person if your device has a phone.

To add a new contact, click 'New'.

Fill in the person's details, email, and phone number. If you need fields for home number, mobile/cell number then click 'add more' and select the field.

Sway

Sway is a presentation tool that allows you to drag and drop files such as images or online videos from social media into presentations, reports, newsletters and personal stories.

You can either use the app on your phone/tablet or using a web browser by navigating to the following website: **sway.office.com**

Once you have signed in, you'll land on the sway home page. From here you can create new sways, open and edit sways, create sways from templates or specific topics, as well as sways from uploaded word and powerpoint documents.

To create a new sway, click 'create new' in the top panel. You'll see the storyline page. This is where you add the content to your sway.

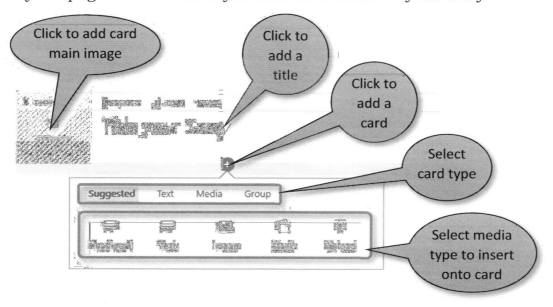

First lets add a heading. To do this click where it says 'title your sway'. Enter a heading. In this example I'm going to enter 'planet earth'.

Next, add a background image. To do this, click 'background'. Click and drag an image to placeholder on the left hand side. Notice how sway has found images according to the title you entered.

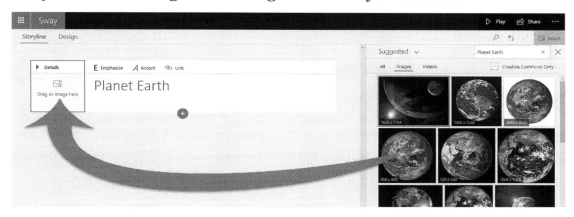

Now lets add a new card. To do this, click the green + sign at the bottom. From the drop down, select the type of media you want to add: text, media (photos, videos, audio), or a group. I'm going to add some text, so select 'text card'.

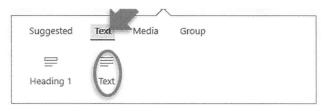

Type your text into the textbox.

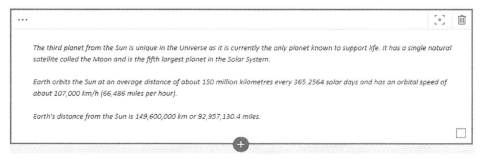

Lets add a video card. Click the green '+' sign on the bottom, select 'media', then click 'video'.

In the top right search field, type what video you're looking for.

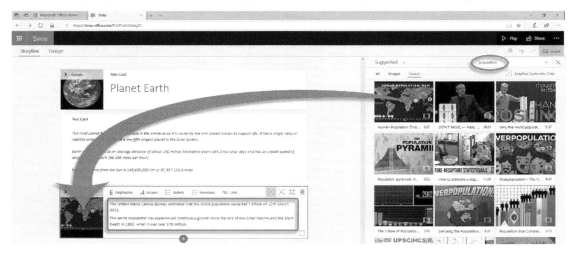

From the pane on the right hand side, click and drag the video you want to the video placeholder on the video card. Add a caption to the video. Add more cards if you want to.

From the panel on the top left of the screen, click 'design'.

To edit the design, click 'styles' on the top right.

Select a style template from the slideout on the right hand side.

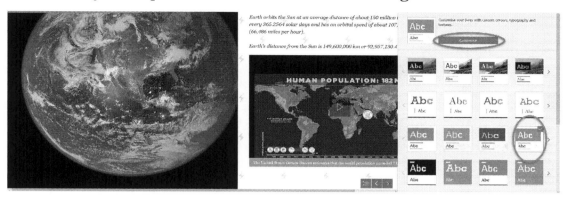

Click 'customise' to edit the styles.

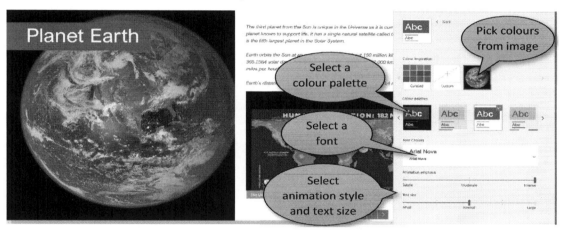

To view your sway, click 'play' on the top right. To share your sway, click 'share'. Select facebook, twitter or linkedin if you want to post on social media. If you want to use email, click 'get visual link' then click 'copy'.

Open up a new email message in outlook, click in the message body, select the 'message' ribbon, then select 'paste'.

OneDrive

OneDrive is online storage you can use as your own personal online hard drive dubbed cloud storage and is part of Office 365 and Microsoft Accounts.

OneDrive is integrated into Windows 8.1 and 10 to allow users to save files to the cloud.

When you create a document with one of the Web Apps, it is saved to your OneDrive. You can store other files there too, such as photos.

Since Web Apps and OneDrive are based in the cloud, you can access them from any device with an internet connection, at any time.

To access your OneDrive from any computer, open your web browser and go to

```
onedrive.live.com
```

From here you can see all your files you have saved to your OneDrive

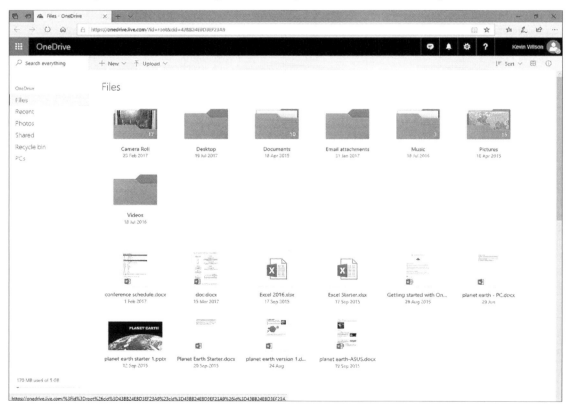

Editing Files

Click on any document to open it in the appropriate office application.

The document will open in a web app, allowing you to edit in your web browser.

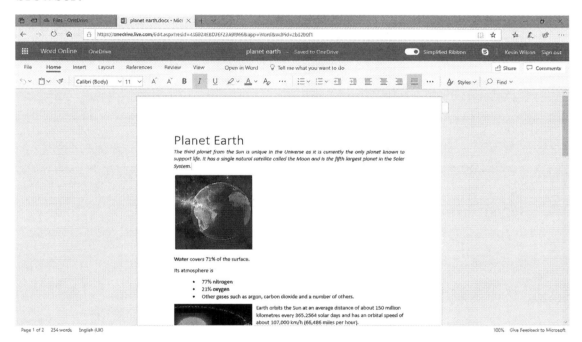

If you have the desktop app installed on your device, in this example Word, you can open the document in this desktop app.

To do this, click 'open in word' on the toolbar along the top of the screen.

Uploading Files

You can upload files from the computer you are using at anytime using OneDrive in your web browser.

To do this click 'Upload'. If you want to upload individual files, select 'files'. If you want to upload an entire folder, select 'folder'. For this example, I am going to upload a file, so select 'files'.

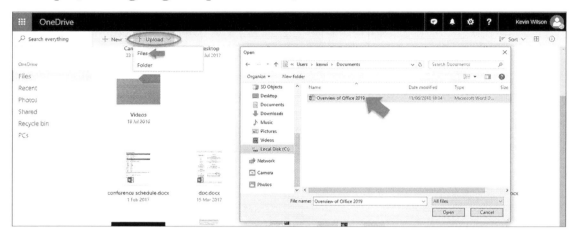

Select the file you want to upload from the dialog box. Hold down the control key to select multiple files. Click 'open' when you're done.

Organising Files

You can organise your files into directories using OneDrive. This helps to keep files together. If you move your mouse over a thumbnail of the file you want, a small check box will appear in the top right, click this box to select the file.

You will also notice along the top, new menu options will appear. These options allow you to open the file, download a copy, share with friends on Facebook, manage your files (rename, move to another folder).

To create a new folder, right click on some empty space and from the pop up menu that appears, select 'Create', then click 'Folder'.

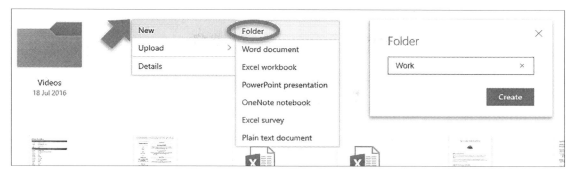

To move files to a folder, just click and drag them over to the folder. To select multiple files, hover your mouse over a document and select the tick box on the top right of each file you want to move.

Now, click one of the selected files and drag them to the folder you want to put the files into. In this example, I'm going to drag my files into my 'work' folder.

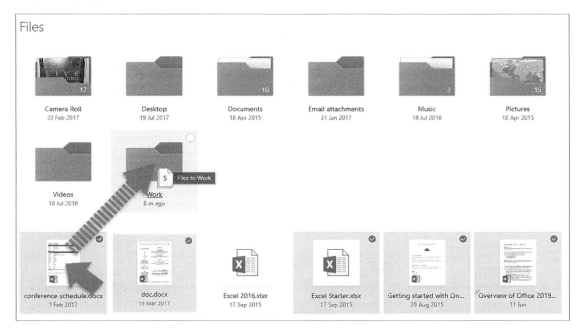

OneDrive on your Desktop

You will be able to access them on your PC or device from the OneDrive folder in file explorer. The file explorer icon is usually on your taskbar.

You can edit your documents, or create new documents and save them to your OneDrive. You'll see your OneDrive folder listed on the left in file explorer. Click this folder to view your files on OneDrive.

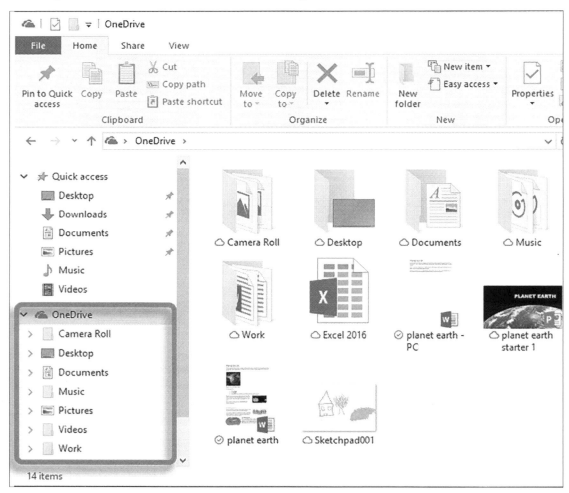

Double clicking on any of the documents in the right hand pane will open them using the Office Apps installed on your PC. You can edit them in the usual way.

Uploading Files

You can upload files from your PC using the file explorer. Locate the file on your computer that you want to upload to your OneDrive. You'll find files stored locally on your computer in the 'this PC' section on the left hand pane. In this example, the file I want to upload is stored on the desktop.

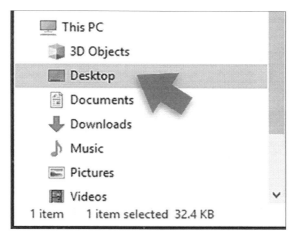

Click and drag the file to the OneDrive folder as shown in the image below.

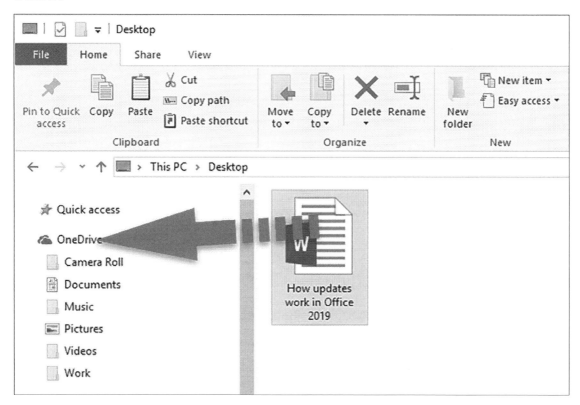

Searching for Files

If you know the names of the documents, you can use the search feature to locate them quickly. Select the location to search in. In this example I want to search for my 'Gideon' files that are stored locally on my computer. So select 'this pc' in the left hand pane as shown below.

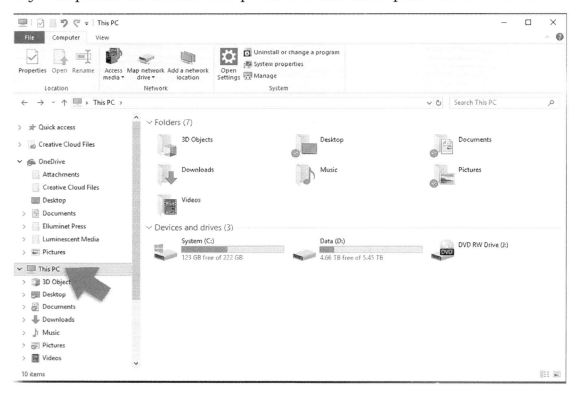

Then type the name of the document in the 'search documents' field, circled below. This will bring up a list of all documents containing the word you typed. To add them to your OneDrive, just drag and drop the file as show below.

Or double click the file name in the search results list to open the file.

Using your iPad

Once you have set up your iPad as in previous chapter, the apps will be available on your home screen

Accessing your Files

To access your files, you can find them using the OneDrive App. This allows you to see all your files and documents you have saved to your OneDrive across all your devices: pc, laptop, tablet or phone.

Tap the OneDrive icon on your home screen. If it's the first time you have used OneDrive, enter your Microsoft account email address and password when prompted.

Once logged in, you will see a screen similar to the following

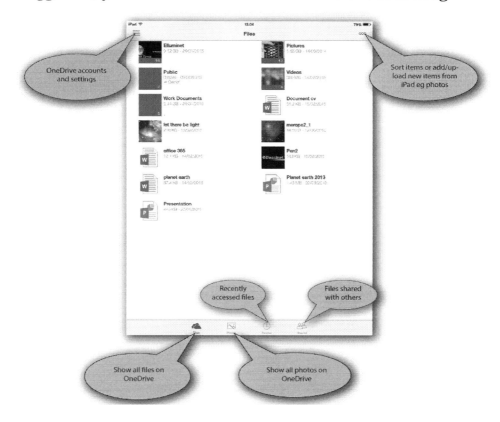

You can open any of your files by tapping on their icons.

Upload Files to OneDrive

You can upload files from your iPad to OneDrive. These are usually photos you have taken with the built in camera. Any documents you create with the Office Apps on your iPad are automatically saved to your OneDrive.

To upload an image tap the **ooo** icon on the top right of the screen then follow the sequence below

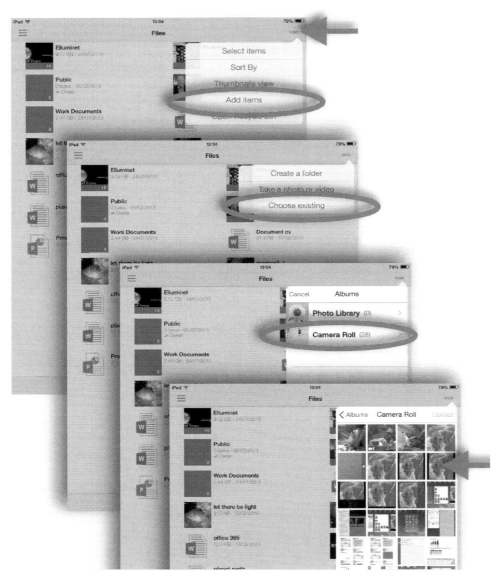

You can select multiple photos by tapping on each of the ones you want to upload.

Editing Files on iPad

If this is the first time using the app, you will need to sign in using your Microsoft Account details. If the sign in box doesn't appear, tap 'sign in' on the top left.

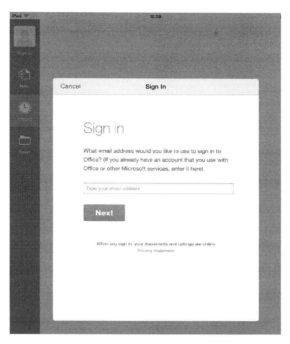

Once you have logged into your account, you will see something similar to the following. This is called the backstage. Here you can open files and create new ones, as well as see a list of your most recently accessed files.

Chapter 2: Using Office on the Web

Once you have selected a saved file to open, or created a new document, you'll be able to edit it in Word for iPad as shown below. Word for iPad is a cut down version of Microsoft Word designed for touch screen mobile devices. You'll be able to do basic edits to the document, insert tables, images and shapes, using the mini ribbon menus along the top.

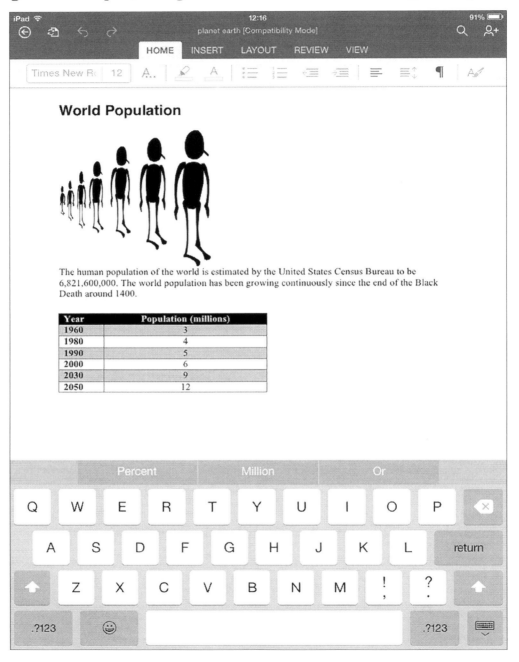

To get back to the 'backstage', click the arrow on the very top left of the screen.

Office Lens

Office Lens turns your smartphone or tablet into a scanner. With this scanner you can scan documents, business cards, receipts, sticky notes, whiteboards and other real-world items and export them to OneNote, OneDrive, Word, PDF or email.

In this example I am going to use an iPhone but you can use Lens on your tablet, or smartphone.

First you need to download the Office Lens App from the App Store. From the search field type 'office lens'. Tap 'office lens' in the list. Tap the Office Lens icon then tap 'get'. Once it has downloaded and installed, tap Office Lens on your home screen.

Once Office Lens has opened, sign in with your Microsoft Account email address and password.

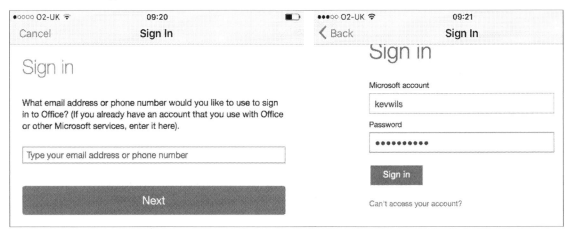

At the bottom of the screen you will see a choice of different objects you can scan. You can scan business cards which automatically extracts and adds the details to your contacts. You can scan photos and documents, which works much like a photocopier/scanner. You can also scan a whiteboard.

In this example I am going to scan a document. Swipe across the list at the bottom of your screen until 'document' is highlighted in orange.

Now take a picture of the document. You'll notice a white box appear on the screen, make sure the whole document fits inside this box, as shown below.

Tap the orange button to take the photo.

If you want to scan another page or document, tap the '+1' icon on the bottom left. Once you are happy that the document is in focus, tap 'done' on the top right of the screen.

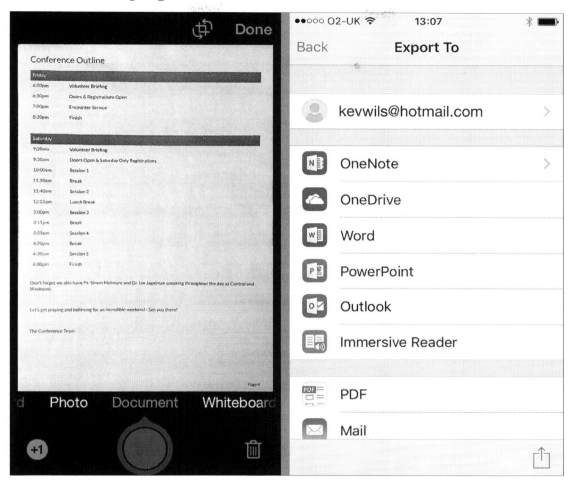

Now from the 'export to' screen, you can send the document to OneNote, you can save as a JPEG image to your OneDrive, you can save it as a Word, or PowerPoint document. If you export to Word or PowerPoint, it's worth installing these apps on your phone, you can download them from your phone's App Store.

You can send the document to someone via email if you have Outlook installed on your phone, you can use 'immersive reader' to read the document aloud.

You can also save as a PDF file or send the document to someone using Apple Mail.

Just tap on the appropriate icon listed on the 'export to' screen.

In this example, I am going to export the scan to Word. If you save the scan to a Word document, you will be able to edit the document in Microsoft Word.

Once Office Lens has exported the file, tap the document in the 'recent uploads' list to open it up in Word.

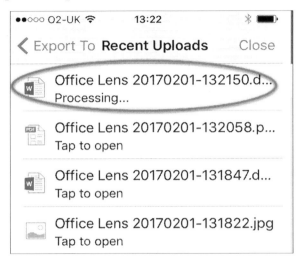

In Word, tap 'duplicate', enter a name for the document, select your OneDrive and tap save.

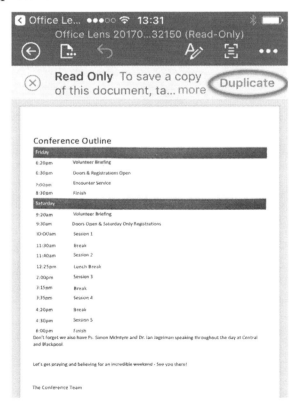

This will save the document to your OneDrive folder where you can load it up in Word on any device connected to the internet and edit it if you need to.

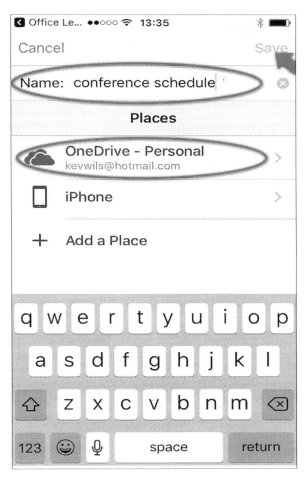

Microsoft Word

Microsoft Word is a word processing application that allows you to create many different types of document, from letters, Resumes/CVs to greetings cards, posters and flyers. You can select from a library of customisable templates or start from scratch and create your own.

Word gives you the ability to do more with your word processing projects, with the introduction of several enhanced features, such as the ability to create and collaborate on documents online using OneDrive.

Before we begin, throughout this book, we will be using the resource files.

You can download these files from

www.elluminetpress.com/office-365-3ed

Go down to the Microsoft Word section and click the icons to download the documents to the documents folder on your PC.

Starting Word

The quickest way to start Microsoft Word is to search for it using the Cortana search field on the bottom left of your task bar. Type "Word". From the search results, click 'word'. You'll also find it on your start menu.

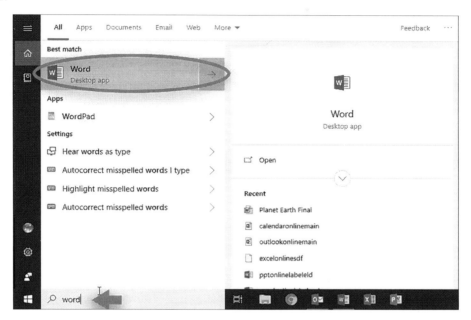

Once Word has started, you'll land on the home screen. On the home screen, you'll see recently used templates along the top, and your most recently saved documents listed underneath.

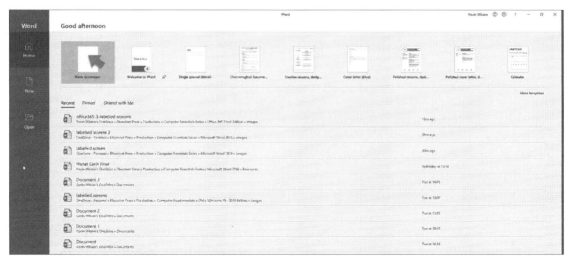

To begin, click 'blank document' to start. This will open up Word with a new document for you.

The Main Screen

Once you have selected a template or created a new document, you will see your main work screen.

On the bottom left of the main window you'll see your page and word counter, as well as your language selection tools.

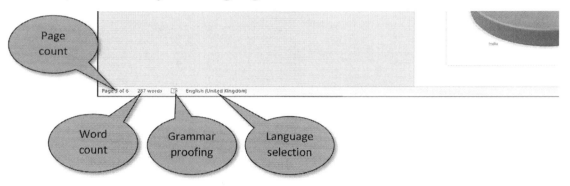

On the bottom right hand side of the screen, you'll see your document display modes: reading, print & web. For normal documents it is best to leave the display mode on print layout.

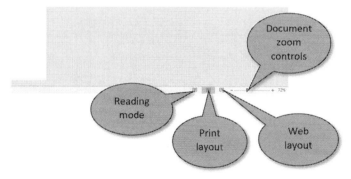

At the end you'll see your document zoom controls. Use these to zoom into the page.

Along the top of the screen, all the tools used in Microsoft Word are organised into a ribbon which is divided into ribbon tabs, each containing a specific set of tools.

The Home Ribbon

You will find your text formatting tools here for making text bold, changing style, font, paragraph alignment etc.

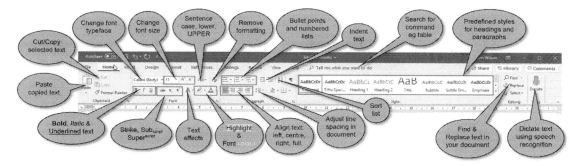

The Insert Ribbon

This is where you will find your clip-art, tables, pictures, page breaks, and pretty much anything you would want to insert into a document.

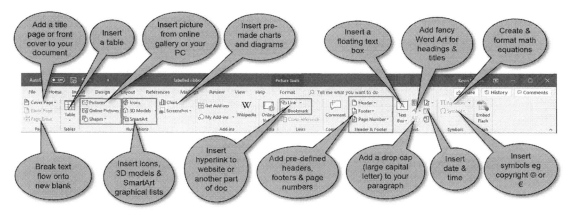

The Design Ribbon

Anything to do with pre-set themes and formatting, such as headings, colours and fonts that you can apply to your document and word will automatically format your document according to the themes.

Just select a theme from the options.

The Page Layout Ribbon

On this ribbon, you will find your page sizes, margins, page orientation (landscape or portrait) and anything to do with how your page is laid out.

The References Ribbon

This is where you can add automatically generated tables of contents, indexes, footnotes to your documents

You can also use reference tools such as researcher and smart lookup to find information about certain topics and phrases used in your documents.

The Review Ribbon

On the review ribbon, you'll find document proofing tools such as word count, spelling, thesaurus and dictionary. As well as language settings, and language translation tools.

The Mailings Ribbon

From the mailings ribbon you can print mailing labels, print on envelopes and create mail-merge documents from a list of names & addresses.

The View Ribbon

On the view ribbon you'll find tools to help you navigate around your document. You can zoom into the document, view as multiple pages side by side, as well as adjusting your page rulers, and the navigation pane.

The Format Ribbon

The format ribbon only appears when you have selected an image in your document.

From here you can remove an image background - this only works if the image has a solid black or white background. You can correct the colours using the brightness and contrast 'corrections'.

You can add picture styles such as borders, shadows and outlines.

You can also wrap your text around your image using the text wrap feature. You can also bring a textbox or image to the front if it falls behind a block of text and rotate an image. Similarly with 'send to back', you can send an image behind a block of text or another image.

You can crop an image and set the height and width of the image if you have an exact size.

File Backstage

If you click 'File' on the top left of your screen, this will open up what Microsoft call the backstage.

Backstage is where you open or save documents, print documents, export or share documents, as well as options, Microsoft account and preference settings.

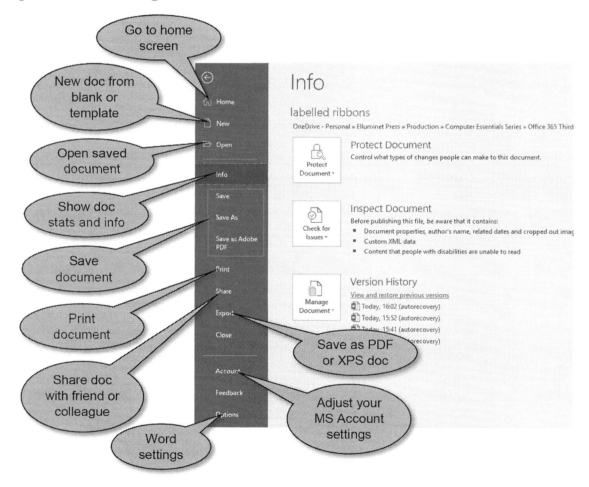

You can also change your Microsoft Account settings, log in and activate your Microsoft Office Suite, change Word's preferences and so on.

Using Paragraph Styles

Word has a number of paragraph styles that are useful for keeping your formatting consistent. The idea is to format all your headings with 'title', 'heading 1', 'heading 2', 'heading 3', your main text as 'normal', and so on. This makes it easier to format your document so you don't have to apply the same font style, size and colour manually every time you want a heading.

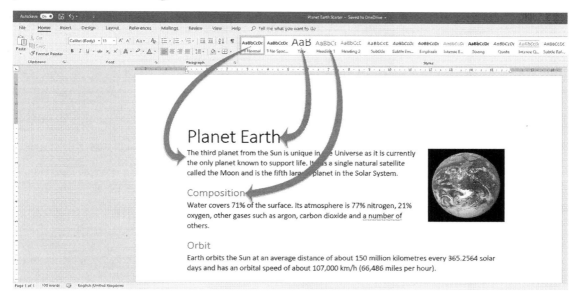

To apply the styles to a heading or paragraph, highlight it with your mouse as shown below.

Select the style from the home ribbon.

Editing Paragraph Styles

To edit a style, right click on the style you want to edit. As an example, I'm going to change the font size of 'heading 1'. First, right click the 'heading 1' style on your home ribbon, then from the drop down menu, click 'modify'.

From the dialog box, under the 'formatting' section, you'll see font typeface and font size. Make your changes here. I'm going with size 16 instead of 18.

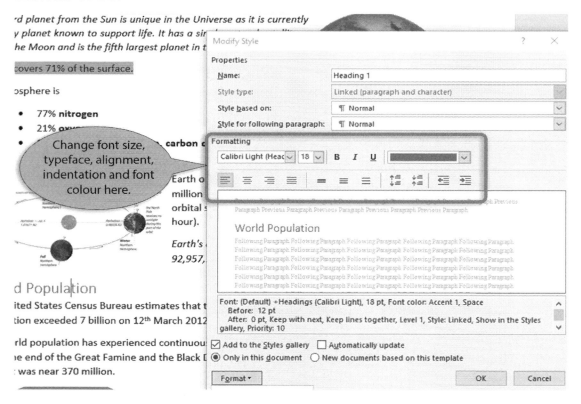

To change anything else, go down to the 'format' button at the bottom left of the dialog box.

From the drop down menu, you can change your paragraph spacing, line spacing, borders and text effects. Select the appropriate option from the menu.

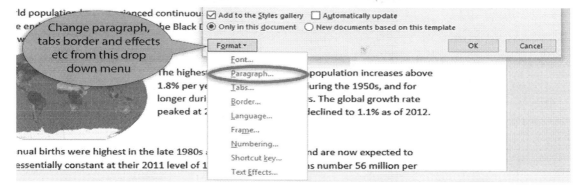

In the example, I am changing the paragraph spacing, ie the spacing before and after the heading.

To change this setting, select 'paragraph' from the drop down format menu, and adjust the settings in the 'spacing' section of the dialog box that appears.

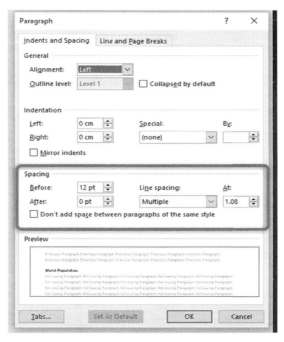

I want 12pts before each heading, so enter 12pt in the 'before' field. This will space out the sections in my document, leaving a gap before each heading.

Try some of the other settings. Try adding a text effect or a border.

Bold, Italic & Underlined

You can use **bold**, *italic* or <u>underlined</u> text to emphasise certain words or paragraphs.

Just select the text you want to apply formatting to and from the home ribbon select one of the icons: **bold**, *italic* or <u>underlined</u>.

For example, I want to make the text "water", "nitrogen" and "oxygen" bold. To do this, double click on the word to highlight it.

Planet Earth

The third planet from the Sun is unique in the Universe as it is currently the only planet known to support life. It has a single natural satellite called the Moon and is the fifth largest planet in the Solar System.

Composition

Water covers 71% of the surface. Its atmosphere is 77% **nitrogen**, 21% oxygen, other gases such as argon, carbon dioxide and a number of others.

Click the bold icon on your home ribbon. Do this for each of the individual words.

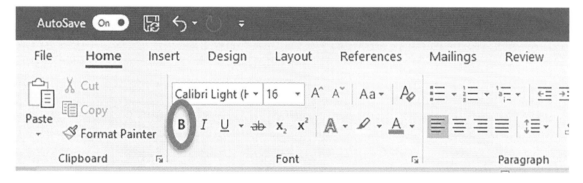

Do the same for <u>underlined</u> and *italic* text, using the appropriate icons on the home ribbon.

Try changing some text to italic or underlined.

Superscript & Subscript

Subscripts appear below the text line and are used primarily in mathematical formulas, to express chemical compounds or footnotes.

For example.

H_2O or CO_2

You can add subscripts to your text. To do this, first highlight the character you want to make into a subscript. In this example, I want to select the '2' in H20.

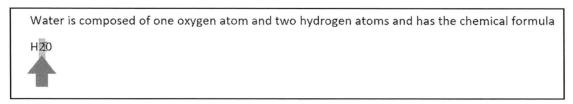

Click your mouse before the '2' and drag over to the right until the '2' is highlighted in grey, as shown above. Click the subscript icon on your home ribbon.

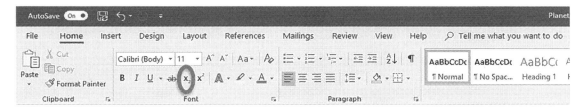

Superscripts appear at the top of the text line and are used primarily in mathematical formulas or to express chemical compounds.

For example:

Temperature was **32°C**, or the area of the circle is = πr^2

For superscripts, it's the same procedure except you select superscript from the home ribbon, instead of subscript.

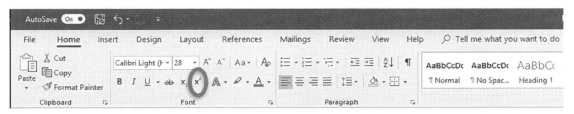

Give it a try.

If the subscript or superscript icons aren't there, click the expand icon at the bottom right of the font section of the home ribbon, circled below at the top of the screen print.

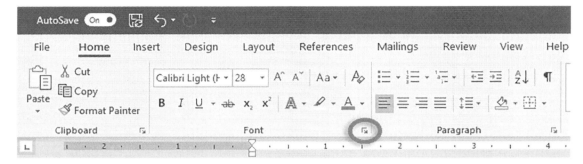

In the dialog box that appears, select subscript or superscipt option under the 'effects' section, then click ok.

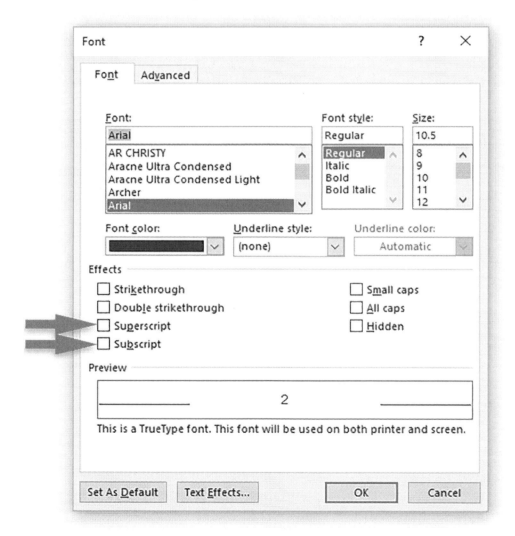

Highlighting Text

To highlight text, first click the small down arrow next to the highlight icon on your home ribbon.

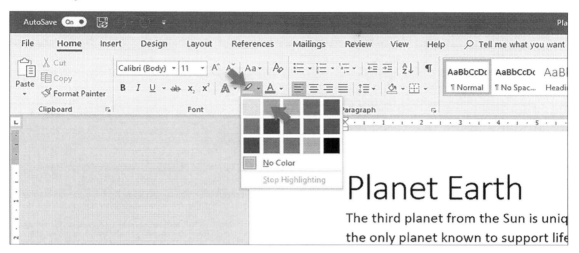

From the drop down menu that appears, select a colour. Usually yellow, green or turquoise show up well.

Now with the highlight tool, click and drag it across the text you want to highlight. In this example, I want to highlight 'Water covers 71% of the surface.'

Planet Earth

The third planet from the Sun is unique in the Universe as it is currently the only planet known to support life. It has a single natural satellite called the Moon and is the fifth largest planet in the Solar System.

Water covers 71% of the surface.

Its atmosphere is

Once you release your mouse, you'll see the text highlight in the colour you chose.

called the Moon and is the fifth largest planet in the Solar System.

Water covers 71% of the surface.

To turn off the highlight tool, click the icon again on your home ribbon.

Text Colour

To change the colour of the text, first highlight it with your mouse. In the example below, I want to change the text colour of the first paragraph. To do this, click before the word 'the' and drag your mouse across the paragraph, to the end after 'March 2012', to highlight it.

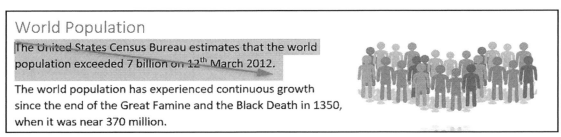

World Population

The United States Census Bureau estimates that the world population exceeded 7 billion on 12th March 2012.

The world population has experienced continuous growth since the end of the Great Famine and the Black Death in 1350, when it was near 370 million.

From the home ribbon, click the small down arrow next to the font colour icon.

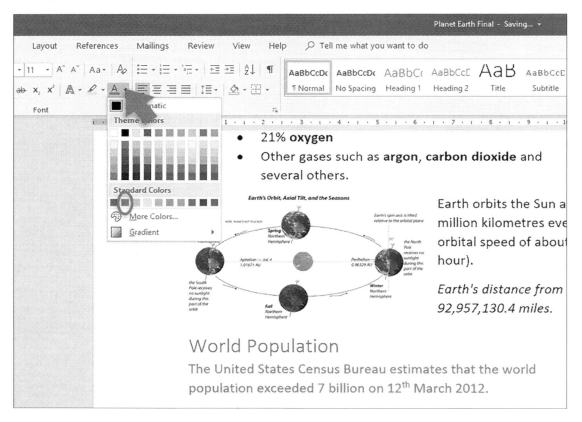

From the drop down menu that appears, select the colour you want from the palette.

Once you click a colour, the selected text will change.

Text Justification

Text justification is the alignment of text relative to the margins on a page. You can align text to the left or right margins, or centred between margins, as shown below.

Most text will be **left aligned** as demonstrated in this paragraph. Only the left margin is aligned, the right margin is not.

Text can also be **right aligned** this is good for addresses on the top of letters

Text can also be **fully justified**. This means that the left and right margins are both aligned. This helps when creating documents with images, as the text will line up neatly around the image.

Text can also be **centre aligned**, as demonstrated by this paragraph and is good for headings, verses, poems and so on.

To justify paragraphs, first select the text you want to apply the formatting to.

In this example, I want fully justify the first paragraph. This means the text is aligned on both the left and right margins.

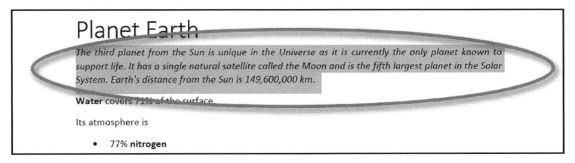

Select the text, then from the home ribbon select the fully justify icon.

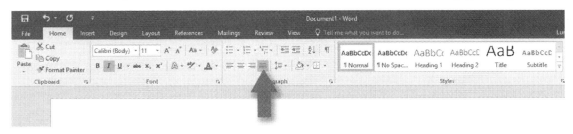

Paragraph Indents

To increase the indent of a paragraph, select the text with your mouse so it's highlighted.

Earth's atmosphere is made up of

77% **nitrogen**, 21% **oxygen** and other gases such as **argon, carbon dioxide** and several others which make up the other 2%.

Earth orbits the Sun at an average distance of about 150 million kilometres every 365.2564 solar days and has an orbital speed of about 107,000 km/h (66,486 miles per hour).

From your home ribbon, click the increase indent icon.

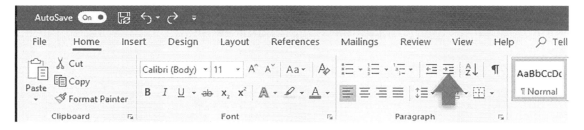

This will produce something like this. This makes it easier to read the information in the document.

Earth's atmosphere is made up of

77% **nitrogen**, 21% **oxygen** and other gases such as **argon, carbon dioxide** and several others which make up the other 2%.

Earth orbits the Sun at an average distance of about 150 million kilometres every 365.2564 solar days and has an orbital speed of about 107,000 km/h (66,486 miles per hour).

To decrease the indent, just use the decrease indent icon instead.

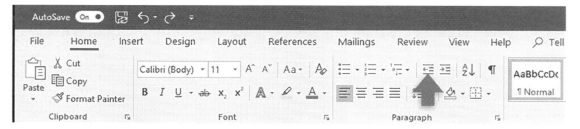

First Line Indent

The first line indent is a good way to begin paragraphs. This helps the reader to process the information and to identify sections in your text.

A first line indent, indents the first line of a paragraph with all other lines of text in line with the left margin.

First, select the paragraph you want to indent. Then click the expand icon under the paragraph section of the home ribbon.

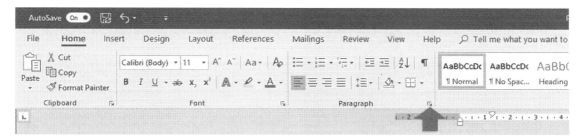

In the paragraph dialog box, go down to 'indentation', and in the 'special' drop down field, select 'first line'.

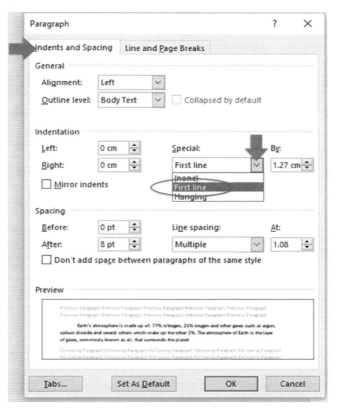

Click OK.

Hanging Indent

A hanging indent, indents all the lines except the first one. These indents are usually used with lists, bullet points or bibliographies.

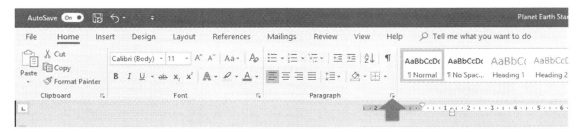

Wilson. K (2016, March 4). Using Microsoft Office 2016: *Getting Started With Word, p34, Chapter 4.* Retrieved from http://www.elluminetpress.com

First, select the paragraph you want to indent. Then click the expand icon under the paragraph section of the home ribbon.

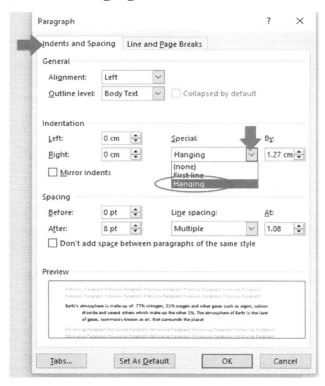

In the paragraph dialog box, go down to 'indentation' and in the 'special' drop down field, select 'hanging'.

Click OK.

Paragraph Spacing

Paragraph spacing is the space before and after a paragraph. Space and font size is measured in points (pt).

First, select the paragraph you want to adjust. Then click the expand icon under the paragraph section of the home ribbon.

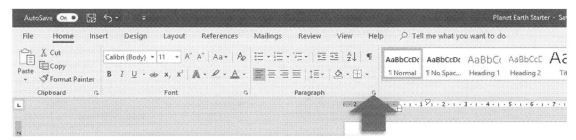

Under the 'spacing' section of the 'indents and spacing' tab, you'll see 'before' and 'after'.

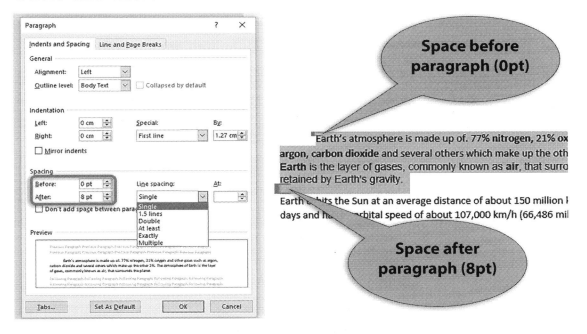

This is where you can adjust the spacing. In this example, I have entered 8pts after the selected paragraph.

This means that there will be an 8pt gap after the paragraph on the page, as you can see above.

These settings are usually applied to the paragraph styles, but you can adjust them here.

Line Spacing

Line spacing is the space between each line. Space and font size is measured in points (pt).

First, select the paragraph you want to adjust. Then click the expand icon under the paragraph section of the home ribbon.

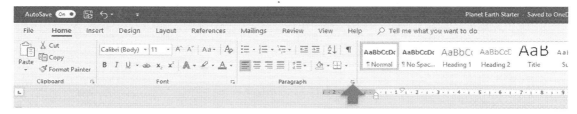

Under spacing on the 'indents and spacing' tab, go down to 'line spacing'.

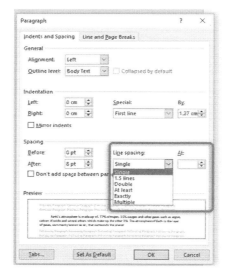

Here you can select single, this is the default. Double, this as its name suggests doubles the space between the lines. 1.5 lines makes the space one and a half times wider. If you select 'at least', you can specify the size of the space between the lines.

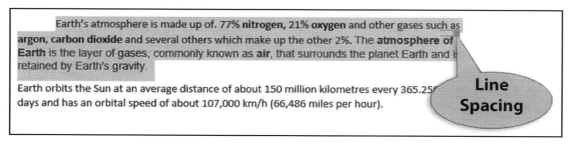

These settings are usually applied to the paragraph styles.

Tabs

To access tab settings, go to your home ribbon and click the expand icon on the bottom right of the paragraph section. From the dialog box that appears, click 'tabs' on the bottom left.

Now from this box, you can add tab stops. If you look along the ruler at the top of the document, you'll see some measurements.

For this particular document, I'm entering finish times and I want all the times to line up in the list (about 5cm across the page should be enough for the first column).

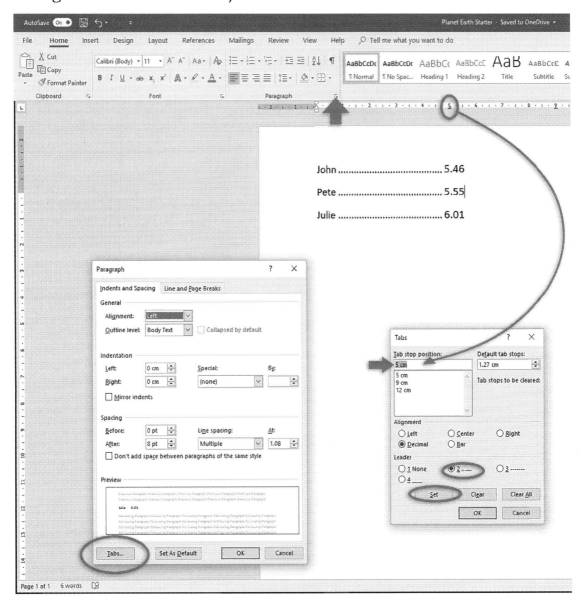

In the 'tab stop position' field enter 5cm. Set the alignment of the tab. Note there are different types of tabs.

Left aligned tabs align all text to the left against the tap stop. **Decimal tabs** align all the decimal points in the numbers, in-line with the tab stop and are good for displaying numbers. **Centre aligned tabs** align all the text centre to the tab stop. **Right aligned tabs** align all text to the right against the tab stop. See the image below.

Decimal tabs would work well for the column of finish times. Click 'decimal' under the alignment section.

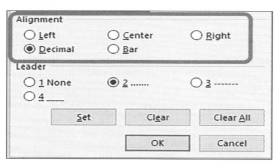

I also want some leading dots to make it easier to read. So in the 'leader' section, click the second option.

Now repeat the process and add the tabs at 9cm and 12cm, noting the different tab alignments (left, decimal, centre, right).

Click OK when done.

Now, every time you press the tab key on your keyboard, your cursor will jump to the tab stop position.

Bullet Lists

Edit the document and change the sentence explaining atmospheric composition to a bullet point list. Select the text using your mouse as shown below.

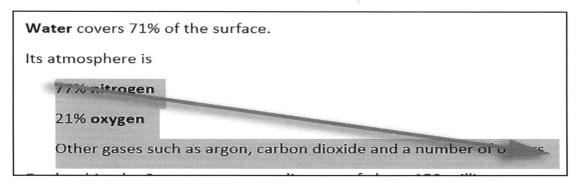

Then from your home ribbon, click the bullet points icon.

You can also have different styles of bullets: ticks, stars, shapes, and so on. To get the drop down menu, click the small down arrow next to the bullet icon.

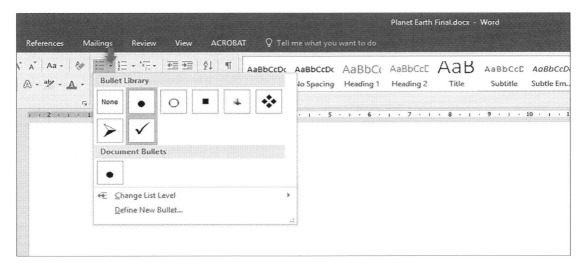

Numbered Lists

Edit the document and change the sentence explaining atmospheric composition to a numbered point list. Select the text using your mouse as shown below.

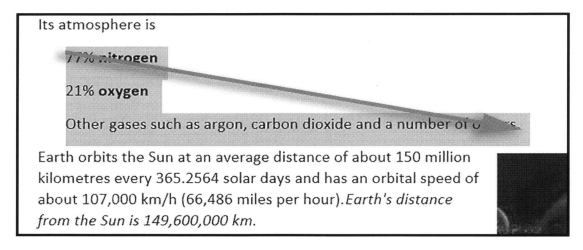

From the home ribbon, click the numbered list icon.

You can also have different styles of numbered lists. To get the drop down menu, click the small down arrow next to the numbered list icon.

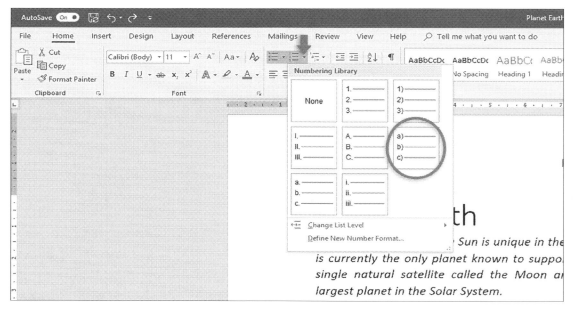

Sorting Text

You can easily sort a list of items into ascending or descending order. For example, I want to alphabetise the list of names below.

First highlight the names as shown above, then click the sort icon on the home ribbon

Now, if we use the default sort settings, the list will be sorted by the first letter of each line of text.

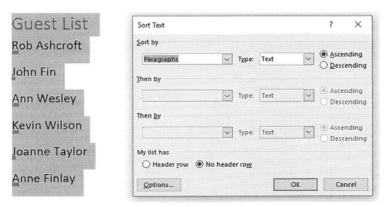

In most cases this is ok, but in this case I want to sort the names by surname. Remember, word sees the list as the first name as word 1 and the surname as word 2.

To change the sort options, click options at the bottom of the dialog box.

Select 'other' and in the small text field enter a space using the spacebar on your keyboard. Then click 'ok'.

Now, in the 'sort text' dialog box, go down to the 'sort by' section, and in the first field, select 'word 2' - remember word 2 is the surname, this is what we want to sort the list by.

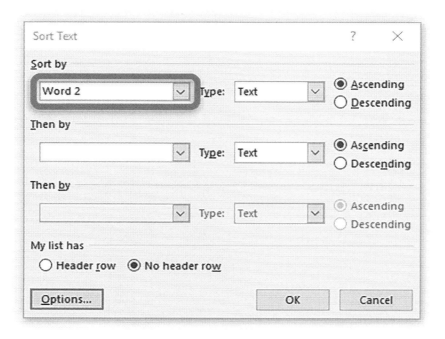

Click 'ok' when you're done.

Cut, Copy & Paste

To ease editing documents, you can use copy, cut and paste to move paragraphs or pictures around in different parts of your document.

First select the paragraph below with your mouse by clicking before the word 'Earth', and dragging your mouse across the line towards the end of the line, as shown below.

The third planet from the Sun is unique in the Universe as it is currently the only planet known to support life. It has a single natural satellite called the Moon and is the fifth largest planet in the Solar System. Earth's distance from the sun is 149,600,000 km.

Click & drag across text to highlight

Once you have done that, click 'cut' from the left hand side of your home ribbon. This will 'cut out' the paragraph.

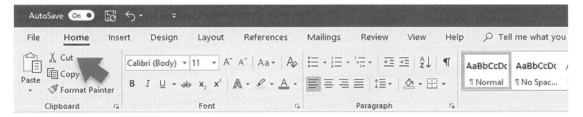

Now click on the position in the document you want the paragraph you just cut out to be inserted.

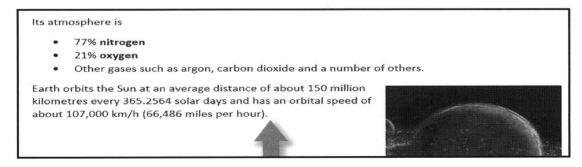

Its atmosphere is

- 77% **nitrogen**
- 21% **oxygen**
- Other gases such as argon, carbon dioxide and a number of others.

Earth orbits the Sun at an average distance of about 150 million kilometres every 365.2564 solar days and has an orbital speed of about 107,000 km/h (66,486 miles per hour).

Once you have done that click 'paste' from the home ribbon. If you wanted to copy something ie make a duplicate of the text, then use the same procedure except click 'copy' instead of 'cut'.

Using the Clipboard

You'll find Word's clipboard on the home ribbon. Just click the small icon under the clipboard section on the left hand side.

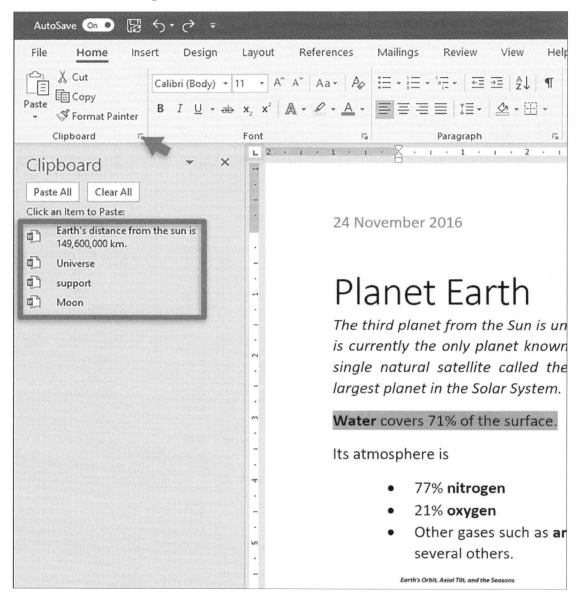

Here you'll see a list of all the parts of the document you've copied or cut. You can click on any of these items on the clipboard to paste into your document. The item will be pasted where your cursor is in your document.

Click 'clear all' to clear the clipboard. Right click on an element and select 'delete' to delete an individual item

Inserting Symbols

First place your cursor in the position you want to insert a symbol.

Select your insert ribbon. From the 'insert' ribbon, select 'symbol'. The most commonly used symbols will show up in the drop down box.

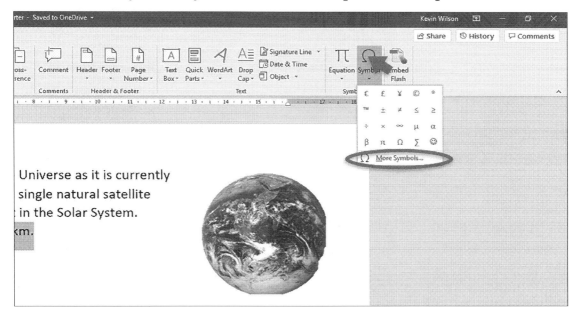

If the symbol you are looking for isn't there, click 'more symbols' at the bottom, and scroll through the list until you find the one you want.

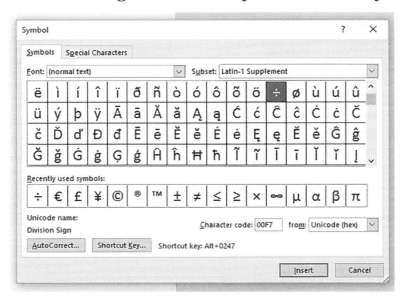

To insert the symbol click on it, then click 'insert'.

Hidden Characters

Word also inserts formatting characters such as carriage returns, spaces, tab characters that are hidden by default, to make editing your document easier for you.

To show these characters, click the 'show/hide special characters' icon on the home ribbon.

You can see in the screen below, the special characters.

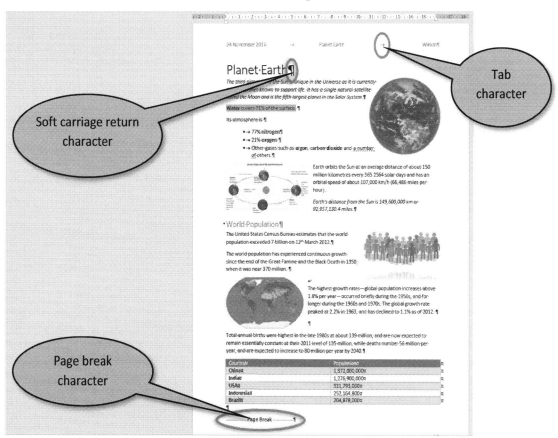

These characters don't print when you print out your document, they are there for formatting purposes.

Equations

Word has built in templates for displaying equations correctly and has some very common ones built in.

$$Speed = \frac{Distance}{Time}$$

$$Volume = \frac{4}{3}\pi r^3$$

You can build equations using the equation tool on the insert ribbon.

If we want to build the second equation first, go to your insert ribbon and click 'equation'

In the box that appears, we can start building the equation.

First type

```
volume =
```

Then we need to insert a fraction, so type

```
4 / 3
```

Now we need to insert a symbol for Pi. So from the design ribbon, scroll down the list of symbols in the centre, until you find Pi (π). Double click to add.

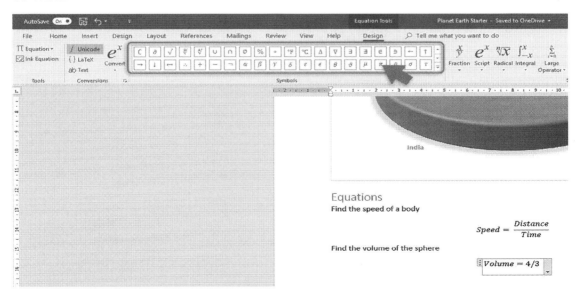

Now click 'script' from the design ribbon and select 'superscript' to add the last part of the equation: r^3

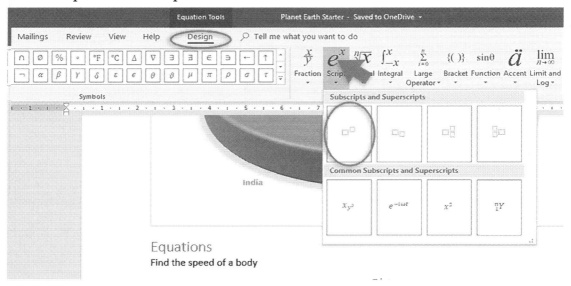

You'll see two little boxes appear on your equation.

$Volume = 4/3\pi\square^\square$

Click the bigger box and type:

r

Then in the smaller box type:

3

This will give you:

r^3

Now we have our equation. Note the formatting of the fraction and font styles.

$$Volume = \frac{4}{3}\pi r^3$$

This is a very simple example to demonstrate the feature. Why not experiment with some of the other equations on the design ribbon such as integrals, radicals and functions.

Saving Documents

To save your work, click the small disk icon in the top left hand corner of the screen.

In the save as screen, you need to tell Word where you want to save the document.

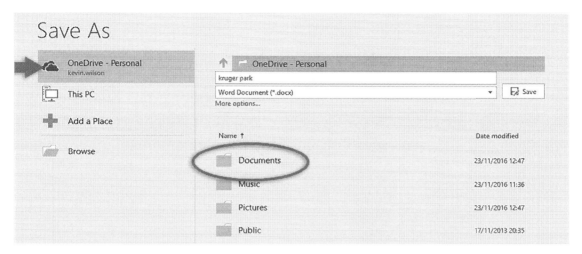

Save it onto "OneDrive Personal", in the documents/word folder created in the previous section. Click OneDrive, Double click 'documents', then double click 'Word'.

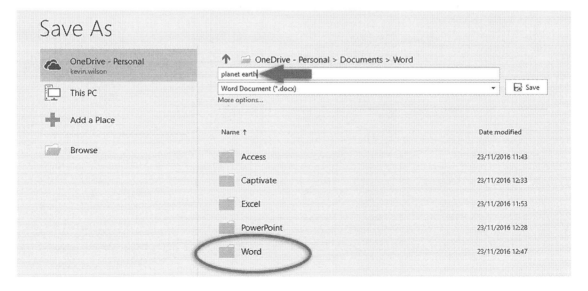

In text box, indicated above with the red arrow, type in a meaningful name describing the work. In this case "planet earth"

Click Save. This will save directly to your OneDrive account.

Saving as a Different Format

Sometimes you'll want to save a document in a different format. This can be useful if you are sending a document to someone that might not be using Windows or have Microsoft Office installed.

Word allows you to save your document in different formats. A common example is saving files as PDFs, which is a portable format that can be read on any type of computer, tablet or phone without the need to have Microsoft Word installed.

With your document open, click File on the top left of your screen. Select 'save as' from the list on the left hand side.

Click 'OneDrive', select the folder you want to save the document into. Eg 'documents'.

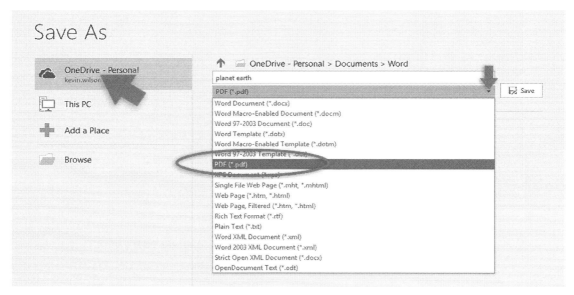

Give your file a name, in this case 'planet earth'

Now to change the format, click the down arrow in the field below and from the list, click PDF

You can also save as a web page, rich text and so on. Bear in mind that you may lose certain formatting and effects if they are not supported in these formats.

Opening Saved Documents

If Word is already open you can open previously saved documents by clicking the FILE menu on the top left of your screen.

From the blue bar along the left hand side click 'open'.

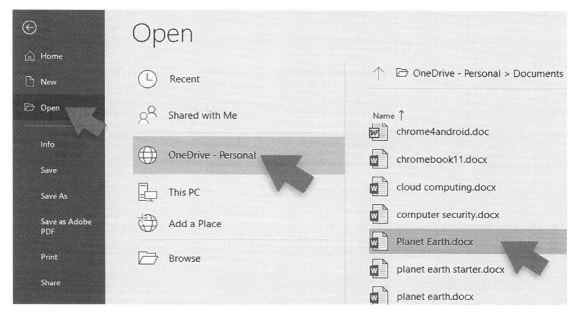

From the list, select the document you want to open. The document from the previous project was saved as 'planet earth.docx', so this is the one I am going to open here.

For convenience, Microsoft Word lists all your most recently opened documents. To do this click 'recent'. On the right hand side, click 'documents' to view recently opened documents, click 'folders' to see recently accessed folders.

Your latest files will be listed first. Double click the file name to open it.

Sharing Documents

Microsoft Word makes it easy to share documents with colleagues or friends.

You can share your document using email and OneDrive's collaboration features.

To do this, click 'file' on the top left of your screen. From the backstage, click 'share'.

In the sharing section, you have a number of options. You can post to a blog or present online. Presenting online works best with PowerPoint presentations and allows you to send links to colleagues or friends so they can see your presentation on the internet.

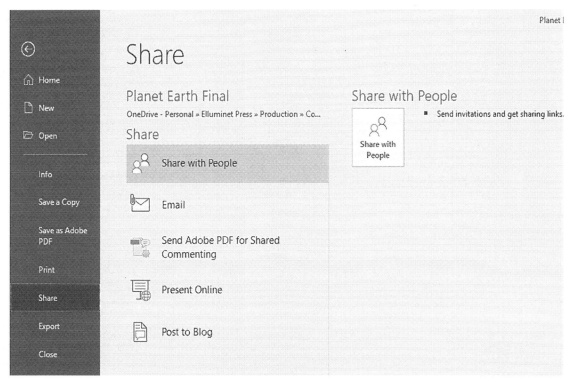

You can also send the file via email using Outlook, or you can 'share with people', which allows you to invite friends or colleagues to view, collaborate on, and edit your document. This is the option we'll look at in this example.

In this example, I'm going to share the document with someone else. To do this, select 'share with people', from the list, then click 'share with people' icon.

On the right hand side of your screen, you'll see some sharing options.

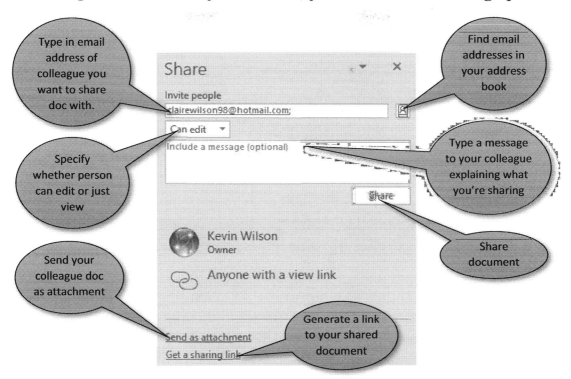

Enter the email addresses of your colleagues/friends, select whether they will be able to edit the document or just view, add a brief message description, then click share. In this example, I'm going to allow edits.

When your friend/colleague checks their email, they will be invited to open the document.

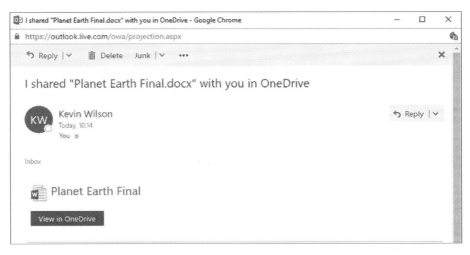

Click 'view in OneDrive' to open.

From here, your colleague/friend can edit or view the document. If they have Word installed on their machine, they can download and work on the document in Word 2019. If they don't, they can work on the document online, within their web browser.

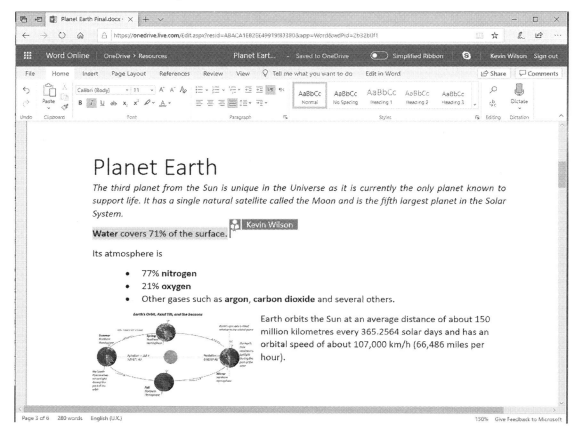

This is useful if you are working on a project with more than one person. Each person you shared the document with can edit and add content.

You can see the other person's edits or where they are in the document as indicated by these markers with their name on it.

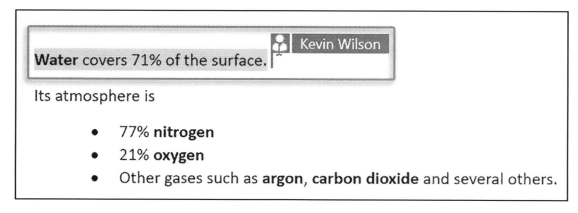

Printing Documents

To print a document, click FILE on the top left of your screen.

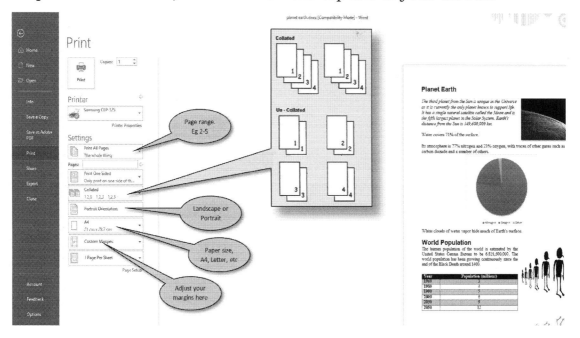

Down the left hand side, you can select options such as number of copies, print individual pages instead of the whole document and adjust layout and margins.

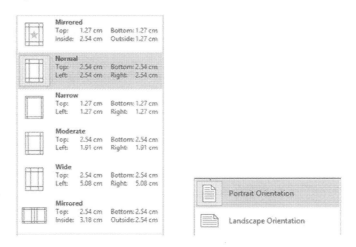

You can adjust margins, and print pages in either landscape or portrait orientation. Portrait tends to be more for documents or letters, while landscape works well with pictures and photos.

Once you have set all your options, click the print button at the top.

Page Setup

Page setup allows you to adjust margins, paper size, orientation (landscape/portrait) and general layout.

To adjust your page setup, go to your layout tab and click the expand icon on the bottom right of the page setup section.

From the dialog box that appears, you'll see your margin, paper and layout tabs.

You can adjust the margins as shown below. The top and bottom margins are colour coded in blue and the left and right margins are colour coded in red.

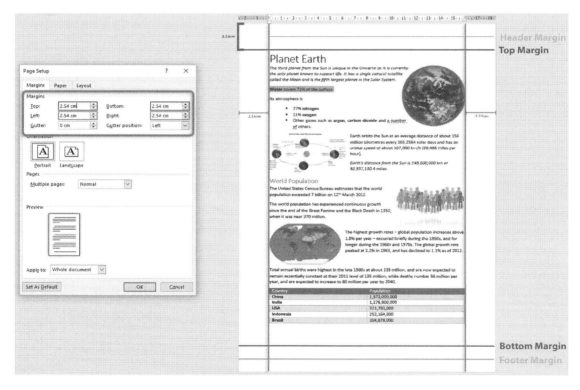

If you look in the margins tab, you'll see these sizes measured in centimetres (or inches). This is the distance from the physical edge of the page. The relevant fields in the margins tab are colour coded accordingly so you can see how it works.

If we move to the next tab 'Paper', we can change the paper size (legal, A4 or A3).

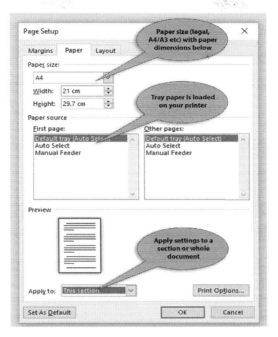

The last tab 'layout', allows you to change the header and footer margins - the distance the header appears from the physical edge of the page.

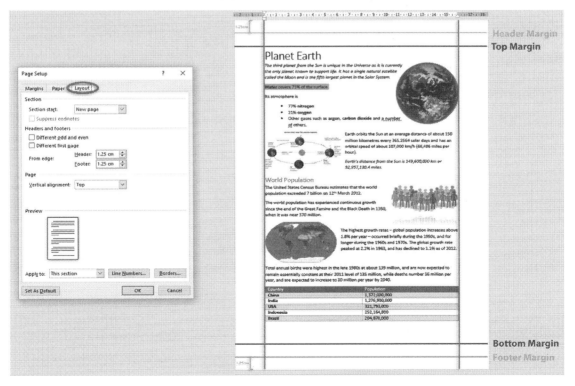

Multiple Documents

If you have multiple documents open at a time, you can easily switch between then on Windows 10. To do this, click the Word icon, on your taskbar.

The documents that are currently open will show up as thumbnails. Just click one of the thumbnails to switch to that document.

You can also display the documents side by side. Go to your view ribbon and click 'side by side'.

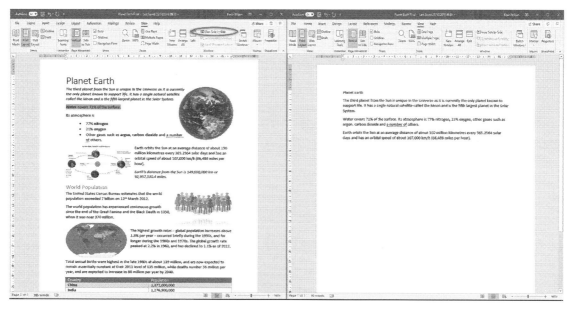

Turn off the synchronous scrolling, otherwise both documents will scroll at the same time, although this feature can be useful if you are comparing two documents.

Headers and Footers

Headers and footers appear at the top and bottom of a page. For example, the header on this page is "Chapter 3: Microsoft Word" and the footer is a page number on the bottom right.

Inserting Headers & Footers

To insert a header, go to your insert ribbon and click 'header'. From the drop down menu, select a header template. The 3 column header is commonly used, allowing you to enter something on the left, center or right of the header.

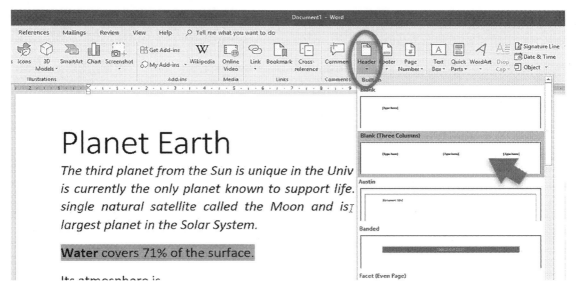

Now fill in the *[type here]* place holders with your information. Double click the place holders to select them, then type your information.

Try inserting a footer. Perhaps a logo on the bottom left? Do the same for inserting a header, except select 'footer' from the insert ribbon. Give it a try.

Editing Headers & Footers

To edit the header, double click in the white space at the top of the document. This is the header space.

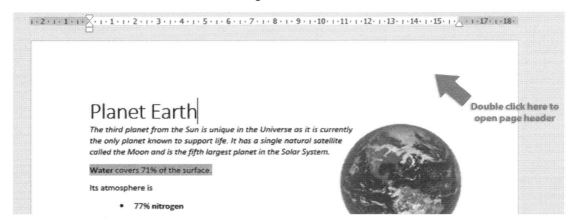

You will see the header & footer design ribbon appear and the header section marked at the top of the document.

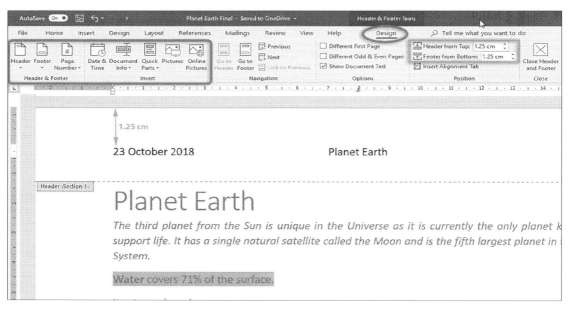

You can insert a date & time field, you can even insert a picture or a logo.

To insert pictures, click 'pictures' to insert a picture stored on your computer, or click 'online pictures' to search Bing. Use the same procedure for inserting images into a document.

Try editing the footer of the document.

Page Numbering

Inserting page numbers are similar to inserting footers. To generate page numbers, go to your insert ribbon and click 'page numbers'.

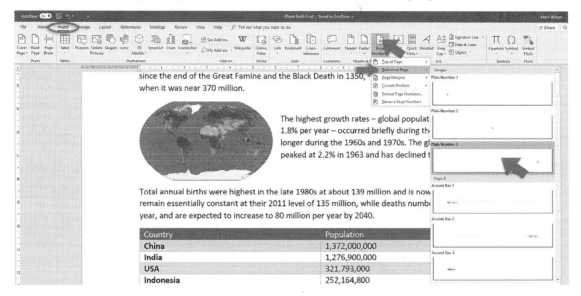

From the drop down menu, select 'bottom of page', which is usually where page numbers are.

From the templates, select 'plain number 3', because we want the page numbers on the bottom right. Similarly if you wanted them in the centre, select 'plain number 2' template.

Why not try some of the other templates, 'accent bar 2' perhaps?

You'll see the page footer open with the page number.

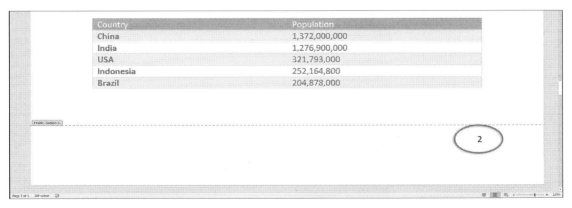

Click 'close header & footer' from the header design ribbon at the top of the screen.

Page Borders

You can add a page border to your documents. To do this, go to your design ribbon and select 'page border'.

From the dialog box that appears, select one of the settings listed down the left hand side. I'm going to select 'shadow'.

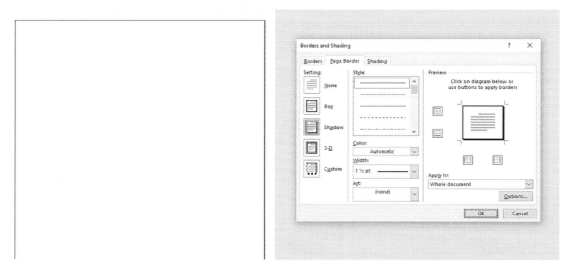

You can adjust the thickness of the lines by adjusting the width.

Or try some border art. Border art as its name suggests allows you to create borders with pre-set clipart images.

Click on the 'art' field and select a design. Since this document is about Earth, I'm going to choose the small planets.

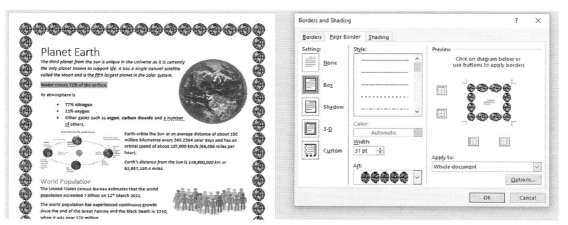

Page Breaks

There may be times where you need to force a new page. Perhaps you are writing a report and you need to start a new chapter or section. Instead of pressing the return key until a new page is created, you should insert a page break.

To do this, make sure you're on the page where the break is to be inserted. Remember breaks are added after the current page.

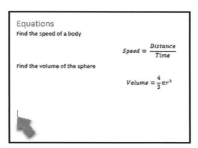

Go to your layout ribbon and click 'breaks'.

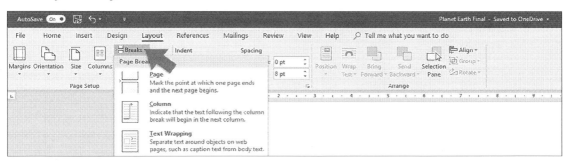

Here you will see a list of different types of breaks. For a simple page break, select the first option, 'page'.

Section breaks divide the document into independent sections. Each section can be formatted independently, meaning you can have different page orientations, sizes and styles.

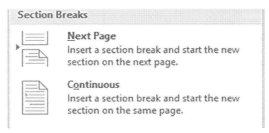

A page break merely forces text to start on a new page of the same section.

Creating Columns

Adding columns to your document arranges your text in a similar fashion to a newspaper.

To do this, go to your layout ribbon and click 'columns'. From the drop down menu, select how many columns you want. In this example, I am going to create a 3 column article.

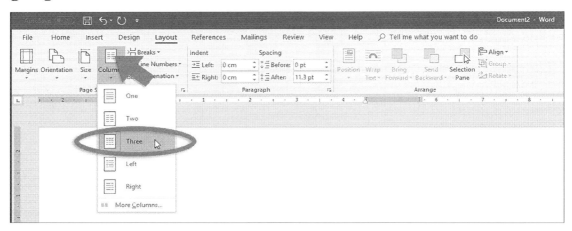

Now, when you start typing your article, Word will arrange your text into columns.

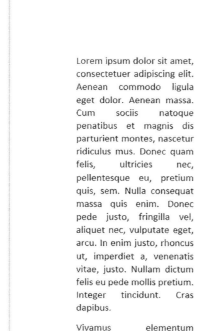

Lorem ipsum dolor sit amet, consectetuer adipiscing elit. Aenean commodo ligula eget dolor. Aenean massa. Cum sociis natoque penatibus et magnis dis parturient montes, nascetur ridiculus mus. Donec quam felis, ultricies nec, pellentesque eu, pretium quis, sem. Nulla consequat massa quis enim. Donec pede justo, fringilla vel, aliquet nec, vulputate eget, arcu. In enim justo, rhoncus ut, imperdiet a, venenatis vitae, justo. Nullam dictum felis eu pede mollis pretium. Integer tincidunt. Cras dapibus.

Vivamus elementum semper nisi. Aenean

orci eget eros faucibus tincidunt. Duis leo. Sed fringilla mauris sit amet nibh. Donec sodales sagittis magna. Sed consequat, leo eget bibendum sodales, augue velit cursus nunc, quis gravida magna mi a libero. Fusce vulputate eleifend sapien.

Vestibulum purus quam, scelerisque ut, mollis sed, nonummy id, metus. Nullam accumsan lorem in dui. Cras ultricies mi eu turpis hendrerit fringilla. Vestibulum ante ipsum primis in faucibus orci luctus et ultrices posuere cubilia Curae; In ac dui quis mi consectetuer lacinia. Nam pretium turpis et arcu.

auctor et, hendrerit quis, nisi. Curabitur ligula sapien, tincidunt non, euismod vitae, posuere imperdiet, leo. Maecenas malesuada. Praesent congue erat at massa. Sed cursus turpis vitae tortor. Donec posuere vulputate arcu. Phasellus accumsan cursus velit. Vestibulum ante ipsum primis in faucibus orci luctus et ultrices posuere cubilia Curae; Sed aliquam, nisi quis porttitor congue, elit erat euismod orci, ac placerat dolor lectus quis orci. Phasellus consectetuer vestibulum elit. Aenean tellus metus, bibendum sed, posuere ac, mattis non, nunc. Vestibulum fringilla pede sit amet augue. In

If you need to adjust the spacing between the columns, from the layout ribbon, click 'columns' then click 'more columns'.

Change the values in the 'width and spacing' section below.

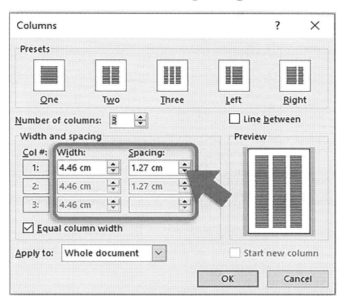

This is what the columns will look like. You can see the column width and column spacing marked on the image below, according to the settings in the dialog box.

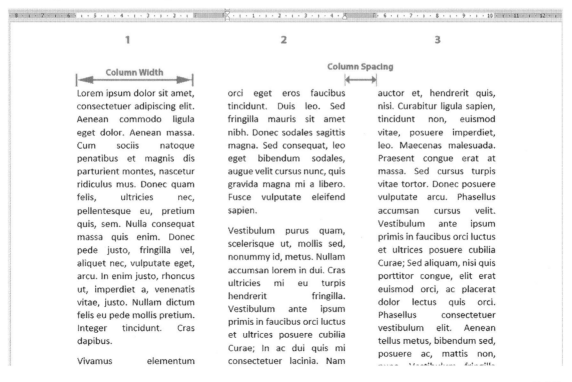

Watermarks

You can add watermarks such as 'confidential', or 'draft' to your documents. To do this, go to your design ribbon and click 'watermark'. From the drop down, select one of the templates.

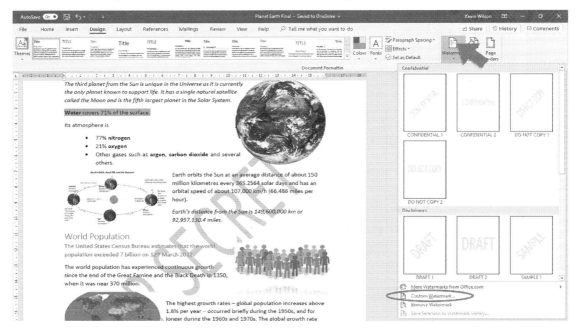

You can also create your own. What if my document was top secret? To do this, click 'custom water mark' from the drop down menu.

Enter your text, 'TOP SECRET' in to the text field. Change the colour to red. Click 'ok' when you're done.

Cover Pages

You can add pre-designed cover pages to your documents. These work well if you are submitting a sales report, a manuscript or something that needs a title page.

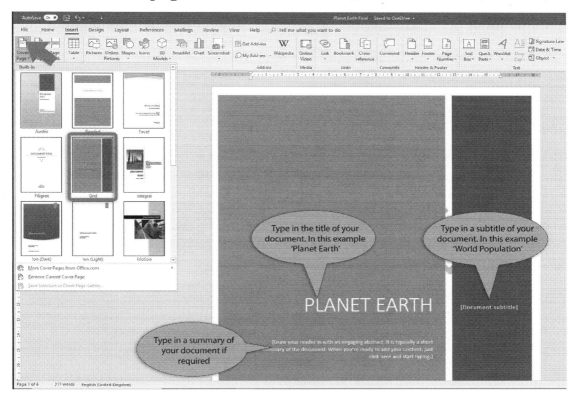

This cover page is looking a bit boring, so I'm going to add an image. For this example, I am going to add an image of the planet earth.

First go to your insert ribbon and click 'online pictures'.

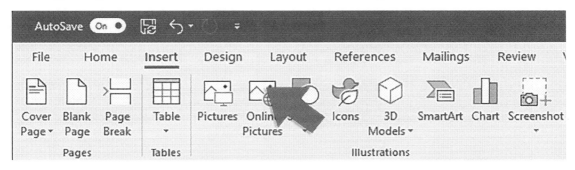

If you want to insert a picture of your own, select 'pictures' instead of 'online pictures', then select the picture you want to insert from the dialog box.

From the dialog box that appears, type what you're looking for into the Bing search, in this example I'm going to type 'earth'.

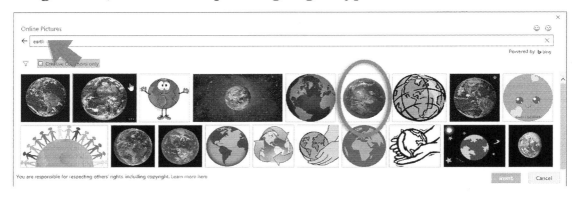

From the list of images that appear, I want one that will blend well with the transparent background. The one circled above works well. Click on it then click 'insert'.

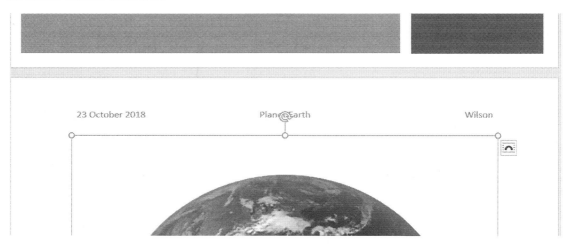

Now the problem is, Word has inserted the image but it isn't in the right place, also the image might be behind something else. First we need to make the image float. To do this, click the image you just inserted, go to the format ribbon and select 'wrap text'. From the drop down, select 'in front of text'.

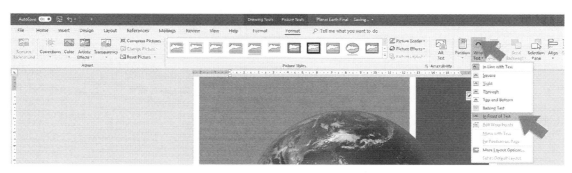

Now click and drag the image into position on your cover page. Drag your image onto the cover page if needed.

Use the resize handles circled in the illustration above, to resize your image.

Drag the image into a position that looks good, as shown in the example above.

Contents Pages

The contents tool works by scanning your document for heading styles. For example, Title, Heading 1, Heading 2, Heading 3 and so on.

To add an automatic table of contents, go to your 'references' ribbon menu and select 'automatic table 2'. This option will scan your document for 'heading 1', 'heading 2' and 'heading 3' styles and add them to the table.

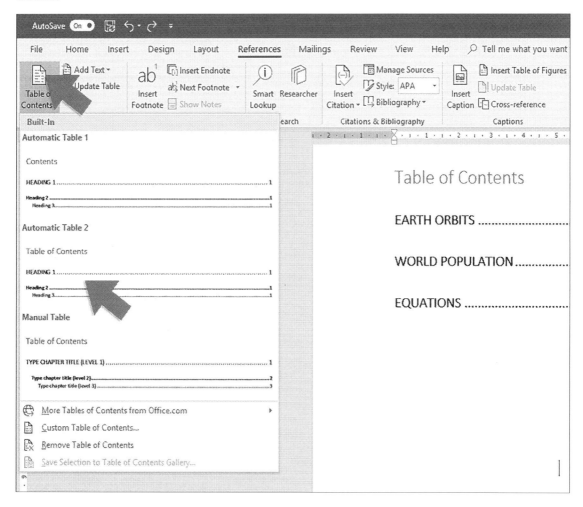

You may notice that in our document we have used a title style which has not been picked up by the table of contents generator.

If you have used styles other than 'heading 1', 'heading 2' and 'heading 3', they won't get picked up.

Remember, we used the 'title' style for the title of our document.

To create a table of contents with other styles, you will need to select 'custom table of contents' from the drop down menu. Then from the dialog box, select 'options'.

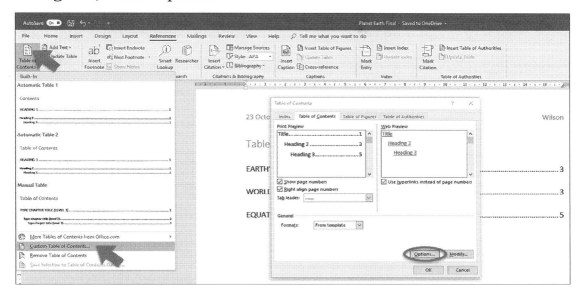

Now in the box that appears, you need to put the heading styles in the order you want them to appear in the table of contents. So in our example document, we have used the 'Title' style for all the chapter headings, so this one needs to appear first, so we scroll down the list until we see the 'Title' style. Enter 1 in the box next to it.

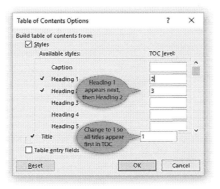

Next we have used Heading 1 for all the subtitles. So again in the list we look for heading 1 style. We want this one to appear second, so enter 2 in the box next to it.

We used Heading 2 for all the sections and we want these included. So find heading 2 in the list and enter 3 in the box next to it.

Click OK when you're done and Word will generate your table of contents.

Indexes

Select the text you want to flag as an index entry. Go to your references ribbon and click 'Mark Entry'.

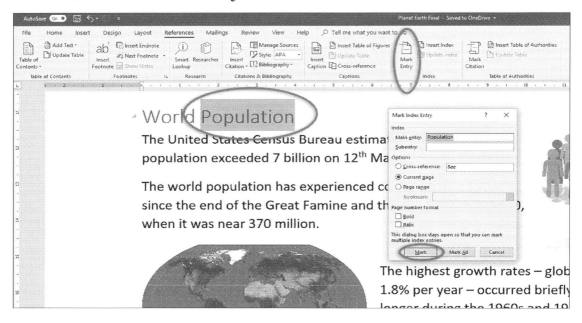

Click 'mark' to mark only that particular occurrence of the word, click 'mark all' to mark every occurrence of the word in your document. Do this with all the words you want to appear in your index - use titles and keywords.

You can have an index that just runs down the left of the page. This is a single column index. You can increase the number of columns for your index. This helps to save space on your page if you are writing long documents. Here's a three column index.

To generate an index, it's a good idea to first insert a blank page or a page break. Click at the top of the page (this is where the index will start). Now from the references ribbon, click 'Insert Index'.

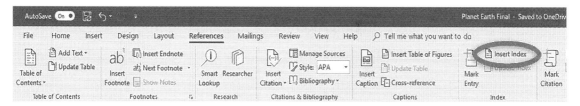

Choose a type: indented or run-in. In an indented style, main headings are followed by indented subheadings, each on its own line. In run-in style, subheadings follow main headings continuously, separated by commas.

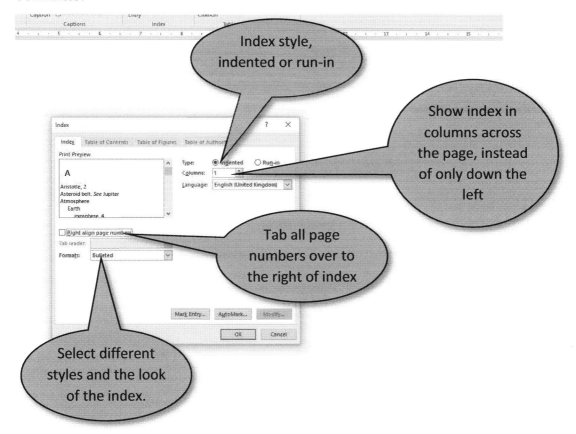

Then specify the number of columns to span the index across.

You can also choose a format if you select the format drop down menu, and select an option. In this example, I am using a 'bulleted' format.

Click OK when you're done.

Adding Images

Adding images to your document is easy.

There are two ways.

- Your own photos and pictures stored on your computer or OneDrive.

- Clipart. This is a large library of images that can be used in your documents.

Click on the line in your document where you want your photograph or image to appear.

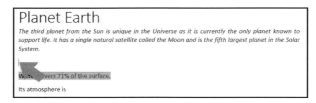

Go to your insert ribbon and click on 'Pictures'

Choose the picture or photo you want from the dialog box that appears. Click insert.

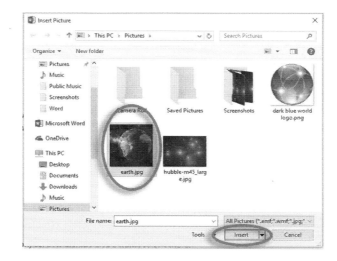

This will insert your photo into your document.

You can move the photo by clicking and dragging it to the position you want it.

You can also search for images on Google. When you download an image, make sure you save them into your pictures folder. Open your web browser and run a google search, then select 'images'.

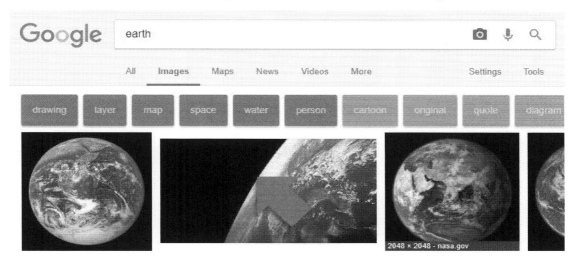

Click on the image thumbnail in the search results to view the full size image. Then right click image, select 'save image as' from the popup menu.

From the dialog box that appears, save the picture into your 'pictures' folder either on your PC or OneDrive folder.

Once your image is saved into your pictures folder, you can import them into your Word document using the same procedure at the beginning of the chapter.

Once imported into Word, you may need to resize the image, as sometimes they can come in a bit big. To do this click on the image, you'll see small handles appear on each corner of the image.

These are called resize handles. You can use them by clicking and dragging a corner toward the centre of the image to make it smaller as shown below. Hold down the shift key as you resize the image to prevent it from being distorted.

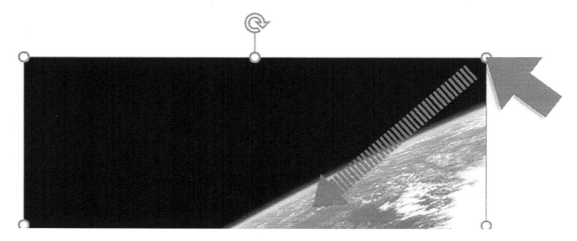

Adding Clipart

Carrying on with our document, I want to add a new section called "World Population" and I want some clipart to illustrate this. 'Office. com' clipart library is no longer supported and has been replaced with Bing images.

First, click the position in your document where you want the clipart to appear.

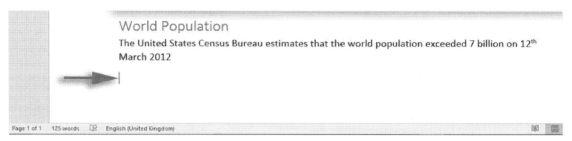

Go to your insert ribbon and click 'online pictures'.

Then, in the dialog box, type in what you are looking for, as shown below. In this example, enter the search term 'population'.

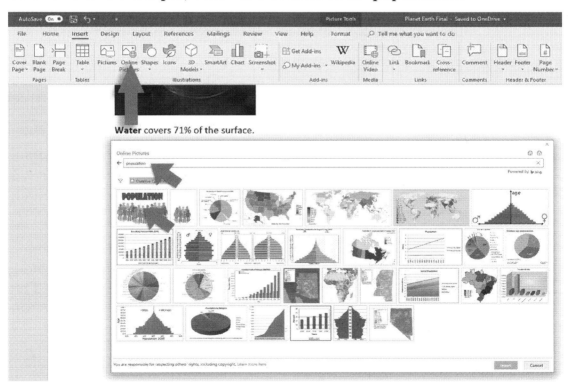

In the search results, click the image you want then click insert.

Word will insert the image in the position where you had your cursor in the document.

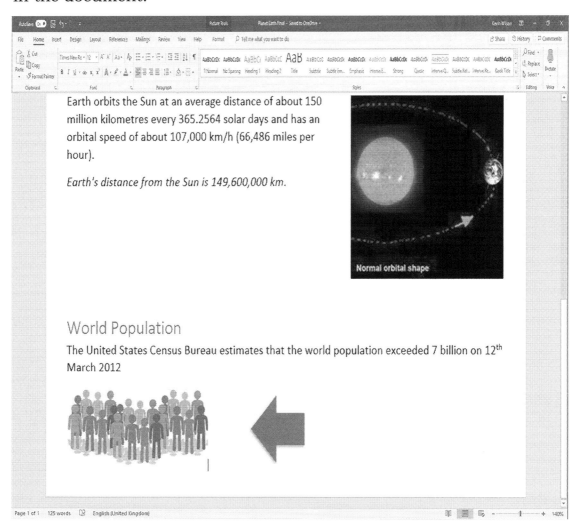

Again, you might need to resize the image. Hold down the shift key as you resize the image to prevent it from being distorted.

Adding Effects to Images

To add effects to your images, such as shadows and borders, click on your image, then select the Format ribbon.

In this example, click on the population image.

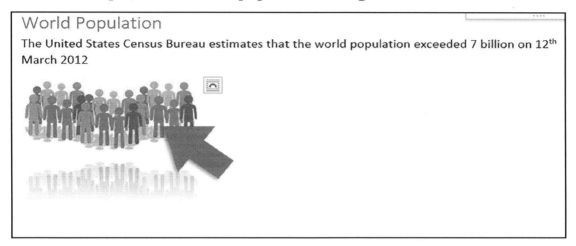

I want to create a nice reflection style to the image. To do this, click 'picture effects', then go down to 'reflection'. Select a variation as shown below.

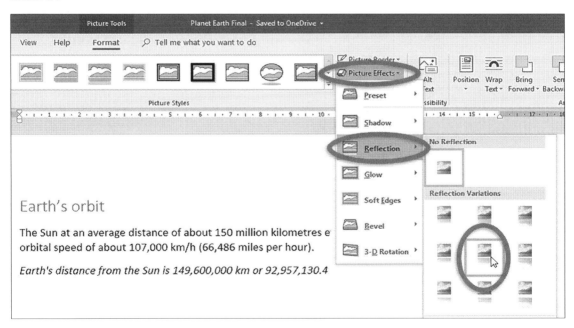

Try different effects, such as 'shadow', 'bevel' or 'glow'.

See what effect they have...

Cropping Images

If you insert an image into your document, and it has unwanted parts, or you want to concentrate on one particular piece of the picture, you can crop the image

First, insert an image from your pictures library into your document.

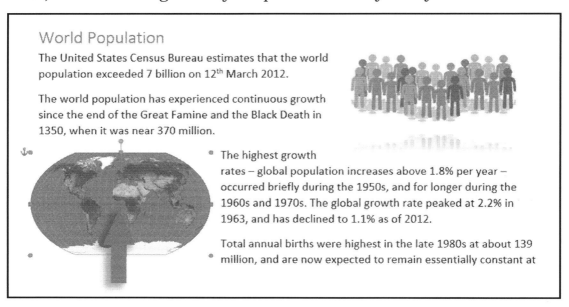

To crop, click on the image, then click the format ribbon. From the format ribbon, click the crop icon.

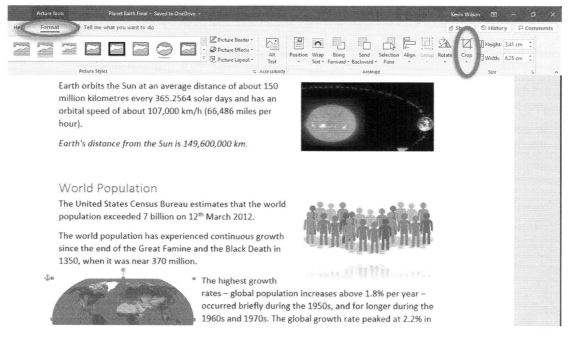

If you look closely at your image, you will see crop handles around the edges, shown circled below.

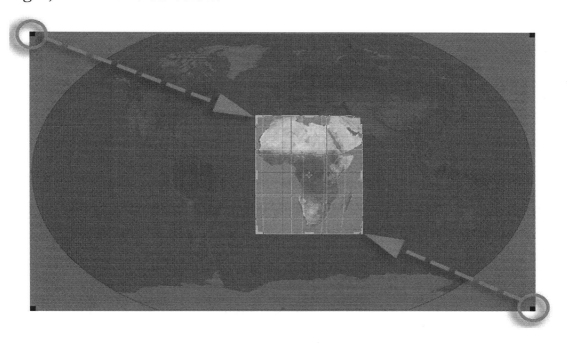

Click and drag these handles around the part of the image you want to keep. Eg, I just want to show Africa in the image.

The dark grey bits will be removed to leave the bit of the image inside the crop square.

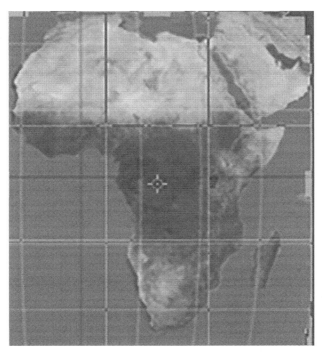

Wrap Text around Images

When you insert an image, the image will be inserted in-line with text, meaning the image will show on one line, with text both above and below.

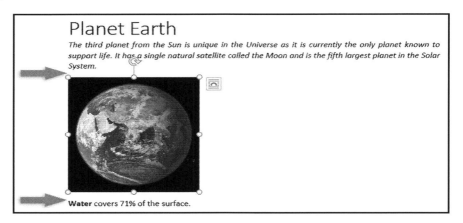

The document would flow much better if you wrapped the relevant text around the image. To change the text wrap, click on the image and from the format ribbon, click 'text wrap'. Select 'square' from the drop down list to align the text squarely around the border of the image.

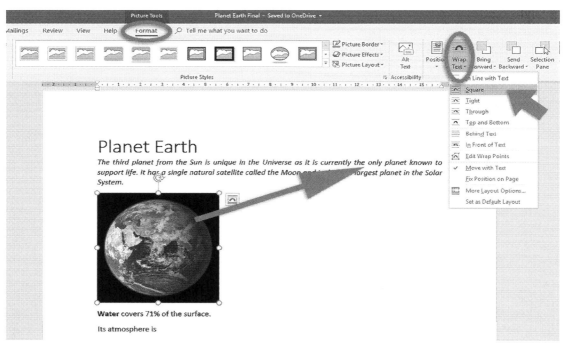

Click and drag the image into position. As you do this, you'll notice the text will arrange itself around the image.

This image, I will align top right, in line with the first paragraph.

If your image has a white background or isn't square, you can wrap your text around the actual image.

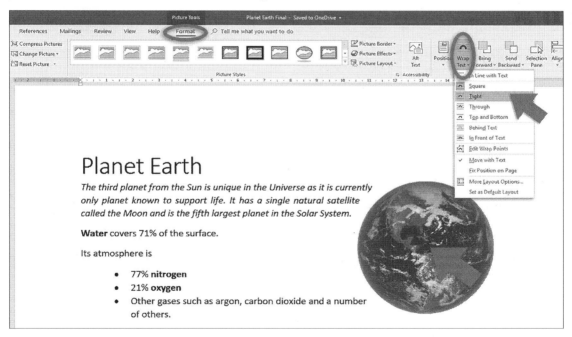

Click on the image and select your format ribbon. Click on 'wrap text' from the drop down menu, and select 'tight'.

Try some of the other text wraps. What happens when you select 'through' or 'behind text'?

Remove Image Backgrounds

If your image has a solid colour background, you can remove it to make it transparent. This can help to blend your image into your document.

Take the example of the image of the planet earth, if you look at it, the image has a black background. This doesn't particularly blend well with the rest of the document.

To remove the black, click the image and select your format ribbon. Click 'remove background'.

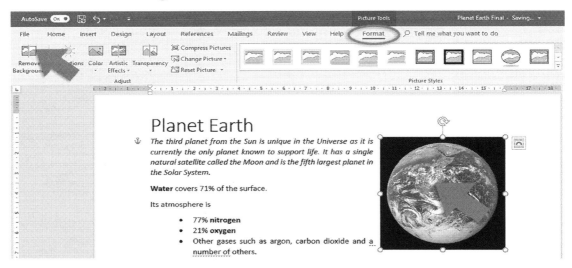

You'll notice a white box with stretch handles appear around your image.

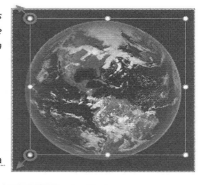

Stretch the box by clicking and dragging the handles outwards until the purple area surrounds the image, and there is no purple spilling over into the image.

The purple bit is a mask, and highlights the bit of the image that will be removed, or 'masked out'.

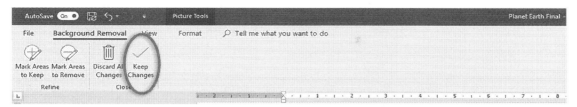

Once you have done that, click 'keep changes' on the top left of your screen.

Planet Earth

The third planet from the Sun is unique in the Universe as it is currently the only planet known to support life. It has a single natural satellite called the Moon and is the fifth largest planet in the Solar System.

Water covers 71% of the surface.

Its atmosphere is

- 77% **nitrogen**
- 21% **oxygen**
- Other gases such as argon, carbon dioxide and a number of others.

You'll see that all the black surrounding the image has been removed, and the image blends in a lot better with the text.

You might want to resize the image and reposition it.

SmartArt

SmartArt allows you to create info graphics, charts and so on. There are a lot of different types of pre-designed templates to choose from.

To insert SmartArt, go to your insert ribbon and click 'SmartArt'.

From the dialog box that appears, select a design. For this example, I am going to select 'picture strips' to display my atmospheric composition data in our document.

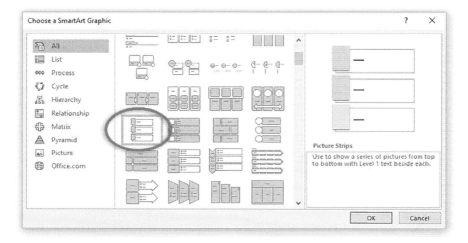

To edit the information, click in the text fields and enter your own data.

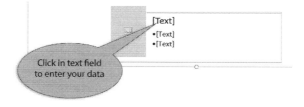

In this particular graphic, you can add images to each of the sections. To do this, double click on the image place holder.

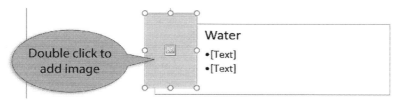

To search for images on line, select 'online pictures' from the options.

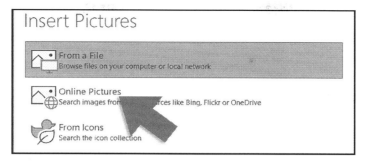

From the dialog box that appears, enter your search term. In this example, the next section is about water, so I'd type water into the search field.

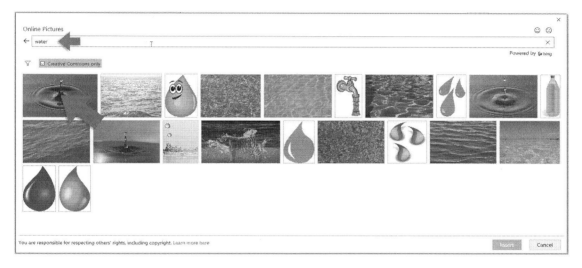

From the search results, select an image that you think best represents 'water'.

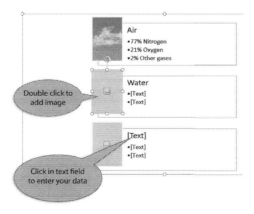

Click insert, to insert the image into the place holder.

You can also change the design of the graphic. For example, change the layout, colour, add some shadows?

To do this, click on the SmartArt graphic and select the design ribbon.

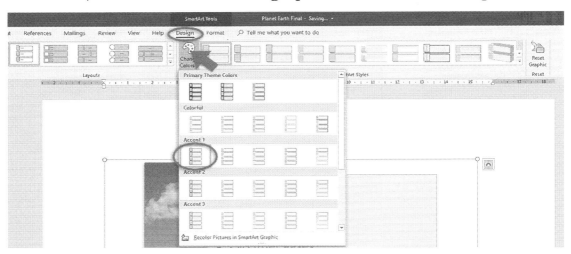

Click the 'change colour' icon and select a colour theme.

You can also change the style. Do this by selecting one of the styles in the 'style' section of the design ribbon.

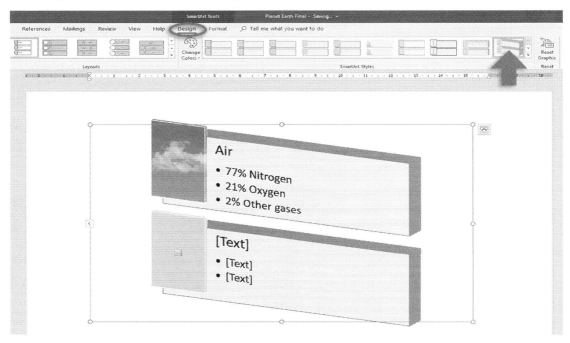

Perhaps some drop shadows to pull the images away from the text? Or even a 3D version of your graphic?

You can also change the layout, if you prefer to use a different one to the one you initially selected.

To do this, go to the layouts section of the design ribbon, and select a layout from the list.

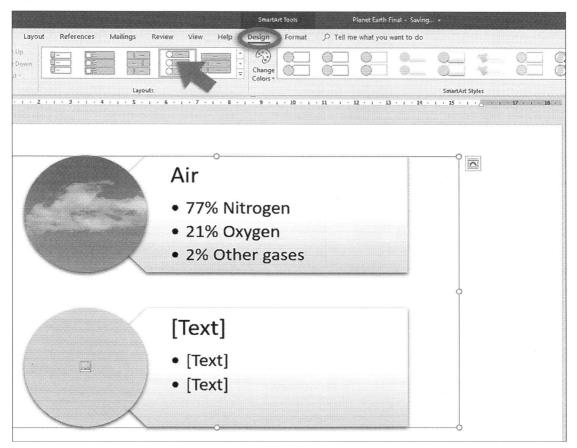

Experiment with some of the other layouts and themes.

Adding Tables

We have added some more text about world population to our document. Now we want to add a table to illustrate our text.

To insert a table click on your document where you want the table to appear. In this example, I want it to appear just below world population paragraph.   Go to your insert ribbon and select table.

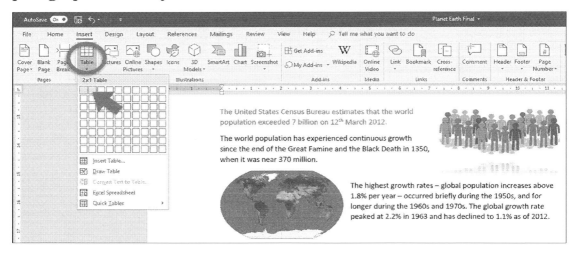

In the grid that appears highlight the number of rows and columns you want. For this table, 1 row and 2 columns.

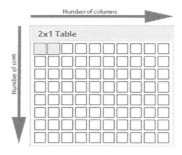

This will add a table with 1 row & 2 columns to your document.

Now just fill in the table. To move between cells on the table press the tab key. When you get to the end of the row, pressing tab will insert a new row.

Country	Population
China	1,372,000,000
India	1,276,900,000
USA	321,793,000
Indonesia	252,164,800
Brazil	204,878,000

Formatting Tables

When you click on a table in your document, two new ribbons appear under 'table tools': design and layout.

The design ribbon allows you to select pre-set designs for your table, such as column and row shading, borders, and colour. In the centre of your design ribbon, you'll see a list of designs. Click the small arrow on the bottom right of the 'table styles' panel to open it up.

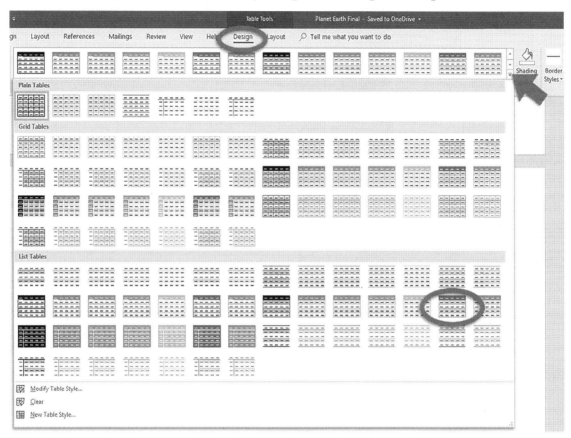

For this table, I am going to choose one with blue headings and shaded rows.

Country	Population
China	1,372,000,000
India	1,276,900,000
USA	321,793,000
Indonesia	252,164,800
Brazil	204,878,000

Add a Column

You can add a column to the right hand side of the table. To do this, click in the end column.

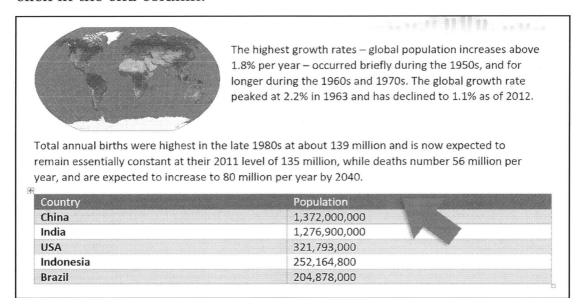

The highest growth rates – global population increases above 1.8% per year – occurred briefly during the 1950s, and for longer during the 1960s and 1970s. The global growth rate peaked at 2.2% in 1963 and has declined to 1.1% as of 2012.

Total annual births were highest in the late 1980s at about 139 million and is now expected to remain essentially constant at their 2011 level of 135 million, while deaths number 56 million per year, and are expected to increase to 80 million per year by 2040.

Country	Population
China	1,372,000,000
India	1,276,900,000
USA	321,793,000
Indonesia	252,164,800
Brazil	204,878,000

Select the layout ribbon under 'table tools', and select 'insert right'.

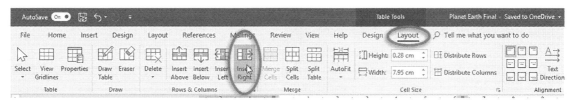

This inserts a column to the right of the one you selected.

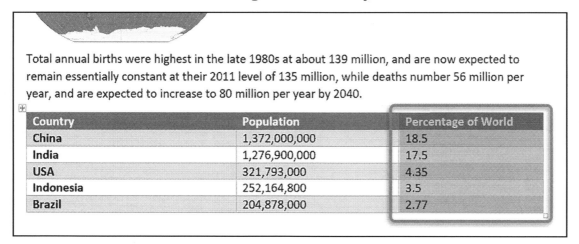

Total annual births were highest in the late 1980s at about 139 million, and are now expected to remain essentially constant at their 2011 level of 135 million, while deaths number 56 million per year, and are expected to increase to 80 million per year by 2040.

Country	Population	Percentage of World
China	1,372,000,000	18.5
India	1,276,900,000	17.5
USA	321,793,000	4.35
Indonesia	252,164,800	3.5
Brazil	204,878,000	2.77

Insert a Row

To add a row, click on the row where you want to insert. For example, I want to add a row between USA and Indonesia. So click on Indonesia, as shown below.

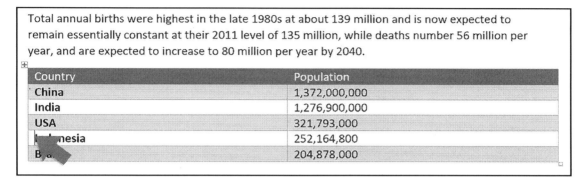

Total annual births were highest in the late 1980s at about 139 million and is now expected to remain essentially constant at their 2011 level of 135 million, while deaths number 56 million per year, and are expected to increase to 80 million per year by 2040.

Country	Population
China	1,372,000,000
India	1,276,900,000
USA	321,793,000
Indonesia	252,164,800
Brazil	204,878,000

Select the layout ribbon from the table tools section.

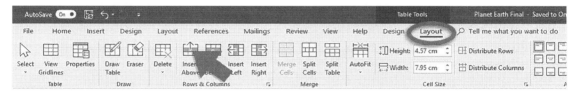

Click 'insert above'. This will insert a row above the one you selected earlier.

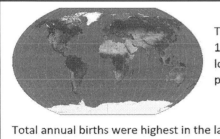

The highest growth rates – global population increases above 1.8% per year – occurred briefly during the 1950s, and for longer during the 1960s and 1970s. The global growth rate peaked at 2.2% in 1963 and has declined to 1.1% as of 2012.

Total annual births were highest in the late 1980s at about 139 million and is now expected to remain essentially constant at their 2011 level of 135 million, while deaths number 56 million per year, and are expected to increase to 80 million per year by 2040.

Country	Population
China	1,372,000,000
India	1,276,900,000
USA	321,793,000
Indonesia	252,164,800
Brazil	204,878,000

Resizing Rows & Columns

You can resize the column or row by clicking and dragging the row or column dividing line to the size you want.

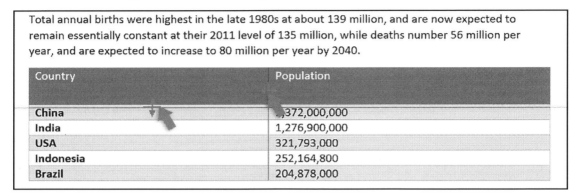

Merge Cells

You can merge cells together. To do this, select the cells you want to merge.

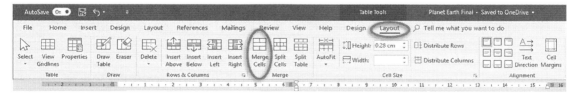

Then select 'merge cells' from the layout ribbon in the table tools section.

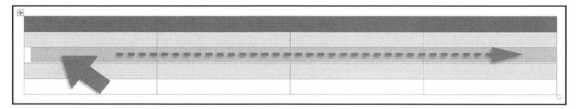

All the selected cells will be merged into a single cell.

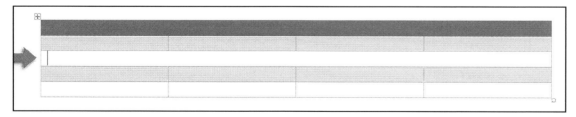

Align Cell Text

You can change text alignment in the cells of the table. To do this, select the cells you want to align. Click and drag...

Country	Population	Percentage of World
China	1,372,000,000	18.5
India	1,276,900,000	17.5
USA	321,793,000	4.35

Select the layout ribbon in the table tools section, as shown below.

From the alignment section, use the nine boxes to select the text alignment you want to apply to the cells.

Here's a quick guide to what the 9 different alignments look like. In the diagram below, note where each box on the left puts the text in the cells in the example on the right.

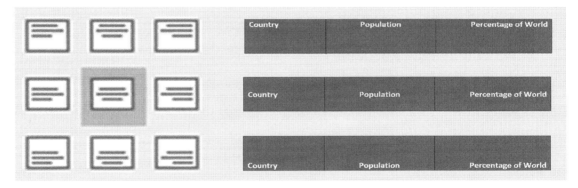

For example, select the center box to align the cells to the middle of the cell.

Country	Population	Percentage of World
China	1,372,000,000	18.5
India	1,276,900,000	17.5
USA	321,793,000	4.35
Indonesia	252,164,800	3.35
Brazil	204,878,000	2.77

Text Direction

Also you can arrange the text vertically, this usually works for headings.

To do this, select the heading rows in your table.

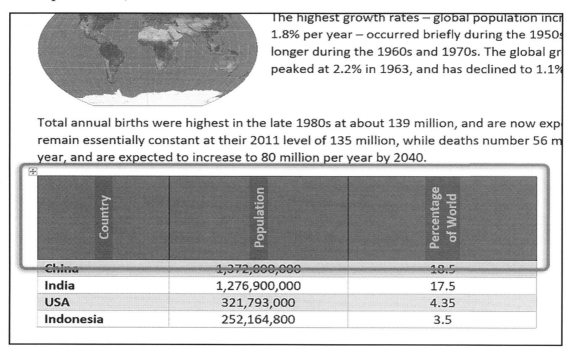

From the layout ribbon click 'text direction'.

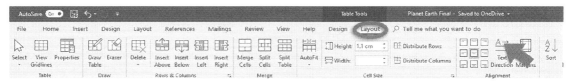

Each time you click 'text direction' the text will change orientation, so you may need to click a couple of times to get the one you want. For the example below, I had to click twice.

The highest growth rates – global population incr
1.8% per year – occurred briefly during the 1950s
longer during the 1960s and 1970s. The global gr
peaked at 2.2% in 1963, and has declined to 1.1%

Total annual births were highest in the late 1980s at about 139 million, and are now exp
remain essentially constant at their 2011 level of 135 million, while deaths number 56 m
year, and are expected to increase to 80 million per year by 2040.

Country	Population	Percentage of World
China	1,372,000,000	18.5
India	1,276,900,000	17.5
USA	321,793,000	4.35
Indonesia	252,164,800	3.5

Adding a Chart

First, click the position in your document where you want your chart to appear. This will place your cursor in that position.

To insert a chart, click the insert ribbon, circled below. From the insert ribbon, click 'chart'.

From the insert chart dialog box, select the type of chart you want to insert. In this example, I am adding a pie chart, so click 'pie' and select a style from the selections.

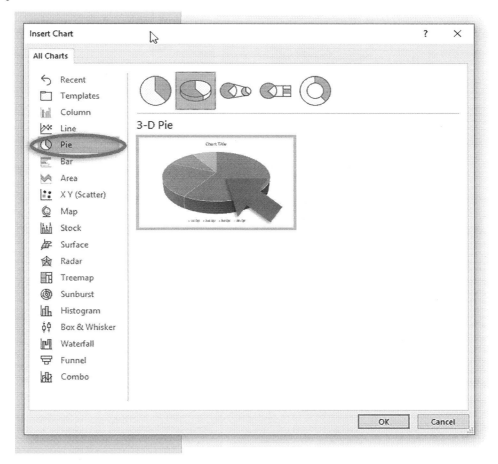

Click 'ok' when you're done.

Chapter 3: Microsoft Word

Now that we have our blank chart, we need to add some data. In this example, I want to create a chart from the population table in the previous section.

You can copy and paste the data from the table into the chart DataSheet. To do this, click your cursor just before the 'C' in country and drag your mouse across the whole table so it's highlighted. Right click on the selection, and from the popup menu select 'copy'.

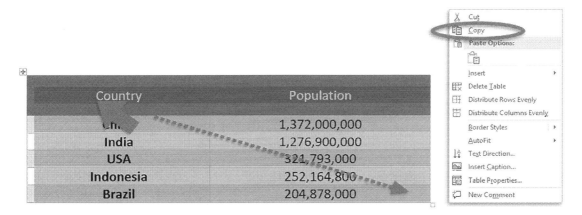

In the chart DataSheet, right click in the cell A1 and select paste.

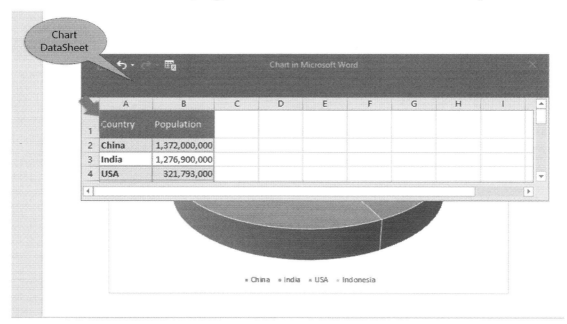

You can also type the data directly into the DataSheet.

Should you need to open up your DataSheet for your chart again, right click on your chart and select 'edit data'.

Chart Styles

To change any of the chart elements, first click on the chart to select it.

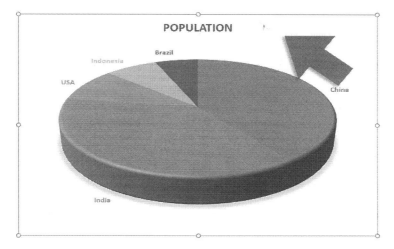

From the icons that appear, select the style icon circled below.

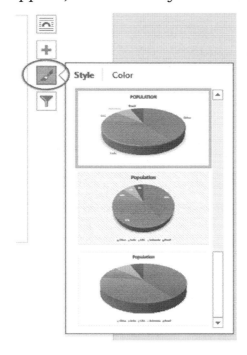

From the popup menu, select a pre-defined style.

You can select a style with a legend or with each segment of the pie chart labelled. You could have your chart with rounded edges or sharp edges, with background shading or not, to name a few examples.

Try a few out and see what they look like.

Finding a Template

When you start Word, you will see a screen containing thumbnails of different templates that are available. To find templates, click 'new' on the left hand side.

The best way to find templates is to search for them.

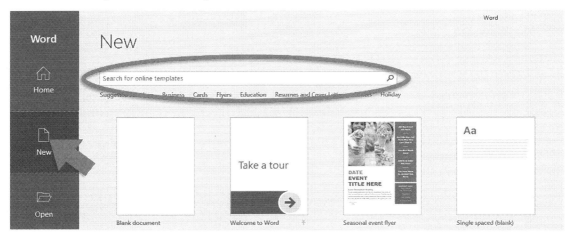

As an example, I am going to build a CV/Resume. So, in the search field I'm going to type...

`resume`

In the search results, you'll see a whole range of different styles and designs. Double click on the template you want to use.

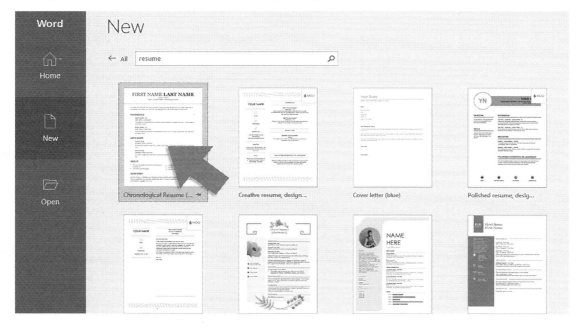

In the document that opens up, notice there are a number of fields. When you click on these fields they will be highlighted in grey. These are just place-holders where you can enter your information

FIRST NAME LAST NAME

Address · Phone
Email · LinkedIn Profile · Twitter/Blog/Portfolio

To replace this text with your own, just click it and start typing. Briefly state your career objective, or summarize what makes you stand out. Use language from the job description as keywords.

EXPERIENCE

DATES FROM – TO
JOB TITLE, COMPANY
Describe your responsibilities and achievements in terms of impact and results. Use examples, but keep it short.

DATES FROM – TO
JOB TITLE, COMPANY
Describe your responsibilities and achievements in terms of impact and results. Use examples,

Click on these and type in your information. You will also be able to fully edit the document as normal.

KEVIN WILSON

Technology Park, Liverpool, L33AF · 01234567890
office@elluminetpress.com · www.elluminetpress.com · #elluminetpress

Lorem ipsum dolor sit amet, consectetur adipiscing elit. Sed tortor ipsum, ullamcorper id viverra eget, luctus vel leo. Quisque at diam sit amet turpis egestas rhoncus ac nec justo. Praesent rutrum metus vitae mi consectetur convallis in vitae justo.

EXPERIENCE

2012 – 2018
DIRECTOR, ELLUMINET PRESS
Mauris luctus lacinia ante, vitae iaculis erat tempus vitae. Maecenas sodales facilisis nulla. Maecenas eu euismod dolor. Vestibulum interdum nibh semper, euismod tellus at, convallis enim.

DATES FROM – TO
JOB TITLE, COMPANY

Chapter 3: Microsoft Word

There are lots of different templates to choose from. Try opening some templates for flyers and brochures.

Why not try making a greeting card for someone you know?

Open Word, click 'new' on the left hand side and type...

`greeting card`

...into the search field.

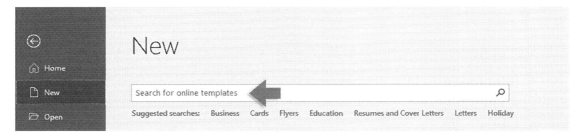

Select a template to use from the search results. How about a nice Christmas card?

Double click the template thumbnail, circled above, to open.

If you scroll down the page, you'll see some place holders where you can enter your own messages.

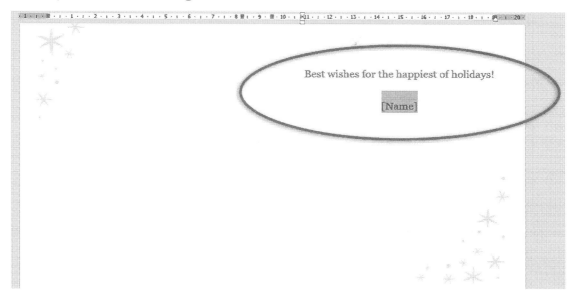

And here...

Just click on the text and enter your own.

Some of these templates need special paper and some need to be printed double sided to work. *You may need to change your printer settings to print on card or glossy paper. Check your printer instructions for specifics.*

Then just fold the printout along the lines, and you have a greeting card.

Making Your Own Template

If you have created your own style, eg heading sizes, fonts and layouts, you can save this as a template, so you can create new documents in the same style.

Before you save your document as a template, you may want to remove the content you have added, if any, and add some detail you want to appear on all your documents you create with this template, for example, the logo in the header.

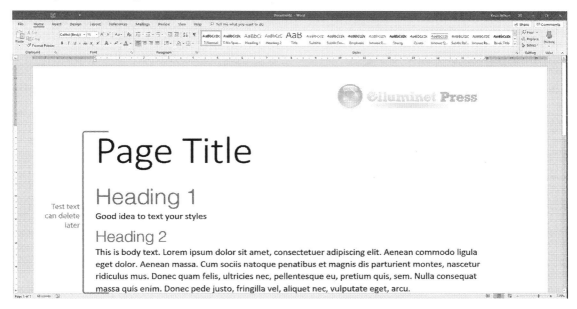

Also make sure your styles for headings and body text are as you want them. You can delete your test text before saving, leaving only what you want to appear in all documents as shown below.

Now my template is ready to save.

To save your template, click 'file' and from the backstage click 'save as'. Click 'OneDrive' or 'This PC'. At the top of the 'save as' window, click 'more options'.

In the dialog box that appears, go down to 'save as type'. Click on the drop down box to open it up. From the drop down box, click 'Word Template (.dotx)'.

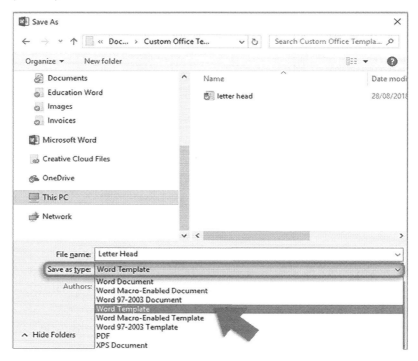

In the 'file name' field, give your template a name (eg letter head). Then click 'save'.

Note that the template is saved in

```
/Users/[your-user-name]/Library/Application Support/
Microsoft/Office/User Templates/My Templates
```

...not in your documents folders.

Create Document from Saved Template

To create a new document from your saved template, select 'new' from the backstage options, then click 'personal' to open your personal templates (the ones you have created yourself).

Double click the template thumbnail to open a new document.

Now we have a new document we can start editing.

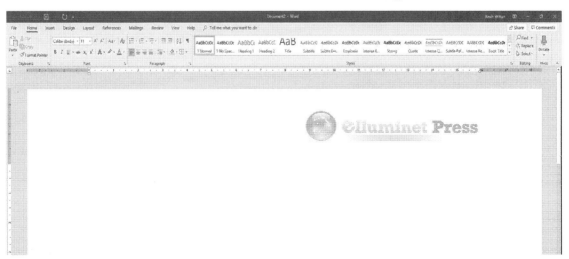

You can add your text and content in the normal way.

Printing on Envelopes

Word has templates for a large number of different size envelopes and has a feature that allows you to print your addresses in the correct position.

To start, click the mailings ribbon and select 'envelopes'

In the dialog box that appears, enter your recipient's address in 'delivery address'. If you want to include your return address, enter it in the 'return address' section, if not, click 'omit'.

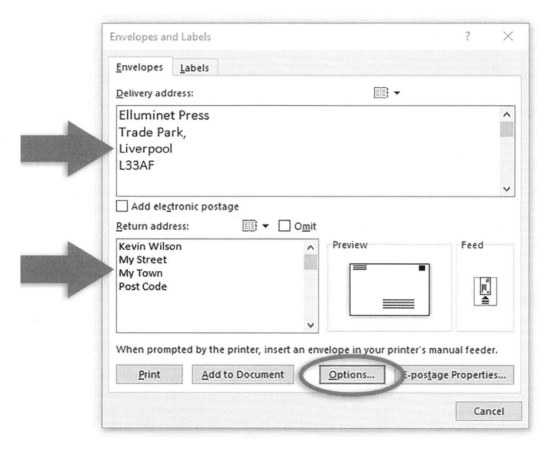

Next you'll need to select the size of your envelope. To do this, click 'options'.

From the dialog box that appears, select the size of the envelope from the drop down list. The sizes will be stated on the packet of envelopes you bought.

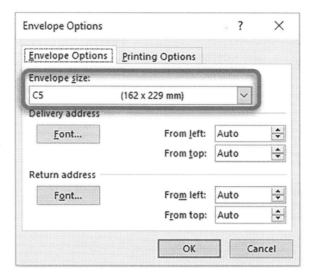

Next, click the 'printing options' tab and select the feed method your printer uses. You might have to read the instructions that came with your printer to find out.

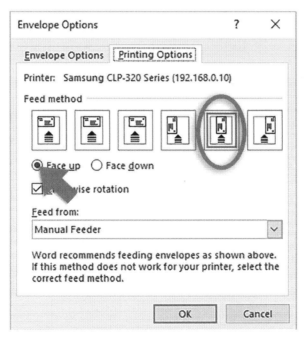

My printer feeds the envelopes from the centre of the main paper tray, face up. So I'll select the 'centre feed method' and select 'face up' option.

Click OK when you're done.

Make sure you have loaded your envelope into your printer. Again, my printer feeds envelopes centred and face up, so this is how I have loaded the envelope into the tray. Note that this particular printer has paper guides that can be moved against the edge of the envelope to keep it in place. Check with your printer instructions for details on your specific printer.

Now back at the main dialog box...

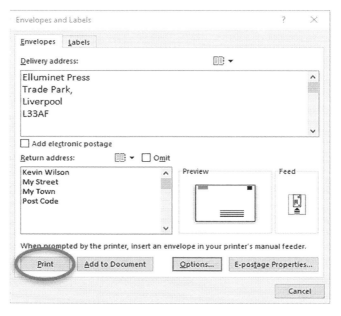

Click 'print' to print the envelope direct to your printer.

If you have a document or letter to go with the envelope, you can click 'add to document'. This will append the envelope to the top of your document.

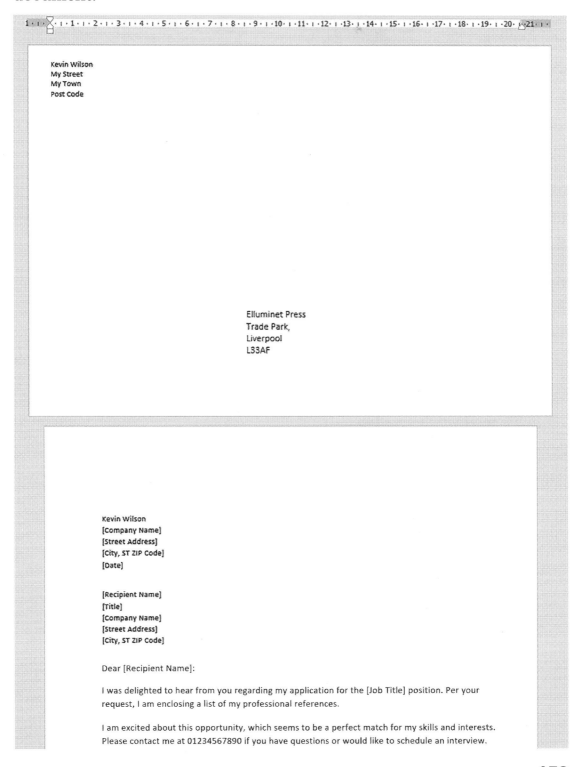

Mail Merge your Envelopes

If you have a lot of recipients, creating an envelope for each of them can be time consuming. This is where mail merge comes in handy.

First you'll need a data source. This is usually a list of names and addresses. A good place to keep names and addresses is in an excel spreadsheet. Also if you have added addresses to your Outlook 2019 contact list, you can import them from that.

I have a client list stored in an excel spreadsheet, so in this example, I will use that option. The procedure is the same if you use your Outlook contacts.

I have included some test data in a spreadsheet called Mail Merge Test Data.xlsx in the downloads section for you to practice with.

To select a data source, go to your mailings ribbon and click 'select recipients'.

From the drop down menu, click 'use an existing list...'.

In the dialog box that appears, find your data source. I'm going to select my excel spreadsheet. Mail Merge Test Data.xlsx

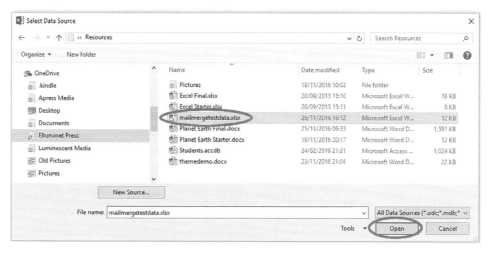

Click 'open'.

Now we can start the mail merge. You can mail merge letters, labels as well as envelopes. In this example I am going to merge envelopes.

From your mailings ribbon, click 'start mail merge' and select 'envelopes'.

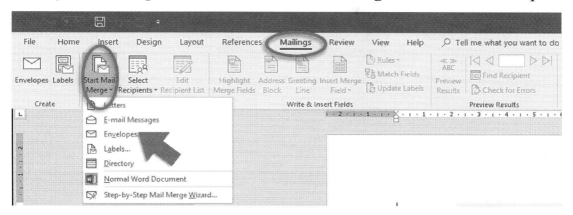

From the dialog box that appears, select the size of envelope from the 'envelope size' drop down list. The sizes are usually printed on the pack of envelopes you bought.

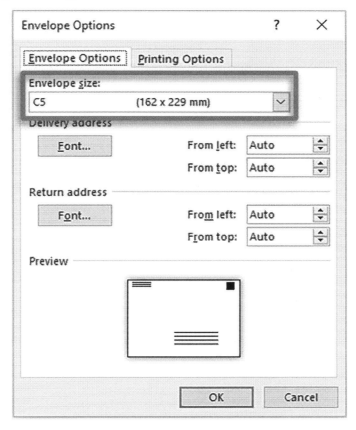

Next, click the 'printing options' tab.

Select the feed method your printer uses. You might have to read the instructions that came with your printer to find out.

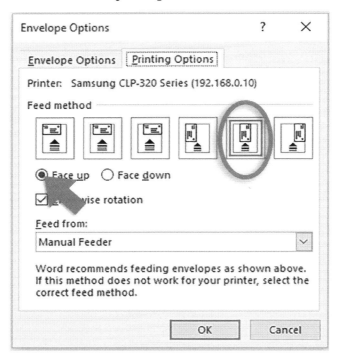

My printer feeds the envelopes from the centre of the main paper tray, face up. So I'll select the 'centre feed method' and select 'face up' option. Click OK when you're done.

Now to create your envelopes. First, find the address field in the template and click inside of it, as shown in the image below. Sometimes this is hidden but will appear once you click inside the field.

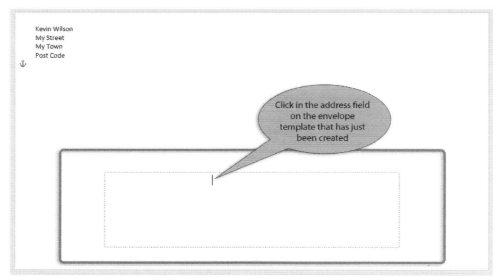

Next, from your mailings ribbon, click 'address block' to add the addresses from your contacts data source (Mail Merge Test Data.xlsx).

Click OK on the dialog box that pops up.

To preview your envelopes, from the mailings ribbon click 'preview results'. You can flip through the envelopes using the next/previous record icons.

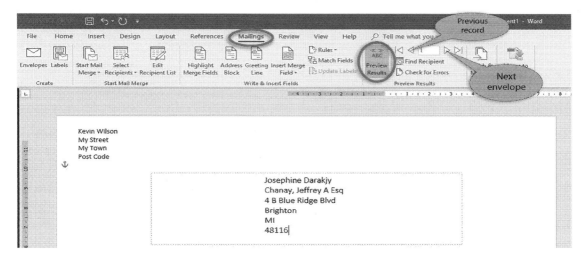

To finish off, from your mailings ribbon click 'finish & merge'. From the drop down menu, click 'print documents' to send the whole lot to the printer, make sure you have your envelopes already loaded into your printer's paper tray.

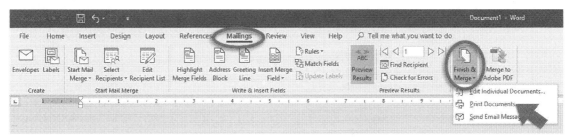

You can also click 'edit individual documents' and Word will generate a document with all your envelopes ready to print. This is useful if you want to make some changes or only print certain addresses.

Select 'all records' from the popup dialog box.

Mail Merge a Letter

Now that we have our envelopes printed, we need to write the letter. Mail merging a letter is a similar process.

First we need to write our letter. Open a blank document or use a letter template and write your letter. I have written an example below, leaving some space at the top for an address we'll add with mail merge.

Dear

We take great pleasure in welcoming your child to our school! I'm excited about the opportunity to get to know you, as well, and I'm looking forward to a happy and productive school year.

This year we will focus on the following curriculum areas:

- Maths
- English
- ICT
- Media
- Sciences
- Physical Education

If you have any questions or concerns, please contact me by email or phone. I also welcome appointments to meet in person. You can contact me on 0151 1234567 or kevin.wilson@anewschool.sch.uk.

Let's work together to make this the best year ever!

Sincerely,

Kevin Wilson
Headmaster

Now that we have our letter, we need to add some fields to address these letters to each recipient.

We need to insert their address on the top right, and their name in the first line of the letter. These names and addresses can be stored in a spreadsheet or database. Just like we did when we mail merged our envelopes, we need to select a data source.

I have included some test data in a spreadsheet called Mail Merge Test Data.xlsx in the downloads section for you to practice with.

To connect your data source, select your mailings ribbon and click 'select recipients'. From the drop down menu, select 'use an existing list'.

Then select your data file. For this example, I'm using Mail Merge Test Data.xlsx.

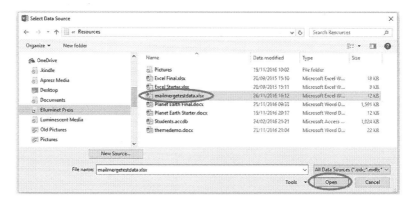

Click 'open' on the dialog box. Now we can start adding our names and addresses to the letter. Click to position your cursor where the address lines will be, eg first name followed by last name will appear top left, so click on the top left of your document to position your cursor.

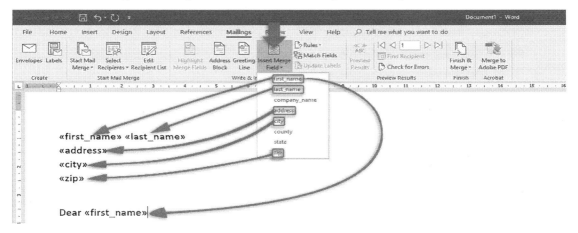

From the mailings ribbon, click 'insert merge field', then from the drop down select 'first_name', press space bar on your keyboard, then click 'insert merge field' and select 'last_name'. Press return and repeat the process to add the rest of the address.

Once you have added all the fields, from the mailings ribbon click 'preview results'. You'll get something like this (a letter for each name and address):

To finish off, from the mailings ribbon, click 'finish & merge'

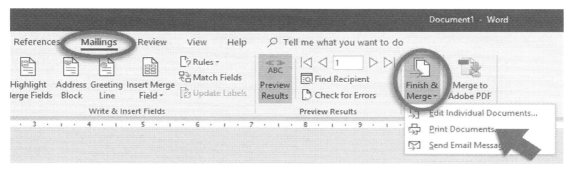

To send all letters to the printer click, 'print documents'. To open all merged letters in a document click 'edit individual documents'.

Check your Spelling & Grammar

To check your document, click the review ribbon and select 'spelling & grammar'.

You'll notice on the right hand side of your screen, Word has found a spelling issue, no grammar issues and one refinement. Refinements are intended to make your document clearer and easier to read.

To review these corrections, click on them in the list. First click 'spelling', you'll see the errors highlighted in your document.

Click on the suggested correction shown in the panel on the right hand side. If the word is a proper noun such as a place name or person's name and the spelling is correct, you can either click 'ignore all' to ignore all uses of the word, or click 'add to dictionary' to add the word to your custom dictionary.

Continuing with the spell & grammar check, Word has found some refinements to make our document clearer. Now this feature isn't 100% accurate but can give some good examples of how to word sentences more clearly. On the editor panel on the right hand side, click 'clarity and conciseness'

You'll see Word has found a better way to write the sentence. Instead of saying "a number of..." we could use the word "several", as shown below.

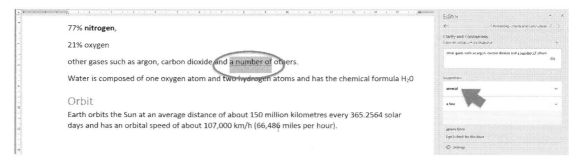

Other gases such as argon, carbon dioxide and <u>a number of</u> others

Can be changed to

Other gases such as argon, carbon dioxide and <u>several</u> others

So, select 'several' from the suggestions on the right hand side of your screen.

You can also check spelling and grammar within the document as you type. Spelling errors are underlined in red, grammar errors are underlined in blue. Possible errors or improvements are usually indicated in dark red dotted line. Notice, there are some errors below.

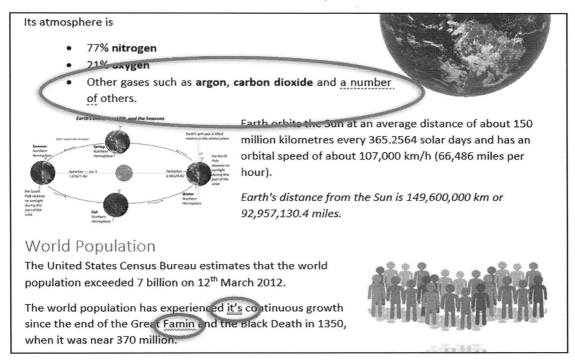

You can quickly correct these. To do this, right click your mouse on the word.

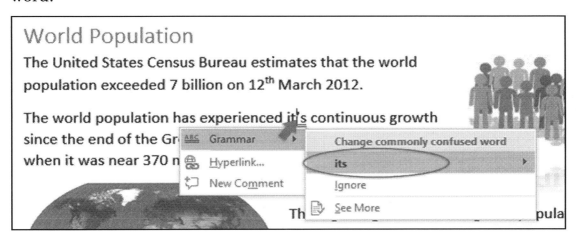

From the popup menu that appears, you'll see Word's suggestion. In this example, the word 'it's' is used instead of 'its' - word used in wrong context. Click the correct word in the suggestions and Word will make the correction.

You can do the same for spelling errors. Right click the error and select the correct word from the suggestions.

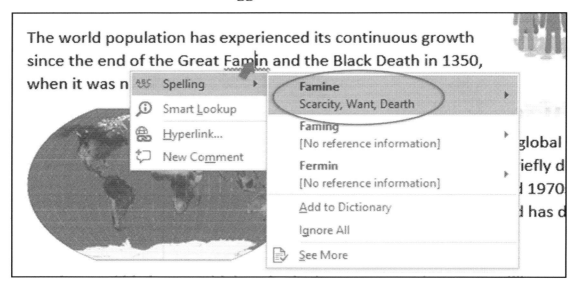

Editing your Custom Dictionary

To edit a custom dictionary, click 'file', then select 'options' from the list on the left hand side.

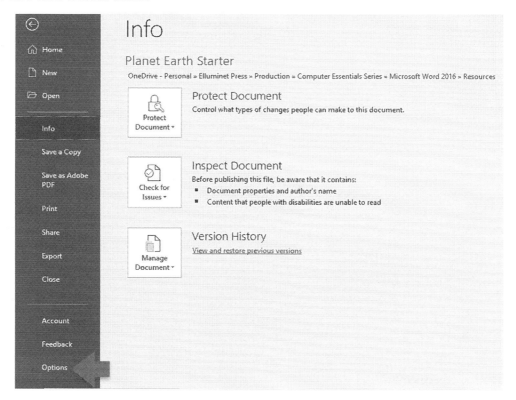

From the dialog box that appears, select 'proofing', then select 'custom dictionaries'.

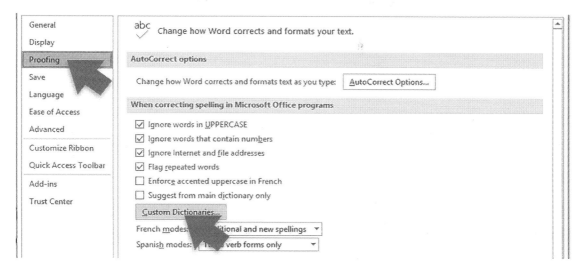

Select your custom dictionary. This is usually called 'custom.dic' or similar.

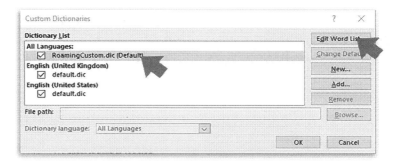

From here, you can delete words - just click the word you want to remove and click 'delete'.

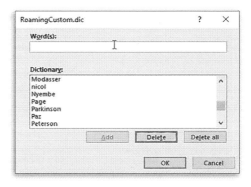

Similarly, to add a word, type the word into the field at the top of the dialog box and click 'add'. Click 'ok' when you're done.

Thesaurus

In our text, if I wanted to find a synonym for the word 'exceeded', I can do that quite easily.

To find a synonym, right click on the word you want and from the popup menu, go down to 'synonyms'.

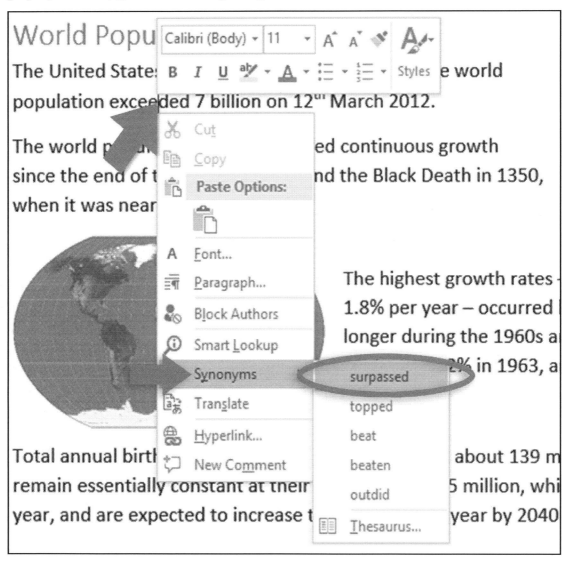

A slide out menu will appear with some suggested synonyms. Click the most appropriate one for your word.

Word will substitute the selected synonym.

Insights

With insights, you can bring information in from online sources right into Word. Word can gather information from online encyclopedias, web searches and other online sources.

You can find insights by navigating over to your references ribbon. To look something up, click on a particular key word, or highlight a name or heading and click 'smart lookup'.

The insights bar will open on the right hand side of your screen. Here you can find images and information about your search.

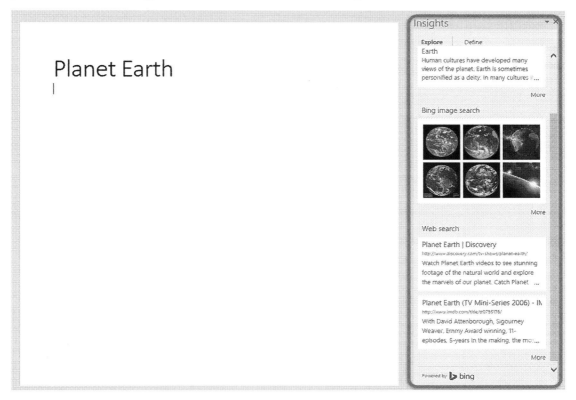

Click and drag the images to your document if you choose to use them. You can also click on the links in the web searches to view more information.

Search & Replace

You can search for any word in your document by clicking the 'find' icon on the home ribbon

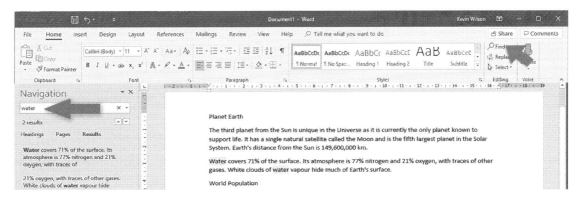

On the side bar that opens up, type the word or phrase you want to search for. In this example, I am searching for the word 'water'. You will see Word has highlighted the words it has found in yellow.

You can also replace a word or phrase. To do this click 'replace' on the home ribbon. In this document, if I wanted to replace all the words 'universe' with 'galaxy'. I'd type in 'universe' in the 'find what' field, and 'galaxy' in the 'replace with' field.

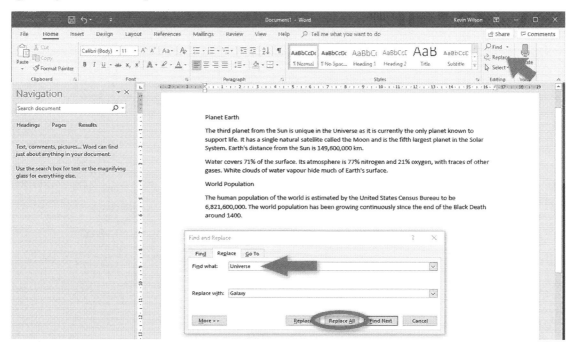

Click 'replace all' to change all the instances of the word.

Zoom Controls

You can quickly adjust your zoom using the controls on the bottom right of your screen. Shift the slider to the right to zoom in, and to the left to zoom out.

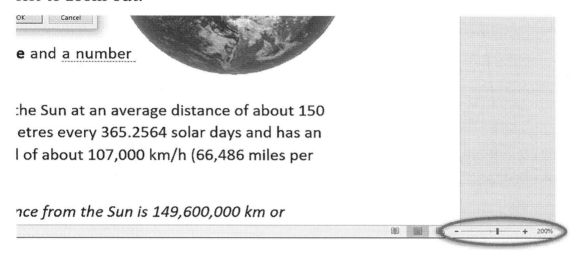

You can also zoom using the controls on the view ribbon. Click 'zoom'.

From the dialog box, select your zoom level: 100%, 200%, etc.

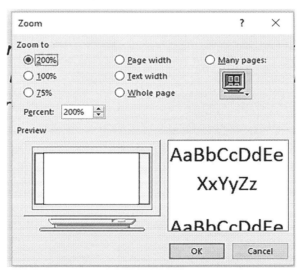

Zoom to 'page width' and 'whole document' are worth keeping in mind.

'Zoom to page width', zooms into your document to the width of the page giving you a clear view of your document and is useful for editing and reading.

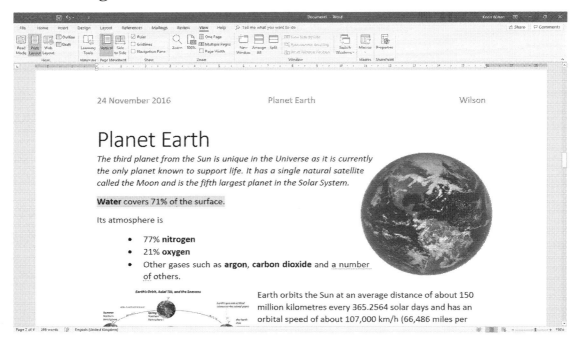

'Zoom to whole document', zooms out to show the whole document on the screen at a time. This helps when you want to see what your document looks like at full page.

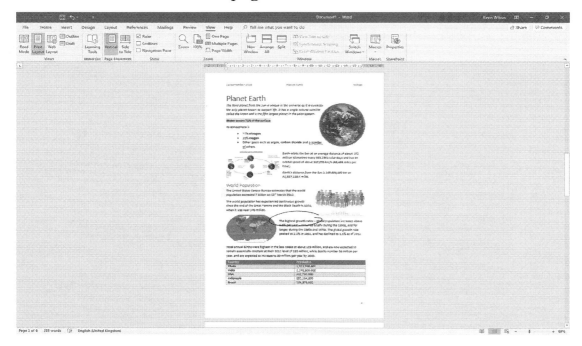

Tell Me Feature

Microsoft have added a feature to Office that allows you to search for commands and tools in any of the Office Applications.

You can find this field on the top right of the screen. Here it is pictured in Word.

Type a command in to the field. For example, if I wanted to insert a picture, type 'insert picture' into the search field.

From the drop down menu that appears, click on the command you were looking for.

This feature can be used in all the Office Apps. If you can't find the tool on the menus or ribbons, just search for it.

The Character Map

The character map is a useful tool to have open if you need to insert symbols.

You can find it if you type in...

`character map`

...into the search field on your task bar.

In the window that appears, you can search for all types of symbols. Select the font typeface from the 'fonts' field, then scroll down all the symbols. When you find the one you want, click on it and click copy.

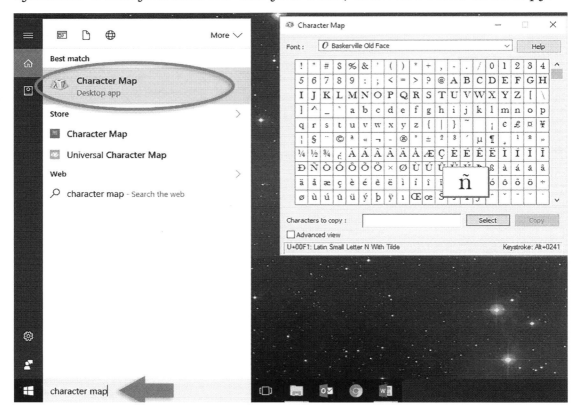

To insert the symbol into your document, open your document in Word, if you haven't already done so.

If your document is open, click the Word icon on your taskbar to switch to Word.

Click the position in the document you want the symbol to appear, go to your home ribbon and click paste.

Office Add-ins

Office has some add-on apps you can download and install directly into Word.

To do this, go to your insert ribbon and click 'get add-ins'.

From the dialog box, you can browse the most commonly downloaded apps, or you can search for specific apps, using the search field, depending on what you're trying to achieve.

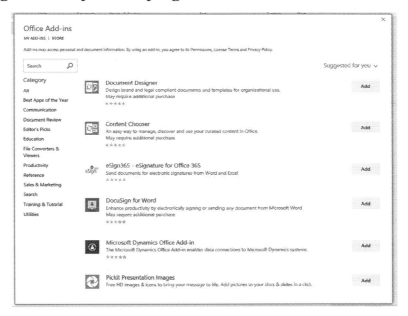

To add an app, just click 'add'.

You'll find all your office add-ins on the 'my add-ins' section. Click 'my add-ins' on the insert ribbon.

To remove any add-ins, right click, select remove from the popup menu.

Microsoft Word Pen Support

In Microsoft Word, you'll see an additional ribbon menu called 'draw'. This has all your drawing tools such as pens, highlighters and an eraser for you to annotate your Word documents.

Select the 'draw' ribbon and select a pen colour from the selections in the centre of the ribbon. From here you can select the colour and thickness of your pen.

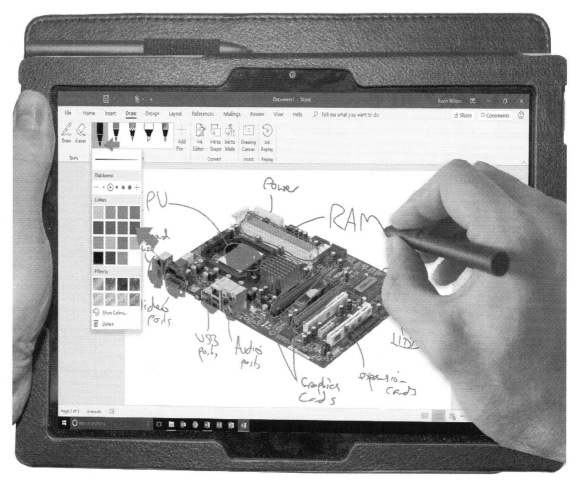

With these tools, you can draw directly onto your Word document, as shown above.

This means you can label diagrams, handwrite notes, make drawings and so on, all using your stylus or finger on your tablet.

You will then be able to save the document including all the annotations or drawings you have made.

Here you can highlight and annotate a typed Word document directly on your tablet using your stylus pen.

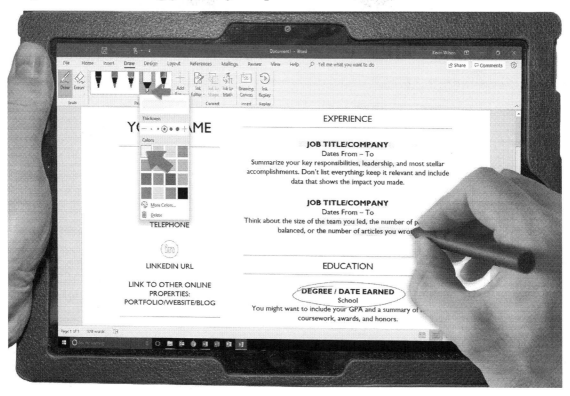

You can then save the document with all the annotations and highlights as well as share these with colleagues or friends.

Either use the share icon on the top right of your screen, or you can email the document over.

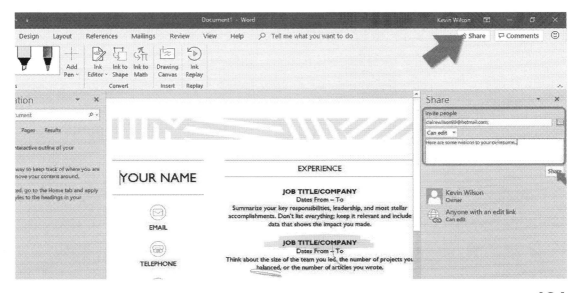

Microsoft Excel

Microsoft Excel is a spreadsheet program that allows you to store, organize, analyse and manipulate numerical data. It allows you to store and present it in tabular form or as a chart.

You can use spreadsheets to create wage slips, company accounts to analyse finance, budgets and present information.

You can create simple personal budgets to keep track of your money, and create score sheets for sports events.

You can display all your data as statistical graphs and charts as well as creating tables.

To begin lets explore what a spreadsheet is.

For this chapter, you'll need to download the resources from:

www.elluminetpress.com/office-365-3ed

What's a Spreadsheet?

A spreadsheet is made up of cells each identified by a reference. The reference is made up by using the column, eg D, and the row, eg 10

[COLUMN] [ROW]

So the highlighted cell would be D10 as illustrated below.

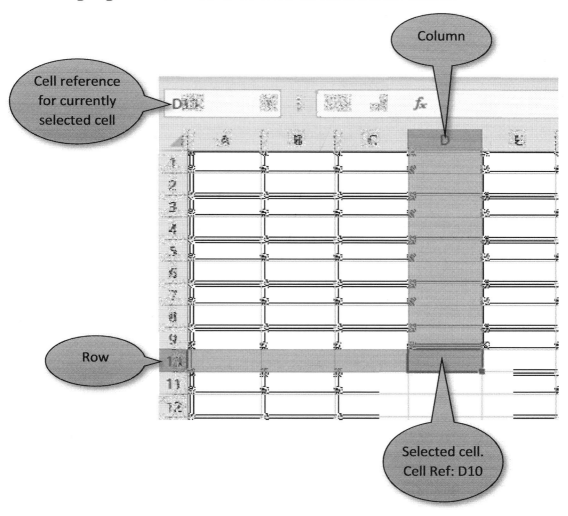

You can also select multiple cells at the same time. A group of cells is called as a cell range.

You can refer to a cell range, using the cell reference of the first cell and the last cell in the range, separated by a colon.

[FIRST CELL in RANGE] **:** [LAST CELL in RANGE]

For example, this cell range would be A1:D10 (firstcell : lastcell).

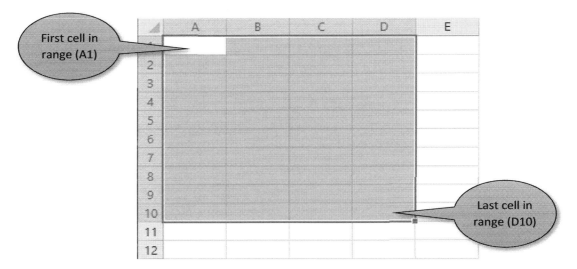

Cell references are used when you start applying functions to the numbers in your cells.

In the example below, to add two numbers together, you can enter a formula into cell C1.

Instead of typing in **=5+5** you would enter **=A1+B1**.

The theory is, if you enter the cell reference instead of the actual number, you can perform calculations automatically and Excel will recalculate all the numbers for you should you change anything.

For example, if I wanted to change it to **5+6**, I would just change the number in cell B1 without rewriting the formula in C1.

Now you can type any number in either cell A1 or B1 and it will add them up automatically.

This is a very basic example but forms the building blocks of a spreadsheet. You can use these concepts to build spreadsheets to analyse and manipulate data, as well as allow changes to the individual data and other parts of the spreadsheet without constantly changing formulas and functions.

Starting Excel

The quickest way to start Microsoft Excel is to search for it using the Cortana search field on the bottom left of your task bar. Type 'excel' into the search field. From the search results click 'excel'. You'll also find Excel on your start menu.

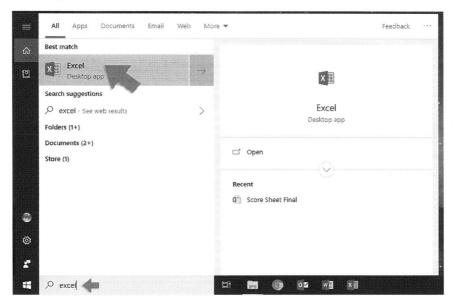

Once Excel has started, you'll land on the home screen. On the home screen, you'll see recently used templates along the top, and your most recently saved spreadsheets listed underneath.

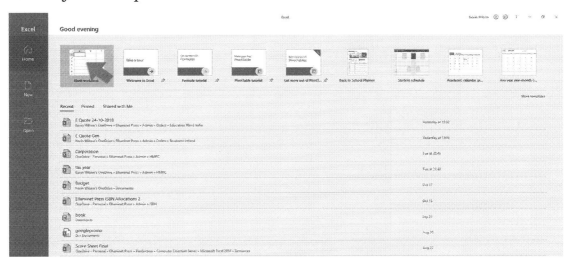

To begin, click 'blank workbook' to start. This will open up Excel with a new spreadsheet for you.

Main Screen

Once you have selected a template, you will see your main screen.

Your columns are labelled across the top of your worksheet with letters and your rows are labelled down the left hand side with numbers. These make up cell references that we'll look at later.

Across the bottom of the screen on the left hand side, you'll see some tabs. This shows you all the worksheets you have created in your workbook - you can click these to switch to that worksheet. You can create a new worksheet here, if you click the small plus icon next to the tabs.

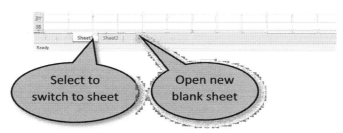

On the bottom right, you can change how Excel displays your worksheet. Grid view is your normal view as shown above, print view shows you how your spreadsheet will look when printed. Further to the right you have your zoom controls. This allows you to zoom in and out of your spreadsheet.

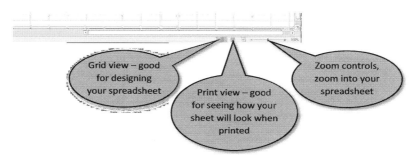

The Ribbon

All the tools used in Microsoft Excel are organised into a ribbon which is divided into ribbon tabs, each containing a specific set of tools.

The most used ribbon tabs are home, insert and formulas. For normal use of Excel, these are the ones you will be looking in the most detail.

The Home Ribbon

This is where you will find your most used tools for basic text formatting, cell borders, cell formatting for text and numbers or currency, etc.

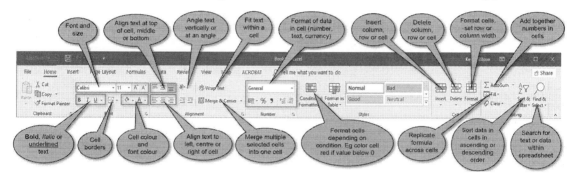

The Insert Ribbon

This is where you will find all your objects that you can insert into your spreadsheet, such as shapes, tables and charts.

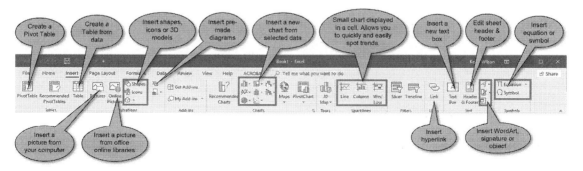

You can also insert equations and symbols, as well as pivot tables and pivot charts.

The Page Layout Ribbon

This is where you will find your page formatting functions, such as size of paper, colours & themes, paper orientation when printed, paper margins, etc.

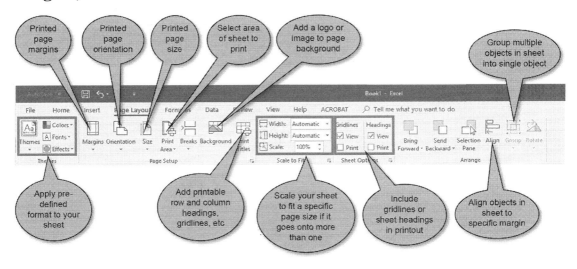

The Formulas Ribbon

This is where you will find your formulas, functions and your data manipulation tools. Sum functions, average, counting tools, etc.

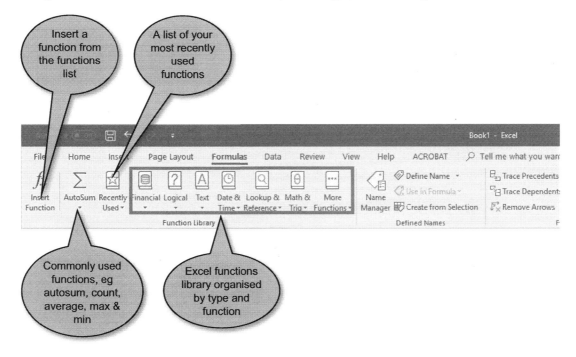

The Data Ribbon

The data ribbon is where you can find tools to connect to external data sources and databases, as well as sort data.

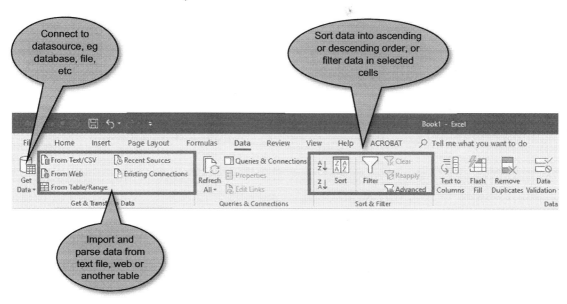

The Review Ribbon

The review ribbon has tools that allow you to add comments as well as check spelling and protect parts of the spreadsheet from making changes.

The View Ribbon

This is where you will find your view layouts, where you can zoom into your spreadsheet etc.

File Backstage

If you click 'File' on the top left of your screen, this will open up what Microsoft call the backstage.

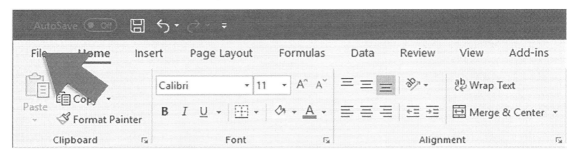

Backstage is where you open or save spreadsheets and workbooks, print, export or share workbooks, as well as options, Microsoft account and preference settings.

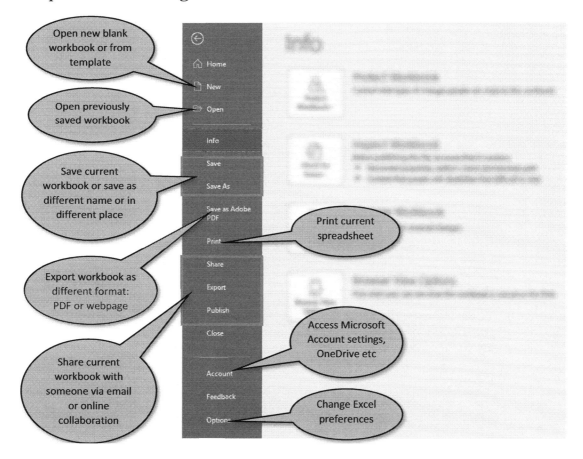

You can also change your Microsoft Account settings, log in and activate your Microsoft Office, change Excel's preferences and so on.

Getting Started

To begin creating your spreadsheet start typing your data into the different cells on the spreadsheet.

Entering Data

In this example we are doing a basic scoring sheet.

	A	B	C	D
1		22-Apr	29-Apr	Total
2	Barbara	21	19	
3	Ann	10	21	
4	Flo	7	7	
5	Rose	9	12	
6	Emily		0	
7	Josie	21	21	
8	Lin			
9	Joan	19		
10	Eva	21	14	
11				

Simple Text Formatting

Sometimes it improves the readability of your spreadsheet to format the data in the cells.

For example, make the heading rows bold.

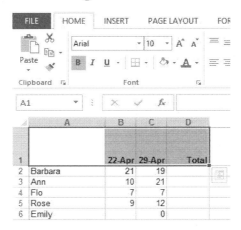

You can do this by selecting the heading row as shown above and click the bold icon.

Text Orientation

Now because the headings are quite long and take up a lot of space, you can change the orientation of the headings to read vertically instead of horizontally. This helps save space and looks better when printed on a page.

To do this, select the cells you want to change the orientation of. Then right click your mouse on the selection. From the menu that appears, select 'format cells'.

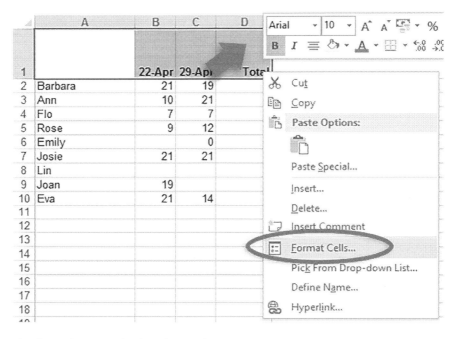

In the dialog box, click the alignment tab. From there, go to the orientation section on the right of the dialog box.

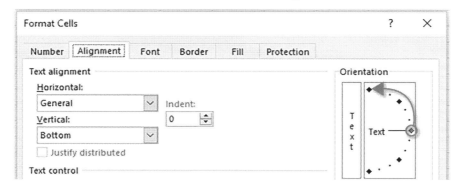

Click the horizontal point (circled above) and drag it up to the top (the vertical point). Or you can enter 90 in the degrees box.

You will see the headings are now oriented vertically.

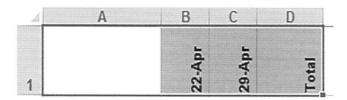

Resizing Rows and Columns

You can resize a column or row by clicking and dragging the column or row divider lines as circled below

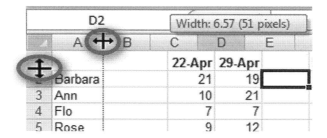

You can also double click on these lines to automatically size the row or column to the data that is in the cell.

Inserting Rows & Columns

To insert a row between Flo and Rose, right click with your mouse on the row Rose is in. In this case row 5

	A	B	C	D
		22-Apr	29-Apr	Total
1				
2	Barbara	21	19	
3	Ann	10	21	
4	Flo	7	7	
5	Rose	9	12	
6	Emily		0	
7	Josie	21	21	
8	Lin			
9	Joan	19		
10	Eva	21	14	
11				
12				

A5   *fx*   Rose

From the menu, click insert. This will insert a blank row above Rose.

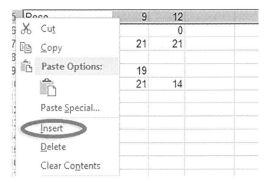

Here we can see Excel has inserted a blank row between the players Flo and Rose.

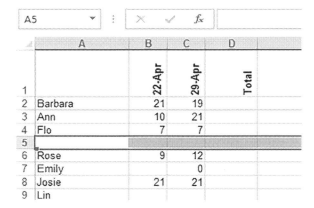

	A	B 22-Apr	C 29-Apr	D Total
1				
2	Barbara	21	19	
3	Ann	10	21	
4	Flo	7	7	
5				
6	Rose	9	12	
7	Emily		0	
8	Josie	21	21	
9	Lin			

Remember, the new row is always added above the one selected, and a new column is always added before the one selected.

To insert a column it is exactly the same procedure, except you select a column instead of a row.

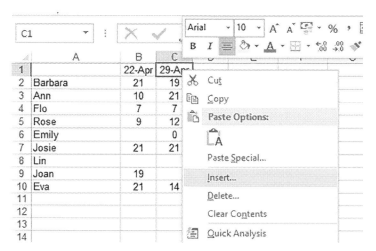

Cut, Copy & Paste

You can copy and paste a cell or cell range and paste it into another worksheet/workbook or in a different location on the same worksheet.

For this example, open **Score Sheet Final.xlsx**. To perform a basic copy, select the cells you want to copy, and from your home ribbon, click copy.

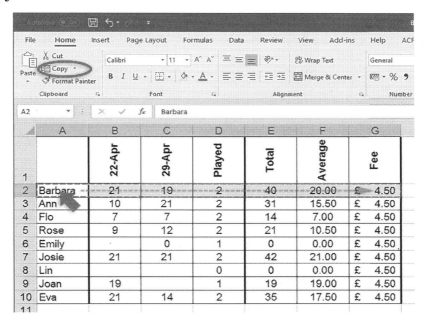

Click the cell where you want the cells to be copied to. I'm going to paste the cells at the end of the table. From your home ribbon, click paste.

	22-Apr	29-Apr	Played	Total	Average	Fee
Barbara	21	19	2	40	20.00	£ 4.50
Ann	10	21	2	31	15.50	£ 4.50
Flo	7	7	2	14	7.00	£ 4.50
Rose	9	12	2	21	10.50	£ 4.50
Emily		0	1	0	0.00	£ 4.50
Josie	21	21	2	42	21.00	£ 4.50
Lin			0	0	0.00	£ 4.50
Joan	19		1	19	19.00	£ 4.50
Eva	21	14	2	35	17.50	£ 4.50
Barbara	21	19	2	40	20.00	£ 4.50

By default, Excel pastes everything copied from the selected cells. Sometimes you only want to paste certain things, such as formatting, or just the text or just the formulas. You can do this with the 'paste special' feature.

To find 'paste special', click the small down arrow under the 'paste' icon, on your home ribbon. You'll see a drop down menu with a few options, shown in the illustrations below.

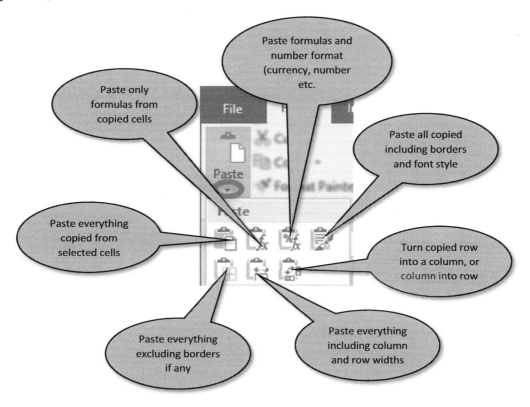

To paste only the formulas, click the second icon across (*fx*).

If you just wanted the values, look further down the drop down menu to the values section, and click '123'.

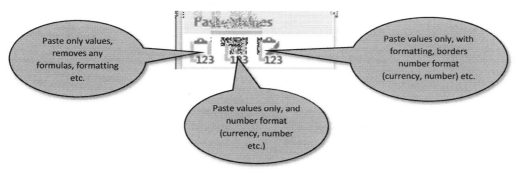

Finally, if you just wanted the formatting, such as the cell borders and number formatting (currency, number, text etc.), then further down the drop down menu, you'll find the 'other paste options' section. To only paste the formatting, click the first option (%).

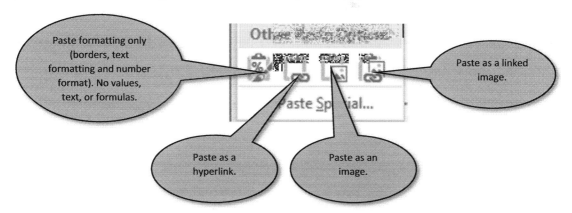

Paste formatting only (borders, text formatting and number format). No values, text, or formulas.

Paste as a linked image.

Paste as a hyperlink.

Paste as an image.

Paste as link can be useful if you are copying and pasting values from a different worksheet to a summarised table. The pasted cells are linked to the copied cells. So if you change the values in the copied cells, they will change in the pasted cells.

	A	B 22-Apr	C 29-Apr	D Played	E Total	F Average	G Fee
1							
2	Barbara	3	19	2	22	11.00	£ 4.50
3	Ann	10	21	2	31	15.50	£ 4.50
4	Flo	7	7	2	14	7.00	£ 4.50
5	Rose	9	12	2	21	10.50	£ 4.50
6	Emily		0	1	0	0.00	£ 4.50
7	Josie	21	21	2	42	21.00	£ 4.50
8	Lin			0	0	0.00	£ 4.50
9	Joan	19		1	19	19.00	£ 4.50
10	Eva	21	14	2	35	17.50	£ 4.50
11							
12							
13	Barbara	3	19	2	22	11	4.5

Using 'cut' is exactly the same, except select 'cut' from the home ribbon, instead of copy. The cut command moves the selected cells rather than copying them.

Sorting Data

To quick sort your data, click on a cell in the column you want to sort the data by. In this example, I want to sort the data by total score so I can see who won this year's player of the year.

Click in the 'total' column. Make sure you click one of the numbers as we want to sort the data, not the title.

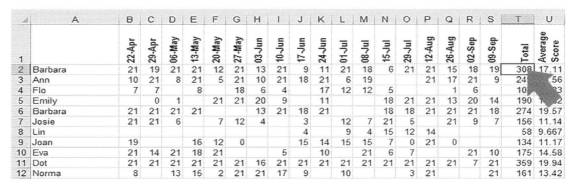

	A	B	C	D	E	F	G	H	I	J	K	L	M	N	O	P	Q	R	S	T	U
1		22-Apr	29-Apr	06-May	13-May	20-May	27-May	03-Jun	10-Jun	17-Jun	24-Jun	01-Jul	08-Jul	15-Jul	29-Jul	12-Aug	26-Aug	02-Sep	09-Sep	Total	Average Score
2	Barbara	21	19	21	21	12	21	13	21	9	11	21	18		6	21	21	15	18	19	308	17.11
3	Ann	10	21	8	21	5	21	10	21	18	21	6	19			21	17	21	9		24	56
4	Flo	7	7		8		18	6	4		17	12	12	5			1	6			10	3
5	Emily		0	1		21	21	20	9		11			18	21	21	13	20	14		190	2
6	Barbara	21	21	21	21			13	21	18	21			18	18	21	21	21	18		274	19.57
7	Josie	21	21	6		7	12	4		3		12	7	21	5		21	9	7		156	11.14
8	Lin									4		9	4	15	12	14					58	9.667
9	Joan	19			16	12	0		15	14	15	15	7	0	21	0					134	11.17
10	Eva	21	14	21	18	21		5		10		21	6	7			21	10			175	14.58
11	Dot	21	21	21	21	21	21	16	21	21	21	21	21	21	21	21	21	7	21		359	19.94
12	Norma	8		13	15	2	21	21	17	9		10			3	21			21		161	13.42

From your home ribbon, click 'sort & filter'. From the drop down menu, click 'Largest to Smallest' (descending order), as we want the highest score listed first.

Looks like Dot won this one...

	A	B	C	D	E	F	G	H	I	J	K	L	M	N	O	P	Q	R	S	T	U				
1		22-Apr	29-Apr	06-May	13-May	20-May	27-May	03-Jun	10-Jun	17-Jun	24-Jun	01-Jul	08-Jul	15-Jul	29-Jul	12-Aug	26-Aug	02-Sep	09-Sep	Total	Average Score	Highest Score	Lowest Score	Played	Won	Lost
2	Dot	21	21	21	21	21	21	16	21	21	21	21	21	21	21	21	21	7	21	359	19.94	21	7	18	16	2
3	Cathy	21	21	21	21	21	21	21	21	13	21	21	21	21	21	21	21	21	9	358	19.89	21	9	18	16	2
4	Barbara	21	19	21	21	12	21	13	21	9	11	21	18	6	21	21	15	18	19	308	17.11	21	6	18	8	10
5	Shirley		20	21	14	13	21	21	16	21	18	21	21		21	21	21	21	21	291	19.4	21	13	15	10	5
6	Barbara	21	21	21	21			13	21	18	21		18	18	21	21	21	21	18	274	19.57	21	13	14	9	5
7	Ann	10	21	8	21	5	21	10	21	18	21	6	19		21	17	21	9		249	15.56	21	5	16	7	9
8	Emily		0	1		21	21	20	9		11		18	21	21	13	20	14		190	14.62	21	0	13	4	9
9	Eva	21	14	21	18	21		5		10		21	6	7		21	10			175	14.58	21	5	12	5	7
10	Norma	8		13	15	2	21	21	17	9		10		3	21		21			161	13.42	21	2	12	4	8
11	Josie	21	21	6		7	12	4		3		12	7	21	5		21	9	7	156	11.14	21	3	14	4	10
12	Joan	19			16	12	0		15	14	15	15	7	0	21	0				134	11.17	21	0	12	1	11
13	Flo	7	7		8		18	6	4		17	12	12	5			1	6		103	8.583	18	1	12	0	12
14	Lin									4		9	4	15	12	14				58	9.667	15	4	6	0	6

The procedure is the same for 'smallest to largest' (ascending order), except click 'Smallest to Largest' from the drop down menu.

Formatting your Spreadsheet

To emphasise certain parts of your spreadsheet such as totals or headings you can apply borders and shading to cells or groups of cells.

Cell Alignment

This helps to align your data inside your cells and make it easier to read. To do this highlight the cells you want to apply the alignment to, then select 'centre' from the alignment icons highlighted above. The top three align vertically in the cell, the bottom three align horizontally in the cell.

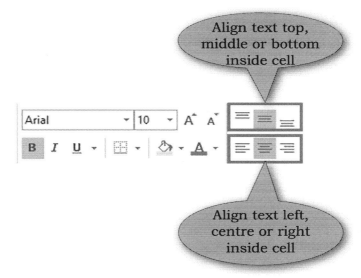

Align text top, middle or bottom inside cell

Align text left, centre or right inside cell

Text Format

As well as aligning the text inside your cell, you can apply bold or italic effects to make certain parts such as headings stand out.

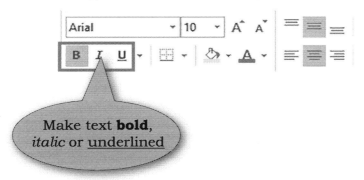

Make text **bold**, *italic* or <u>underlined</u>

You can also change the font and size.

To do this in our spreadsheet highlight the headings ('22-Apr' to 'Fee Paid') and then click the bold icon highlighted below.

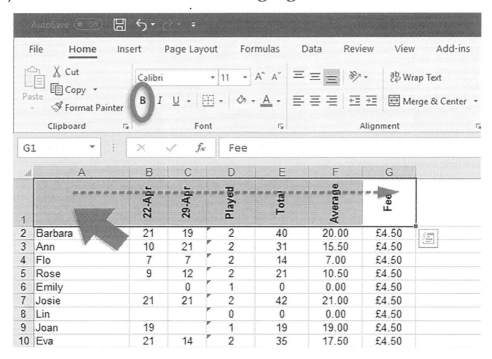

To align your text in the cells in the centre, select the cells you want then click the centre icon as highlighted below. *The top three icons align the text vertically, and the bottom three icons align the text horizontally.*

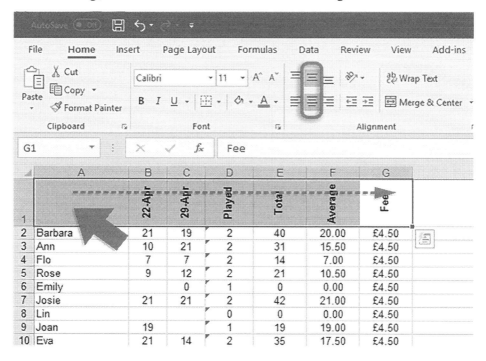

Cell Borders

To apply borders to your spreadsheet, select with your mouse the cells you want to format. In this case, I am going to do the whole table. Right click on the selected cells and select 'format cells' from the menu.

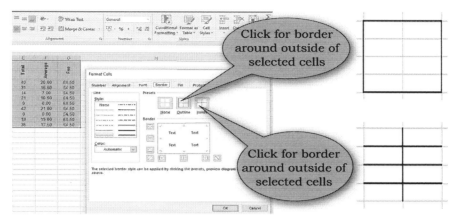

I want the borders around all the cells both inside and the outline. So from the dialog box click 'outline' & 'inside'.

Now you can tweak the borders around the cells. It would make our spreadsheet easier to read if we divided the table into sections. Player name can be one section, scores can be the second section, total, average, and fee can be the third section. We can divide the table with a thicker line. First, highlight the total, average and fee paid columns, because this is one section. Right click, select 'format cells'.

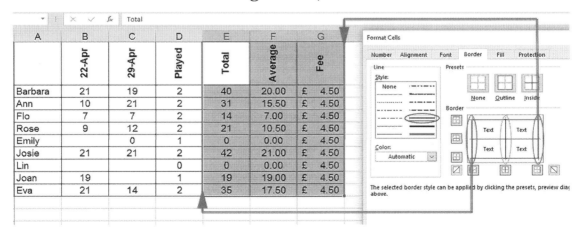

From the dialog box, under the style section, select the size of your line, circled above in blue. Under the 'border section', select the left line and the right line, circled in red above, to apply the border to these edges.

Do this with the player names column too.

First, highlight the column as shown below. Right click on the grey selection and select 'format cells' from the menu...

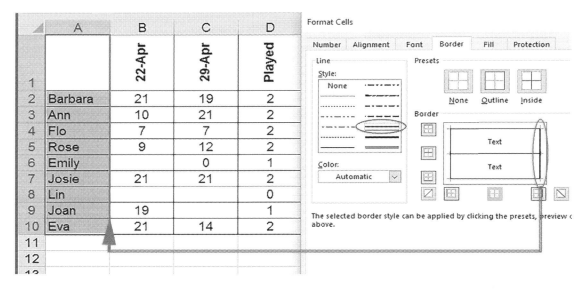

From the 'style' section of the dialog box, select the style of line, eg dotted line, solid line, thick line etc. I'm going to click the thicker line in this example, circled above in blue.

Then from the 'border section', select the right line, circled in red above, to apply the border to the right edge of the selected column.

You can quickly apply borders using the borders icon on the home ribbon. This allows you to apply common border presets. Select your cells, then click the small down arrow next to the borders icon, indicated with the red arrow below, to reveal the drop down menu.

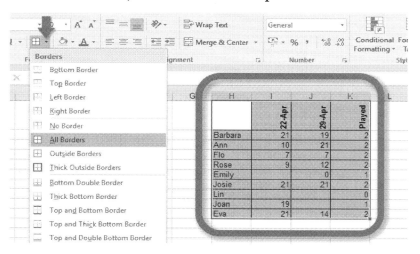

From the drop down menu select the border you want.

Opening a New Sheet

Within your excel workbook, you can open more then one spreadsheet. To do this, click the '+' icon on the bottom left of your screen.

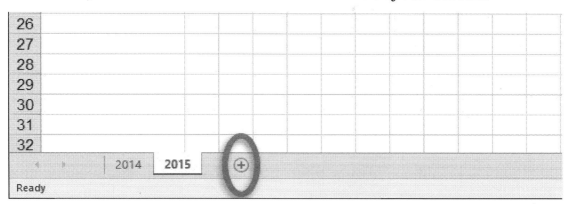

You'll see another blank tab appear along the bottom

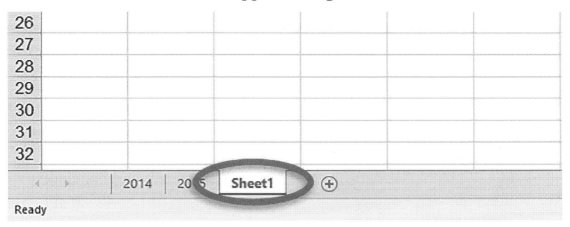

Double click on the name of the sheet, 'sheet1' in this case, and enter a meaningful name.

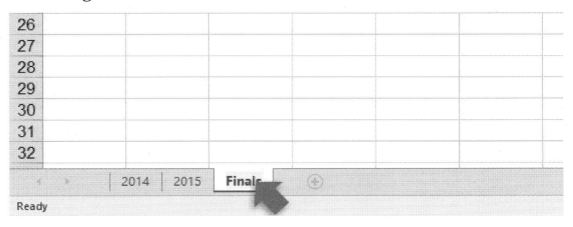

Copy Data Between Sheets

You can copy data between sheets using simple copy and paste. This works with simple data such as a name or number.

If you have formulas in the cells you want to copy, this poses more of a problem, as standard copy and paste will only copy the formula itself and you will get a "!REF" error. To get around this problem, you need to use the paste link feature.

To demonstrate this, I'm going to copy the list of names using standard copy and paste from one sheet to another. We're going to use the sample **Score Sheet Final.xlsx**.

First highlight the list of names.

	A	22-Apr	29-Apr	06-May	13-May	20-May	27-May	03-Jun	10-Jun	17-Jun	24-Jun	01-Jul	08-Jul	15-Jul	29-Jul	12-Aug
		B	C	D	E	F	G	H	I	J	K	L	M	N	O	P
2	Barbara	21	19	21	21	12	21	13	21	9	11	21	18	6	21	21
3	Ann		21	8	21	5	21	10	21	18	21	6	19			21
4	Flo		7		8		18	6	4			17	12	12	5	
5	Emily		0	1			21	21	20	9		11		18	21	21
6	Barbara	21	21	21	21			13	21	18	21			18	18	21
7	Josie	21	21	6		7	12	4		3		12	7	21	5	
8	Lin									4		9	4	15	12	14
9	Joan	19			16	12	0			15	14	15	15	7	0	21
10	Eva	21	14	21	18	21			5			10		21	6	7
11	Dot	21	21	21	21	21	21	16	21	21	21	21	21	21	21	21
12	Norma	8		13	15	2	21	21	17	9		10			3	21
13	Shirley		20	21	14	13	21	21	16	21	18	21	21			21
14	Cathy	21	21	21	21	21	21	21	21	13	21	21	21	21	21	21

From the home ribbon, select 'copy'.

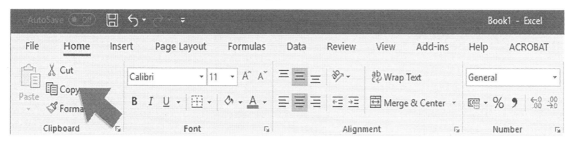

Switch to the other sheet. Select the tab along the bottom of the screen.

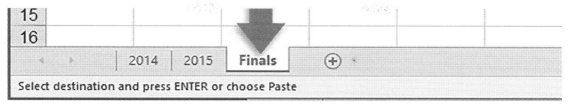

Select cell A1 (where you want the names to appear).

Select 'paste' from the home ribbon.

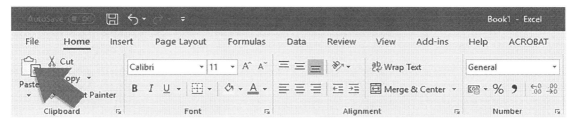

Now, I want to add a second column to contain the total scores. I don't just want to copy the values, I want to copy the formulas, so the values update as the spreadsheet is updated.

	A	B	C
1	Barbara		
2	Ann		
3	Flo		
4	Emily		
5	Barbara		
6	Josie		
7	Lin		
8	Joan		
9	Eva		
10	Dot		
11	Norma		

To do this, go back to the '2015' sheet, in the example workbook **Score Sheet Final.xlsx**.

Highlight the totals as shown below and select copy from the home ribbon.

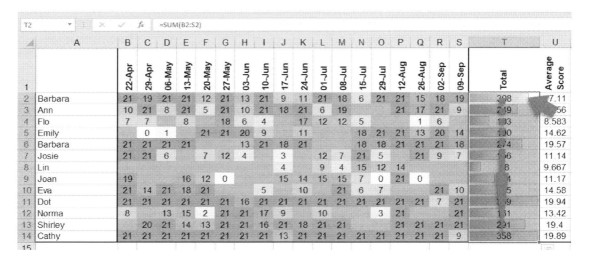

	A	22-Apr	29-Apr	06-May	13-May	20-May	27-May	03-Jun	10-Jun	17-Jun	24-Jun	01-Jul	08-Jul	15-Jul	29-Jul	12-Aug	26-Aug	02-Sep	09-Sep	Total	Average Score
2	Barbara	21	19	21	21	12	21	13	21	9	11	21	18	6	21	21	15	18	19	308	7.11
3	Ann	10	21	8	21	5	21	10	21	18	21	6	19			21	17	21	9	249	56
4	Flo	7	7		8		18	6	4		17	12	12	5			1	6		103	8.583
5	Emily		0	1		21	21	20	9		11			18	21	21	13	20	14	190	14.62
6	Barbara	21	21	21	21			13	21	18	21			18	18	21	21	21	18	274	19.57
7	Josie	21	21	6		7	12	4		3		12	7	21	5		21	9	7	156	11.14
8	Lin									4		9	4	15	12	14				8	9.667
9	Joan	19			16	12	0			15	14	15	15	7	0	21	0			4	11.17
10	Eva	21	14	21	18	21		5			10		21	6	7			21	10	5	14.58
11	Dot	21	21	21	21	21	21	16	21	21	21	21	21	21	21	21	21	7	21	109	19.94
12	Norma	8		13	15	2	21	21	17	9		10			3	21			21	151	13.42
13	Shirley		20	21	14	13	21	21	16	21	18	21	21			21	21	21	21	291	19.4
14	Cathy	21	21	21	21	21	21	21	21	13	21	21	21	21	21	21	21	21	9	358	19.89

Switch to your other sheet: 'finals' and select the cell you want the values to start. In this case cell B1.

Click the down arrow under the 'paste' icon and select 'paste special'.

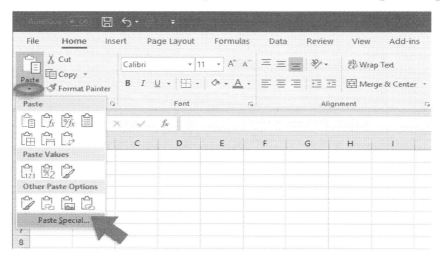

From bottom left of the dialog box select 'paste link'.

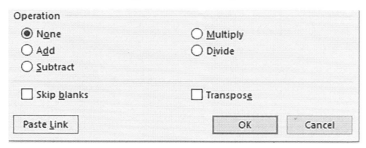

Freeze Panes

Large tables or long lists of data can often be difficult to read on a computer screen, sometimes scrolling down the list you can lose track of headings. To combat this, Excel has a feature that allows you to freeze a row or column, meaning the row/column will be on the screen at all times while you scroll down or across your screen. This is called 'freeze panes'.

If we have a look at our imported bank statement, **statement final.xls**, from the previous section, the list is quite long. Download and use the file **statement example.xls** if you haven't done the previous section.

It would be far easier to read if we froze the top row. To do this, go to your view ribbon and click 'freeze panes'. From the drop down menu, select 'freeze top row'. The top row of the list contains the headings.

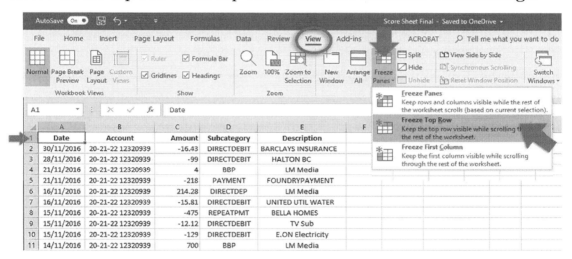

Now when you scroll down the list, the top row remains visible.

You can do the same with the first column. Click 'freeze first column' instead, from the drop down menu.

In the score sheet example, if I wanted the column with the player names as well as the dates to remain visible, you can do this with freeze panes.

I have included the file **score sheet final.xls** for you to practice with. You can download the file from

www.elluminetpress.com/office-365-3ed

When you click 'freeze panes' from the 'freeze panes' drop down menu, Excel will apply the freeze to the <u>rows above</u> and the <u>columns to the left</u> of the cell you have selected.

	22-Apr	29-Apr	06-May	13-May	20-May	27-May	03-Jun	10-Jun	17-Jun	24-Jun	01-Jul	08-Jul
Barbara	21	19	21	21	12	21	13	21	9	11	21	18
Ann	10	21	8	21	5	21	10	21	18	21	6	19
Flo	7	7		8		18	6	4		17	12	12
Emily		0	1		21	21	20	9		11		
Barbara	21	21	21	21			13	21	18	21		
Josie	21	21	6		7	12	4		3		12	7
Lin									4		9	4
Joan	19			16	12	0			15	14	15	15

So in the example below, I have selected the cell B2 because I want to freeze the row above this cell (the dates), and freeze the column to the left of the cell (the names), as you can see in the screen print below.

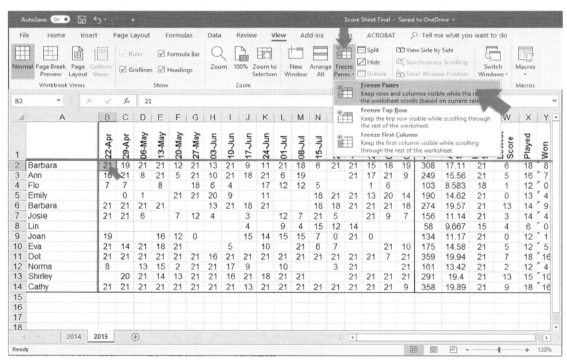

Once you have selected the cell. From your view ribbon, click 'freeze panes' then from the drop down menu click 'freeze panes'.

Importing Data

You can import data into Excel. These could be lists of names and addresses or bank statement data you can download from your Bank. Make sure you download your data as comma separated, either a TXT file or CSV file.

You can import the data using Excel's import wizard. As an example, I have included some test data from a sample bank statement for you to practice with.

You can download the test data file **statement test data.csv** from

www.elluminetpress.com/office-365-3ed

To import the data, open a new spreadsheet and from the data ribbon, click 'From Text/CSV'.

In the dialog box that appears, select your data file. In this example **statement test data.csv**.

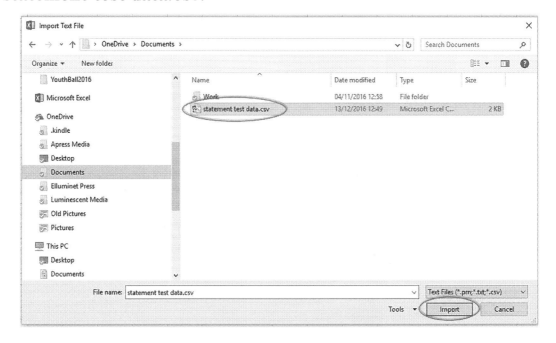

When you have done that, click import.

Now you have to tell Excel how your data is 'delimited' or separated from each other. To show you what this means, if we open the file in notepad, you can see we have a list of transactions. The data in each transaction in the list is separated or 'delimited' with a comma: Date, Account Number, Amount, Sub Category, Description.

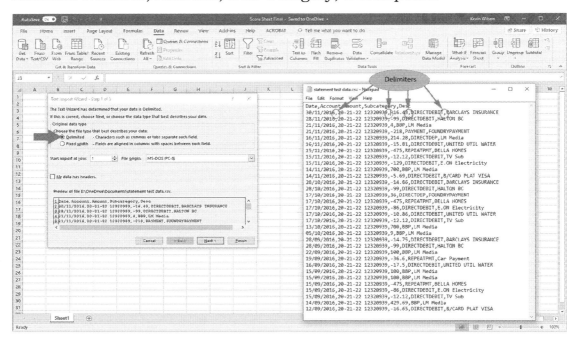

So in the dialog box, select 'delimited' and click next.

The data is separated, or delimited by a comma. So in the 'delimiters' section, uncheck 'tab' and click the check box next to 'comma'.

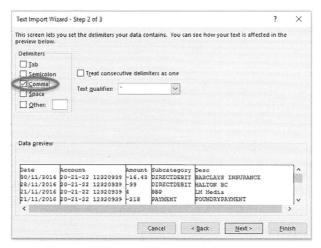

Notice the data in the preview has now been separated into Excel columns. Click 'finish'.

Select the first cell where you want to insert the data. Cell A1 is usually a good start on a blank sheet.

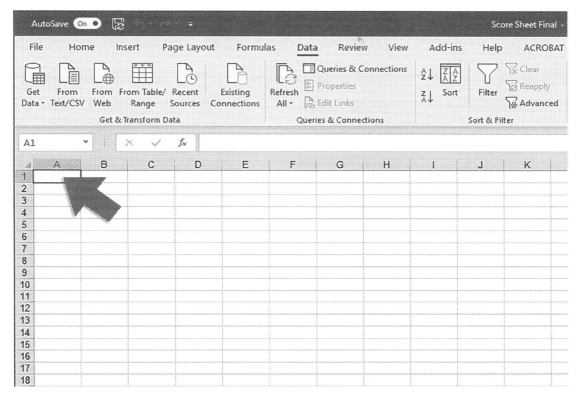

If you want the data to be imported into a new worksheet, just click the radio button next to 'new worksheet' at the bottom of the dialog box.

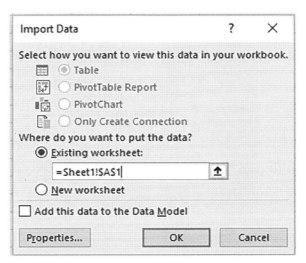

Click OK when you're done.

Save your spreadsheet as **statement final.xls**

Conditional Formatting

Conditional formatting allows you to change the format of a cell depending on the cell's contents or value. For example, in our score sheet, I want to highlight all the wins for each player. In this particular sport a score of 21 is a win, so we can apply some conditional formatting to change the colour of each cell with the number 21.

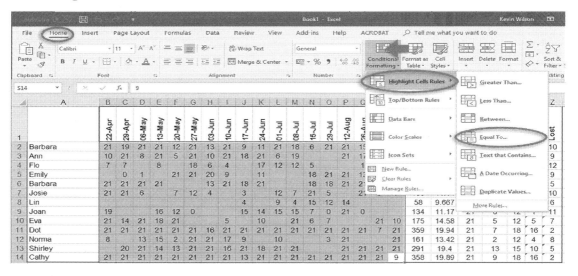

First, highlight the range of cells you want to apply the conditional formatting to. In this example, it's the range B2 to S14 - all the player's scores.

Next, from your home ribbon, click 'conditional formatting'. You'll see a drop down menu with some options. We want to highlight the cells that have a score of 21, so in the menu, go to 'highlight cell rules'. From the slide out, you can select your conditions. In this example, we're highlighting cells with a value equal to 21, so click 'equal to...'

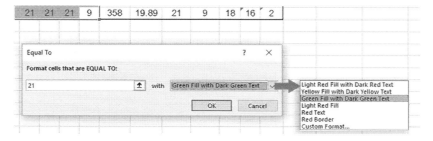

In the 'equal to' dialog box, enter the number your cells must be equal to, in this example, '21'. In the drop down box, select a format. Green is usually good to indicate positives like a win, so select 'green fill with dark green text'. Click OK when you're done.

Taking it a step further, you can also apply different pre-set effects to the cells according to their value. For example, in our scoring sheet, you could have a different shade for each value. 21 being the highest score and a win could be dark green, and each value below 21 could have a lighter shade as the number decreases. So you end up with a very light green at the lowest scores.

You can do this with colour scales. From your home ribbon, click 'conditional formatting', select 'colour scales', then from the slide out menu, select a style. I'm going to go for the bottom left option with a dark to green colour scale.

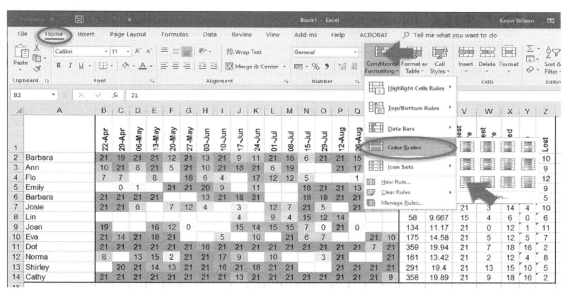

Any blank cells in the table are when a player was either absent or didn't play. We could highlight these in light red. For this one, select 'conditional formatting' from your home ribbon, go to 'highlight cell rules' and from the slide out menu, click 'more rules'.

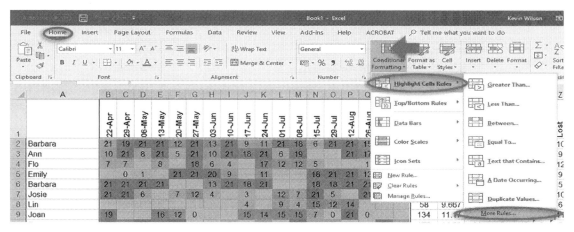

From the dialog box, in the 'select a rule type' section, select 'format only cells that contain', because we are formatting according to a specific value or condition (ie blank cells).

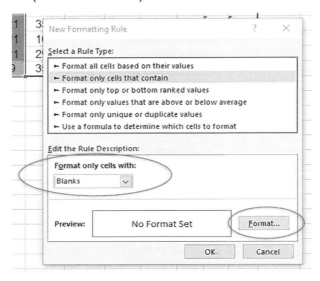

Then in the 'edit the rule description' section, change this to 'blanks' because we are checking for blank cells.

Next click 'format', then select a colour to shade the cell when Excel finds a blank. In this example, I'm choosing a light red.

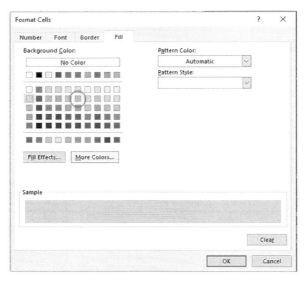

Click 'ok' on both dialog boxes.

For the totals column you could add data bars. You'll need to widen the totals column a bit to see the effect.

Select the total column, from your home ribbon click 'conditional formatting'.

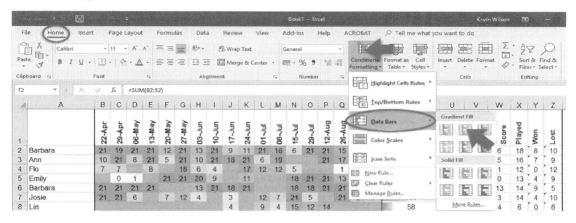

Go down to 'data bars' and select a gradient fill from the slide out menu.

You should end up with something like this. As you can see the higher the final score, the longer the data bar. This is useful for making totals at a glance easier to process.

	22-Apr	29-Apr	06-May	13-May	20-May	27-May	03-Jun	10-Jun	17-Jun	24-Jun	01-Jul	08-Jul	15-Jul	29-Jul	12-Aug	26-Aug	02-Sep	09-Sep	Total
Barbara	21	19	21	21	12	21	13	21	9	11	21	18	6	21	21	15	18	19	308
Ann	10	21	8	21	5	21	10	21	18	21	6	19			21	17	21	9	249
Flo	7	7		8		18	6	4		17	12	12	5			1	6		103
Emily		0	1		21	21	20	9		11			18	21	21	13	20	14	190
Barbara	21	21	21	21			13	21	18	21			18	18	21	21	21	18	274
Josie	21	21	6		7	12	4		3		12	7	21	5		21	9	7	156
Lin							4		9	4	15	12	14						58
Joan	19			16	12	0			15	14	15	15	7	0	21	0			134
Eva	21	14	21	18	21			5		10		21	6	7			21	10	175
Dot	21	21	21	21	21	21	16	21	21	21	21	21	21	21	21	21	7	21	359
Norma	8		13	15	2	21	21	17	9		10			3	21			21	161
Shirley		20	21	14	13	21	21	16	21	18	21	21			21	21	21	21	291
Cathy	21	21	21	21	21	21	21	21	13	21	21	21	21	21	21	21	21	9	358

Using Formulas

If I wanted to add up all the scores in my score sheet, I could add another column called total and enter a formula to add up the scores for the two weeks the player has played.

To do this, I need to find the cell references for Barbara's scores.

Her scores are in row 2 and columns B and C circled below.

	A	B	C	D
1		22 Apr	29 Apr	Total
2	Barbara	21	19	
3	Ann	10	21	
4	Flo	7	7	
5	Rose	9	12	
6	Emily		0	
7	Josie	21	21	
8	Lin			
9	Joan	19		
10	Eva	21	14	

Enter formula in this cell

So the cell references are B2 for her score of 21, and C2 for her score of 19.

So we enter into the cell under the heading 'total'

    = B2+C2

Remember all formulas must start with an equals sign **(=)**.

To save you entering the formula for each row, you can replicate it instead.

If you click on the cell D2, where you entered the formula above, you will notice on the bottom right of the box, a small square handle.

I've enlarged the image so you can see it clearly.

40

Drag this handle down the rest of the column. You can also double click this handle to fill the rest of the column automatically.

D2	▼ ⋮	✕ ✓	*fx*	=C2+B2

◢	A	B 22-Apr	C 29-Apr	D Total
1				
2	Barbara	21	19	
3	Ann	10	21	
4	Flo	7	7	
5	Rose	9	12	
6	Emily		0	
7	Josie	21	21	
8	Lin			
9	Joan	19		
10	Eva	21	14	
11				

Excel will automatically copy the formula and calculate the rest of the totals for you, without you having to enter the formulas for each row.

BIDMAS Rule

BIDMAS (sometimes BODMAS) is an acronym commonly used to remember mathematical operator priority.

Brackets ( )
Indices (square roots: $\sqrt{}$, exponents: squared^2 or cubed^3)
Divide /
Multiply *
Add +
Subtract -

For example, if you wanted to add 20% sales tax to a price of £12.95, you could do something like this...

$$Total = 12.95 + \left(12.95 * \frac{20}{100} \right)$$

Do the bit circled in red first [multiply & divide], then the addition.

Using Functions

A function is a pre-defined formula. Excel has hundreds of different functions all designed to make analysing your data easier. You can find most of these functions on the formulas ribbon.

Count

Say I wanted to count the number of games played automatically. I could do this with a function.

Insert a new column after "29 Apr" into the spreadsheet and call it "Played". To do this, right click on the D column (the 'Total' column) and from the menu click insert.

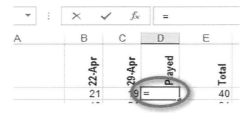

Make sure you have selected the cell you want the formula to appear in, then click 'insert function' (*fx*).

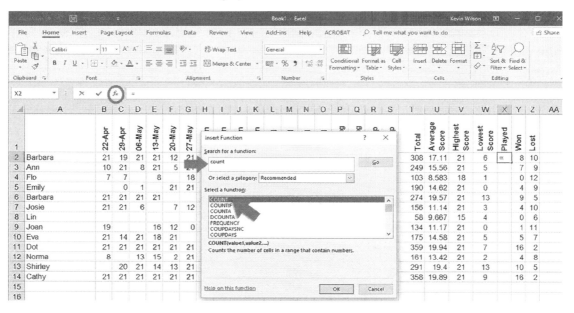

In the insert function dialog box, select the count function from the list then click OK. Type it into the 'search for a function' field if it isn't listed.

Now we need to tell the count function what we want it to count. We want to count the number of games played.

Barbara's scores are in cells B2:S2, so highlight these by dragging your mouse over them, as shown below

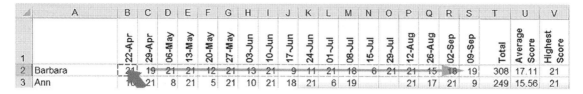

Click OK in the dialog box.

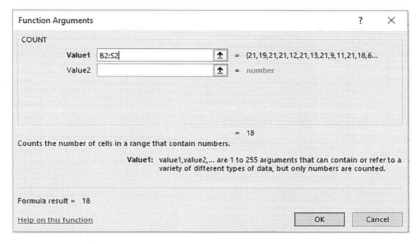

You can see she has played 18 games. Now we can replicate the formula as we did before. Click and drag the small square handle on the bottom right hand side of the cell.

Played	Won	Lost
18	8	10
	7	9
	0	12
	4	9
	9	5
	4	10

Drag it down to fill the rest of the column.

219

CountIf

Counting the number of wins gets a little bit more tricky. In this particular sport, a win is the first to 21 points. So we can count the '21s' in the players' scores.

To do this, we use the 'CountIf' function. This function counts a value depending on a certain condition, in this case if the value is 21 or not.

I have inserted another column called 'won'. Click in the first cell of that column. This is where we want the result to appear.

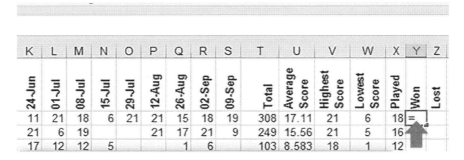

To insert a CountIf function, click the insert function icon on your ribbon (*fx*).

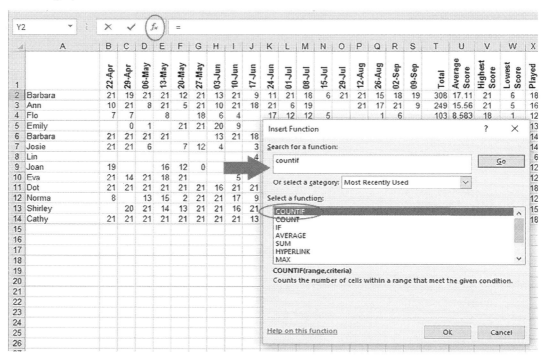

From the dialog box that appears, select 'CountIf'. If it isn't listed, type countif into the search field. Click OK.

Select the range of values you want to count. For Barbara's scores, the range is B2:S2. To do this, click on the cell B2 and drag your mouse over to S2.

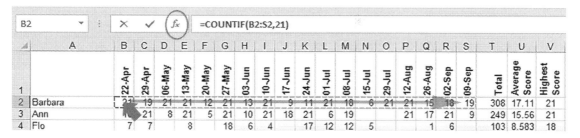

	A	22-Apr	29-Apr	06-May	13-May	20-May	27-May	03-Jun	10-Jun	17-Jun	24-Jun	01-Jul	08-Jul	15-Jul	29-Jul	12-Aug	26-Aug	02-Sep	09-Sep	Total	Average Score	Highest Score
1																						
2	Barbara	21	19	21	21	12	21	13	21	9	11	21	18	6	21	21	15	18	19	308	17.11	21
3	Ann		21	8	21	5	21	10	21	18	21	6	19			21	17	21	9	249	15.56	21
4	Flo	7	7		8		18	6	4		17	12	12	5			1	6		103	8.583	18

In the criteria field enter the number 21, because we want to count the number of '21s' in the range.

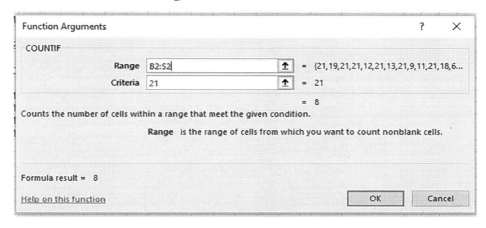

Click OK.

Now replicate the function down the rest of the column. Drag the square handle on the bottom right of the cell.

Played	Won	Lost
18	8	
16		
12		
13		
14		
14		
6		
12		
12		

Auto Sum

Auto sum, as its name suggests, adds up all the values in a row or column.

To add up a row, click on the cell you want the total to appear in. In this example, I have created a column for totals, and I want the total for the first player to appear in cell T2, circled below in the illustration.

Next, add the auto sum function. You'll find this on your home ribbon. Click on the 'auto sum' icon.

You'll notice, the auto sum function has highlighted the row I want to add up. Press the enter key on your keyboard to execute the function.

Now replicate the function to fill the rest of the column by dragging the handle down, as shown below.

	E 13-May	F 20-May	G 27-May	H 03-Jun	I 10-Jun	J 17-Jun	K 24-Jun	L 01-Jul	M 08-Jul	N 15-Jul	O 29-Jul	P 12-Aug	Q 26-Aug	R 02-Sep	S 09-Sep	T Total	U Played	V Won	W Lost
2	21	12	21	13	21	9	11	21	18	6	21	21	15	18	19	308	18	8	10
3	21	5	21	10	21	18	21	6	19			21	17	21	9		16	7	9
4	8		18	6	4		17	12	12	5			1	6			12		12
5		21	21	20	9		11			18	21	21	13	20	14		13	4	9
6	21			13	21	18	21			18	18	21	21	21	18		14	9	5
7		7	12	4		3		12	7	21	5		21	9	7		14	4	10
8				4			9	4	15	12	14						6		6
9	16	12	0		15	14	15	15	7	0	21	0					12	1	11

Average

Average finds the middle number in a row or column. To find the average, click on the cell you want the result to appear in. In this example, I have inserted a column for average score, and I want the average for the first player to appear in cell U2, circled below left in the illustration.

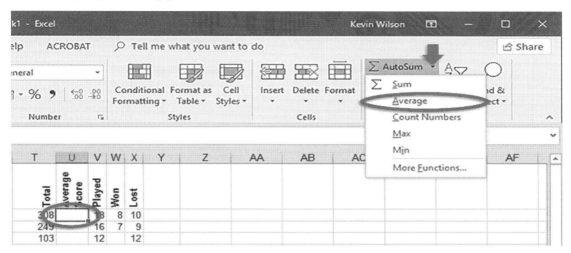

Next, add the average function. You'll find this on your home ribbon. Click on the small down arrow next to the auto sum icon. From the drop down menu, select 'average'. Now, you'll notice that the average function includes the totals column. This is not what we want to average, so you'll need to select the range B2:S2. Click on the cell B2 and drag the box across to S2. Hit return to enter the function.

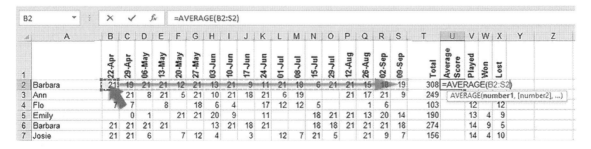

Now replicate the function down the rest of the column.

08	15	29	12	26	02	09	Tc	A\ Sc	Pl	W	Lc
18	6	21	21	15	18	19	308	17.1	18	8	10
19			21	17	21	9	249	15.6	16	7	9
12	5			1	6		103	8.58	12		12
		18	21	21	13	20	14	190	14.6	13	4	9
	18	18	21	21	21	18	274	19.6	14	9	5
7	21	5		21	9	7	156	11.1	14	4	10

Max & Min

Max returns the largest number in a selected range of values, and min returns the smallest number.

Select the cell you want the result to appear in. I have added two new columns, one for highest score and one for lowest score. I'm going to use the max function in the 'highest score' column.

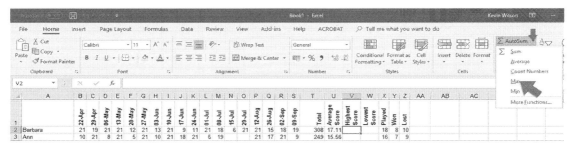

From your home ribbon, click the small down arrow next to the auto sum icon, and from the drop down menu, select 'max'.

Now, you'll notice that the max function has included 'total' and 'average score', this is not what we want. Select the range B2:S2 - click on the cell B2, then drag your mouse pointer over to S2.

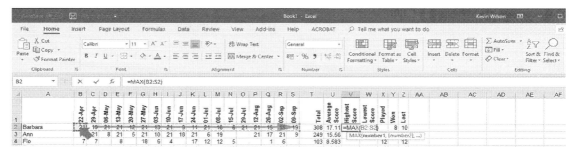

Hit enter to execute the function, then drag the square handle on the bottom right of the cell to replicate the function down the rest of the column.

Total	Average Score	Highest Score	Lowest Score
308	17.1	21	
249	15.6		
103	8.58		
190	14.6		

The procedure is exactly the same for the Min function, except from the auto sum drop down menu select 'min' instead of 'max'. Give it a try.

IF Function

If functions are called conditional functions and test whether a condition is true or false. The function returns a different result for the true condition and another result for false.

```
= (IF condition, result-if-true, result-if-false)
```

Can be read as

```
If test condition is true,
    execute result-if-true
else
    execute result-if-false
```

In the example **IF function demo.xlsx**, we are going to apply a conditional function to calculate our shipping cost. The rule is, free delivery for orders over £25, otherwise a shipping charge of £3.99 applies.

To insert an IF function, click on the cell you want the calculation to appear in (D12).

Then go to your formulas ribbon and click 'insert function'.

From the dialog box that appears, select IF. *If the function isn't in the list, type IF into the search field and click 'go'.*

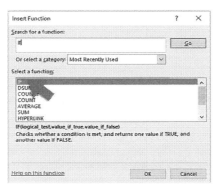

Click OK when you're done.

Now to build the IF function. First, we need to find out if the total is greater than or equal to 25.

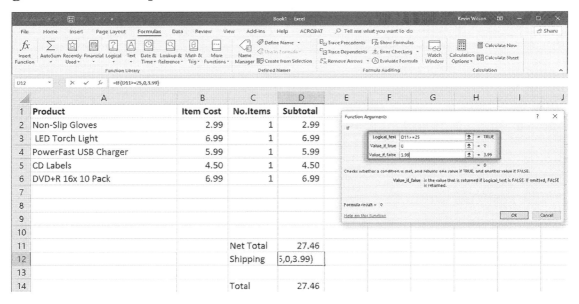

In the function arguments dialog box, click in the 'logical test' field, then click cell D11 to add this field to the logical test.

The net total is in cell D11.

Click back in the logical test field and add the following

>=25

In the 'value if true' field type 0, because if the net total is over 25, the logical test condition is true, so it's free delivery over £25

In the 'value if false' type 3.99, because if it's under £25 we charge the fee.

Click OK.

Because the net total is £27.46, this is over 25, so the shipping is 0.

Try adjusting the number of items and see what happens when the total goes below £25.

VLookup

VLOOKUP searches for a value in the first column of a specified table, and returns a value from the specified adjacent column.

```
=VLOOKUP (value to look for,
          table to retrieve value from,
              column number with value to return,
                  true for exact/false for approx)
```

In the example **VLOOKUP function demo.xlsx**, we are going to apply a lookup function to calculate our shipping cost according to the shipping rates table (F15:G20).

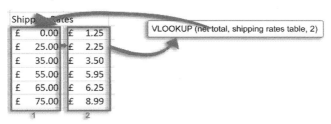

To insert a VLOOKUP, click on the cell you want the calculation to appear in (D12), then go to your formulas ribbon and click 'insert function'.

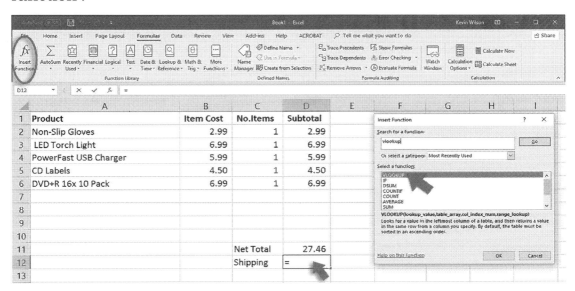

From the dialog box that appears, select VLOOKUP.

If the function isn't in the list, type VLOOKUP into the search field and click 'go'.

Click OK when you're done.

In the 'function arguments' dialog box, click in the first argument box, 'lookup value'. This is the value we want to look up in the shipping rates table. In this case the net total is in cell D11, so click D11 to add the cell to the 'lookup value' field.

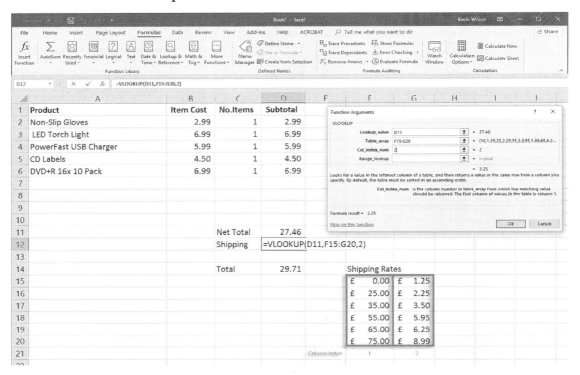

Next click in the 'table array' field. In this field, we want to specify the table of values we are looking up. In this case the table array is the shipping rates table (highlighted in red, above). So click on F15 and drag your mouse over to G20, to select the table.

Now click in the 'col index num' field. This is the column in the table that contains the values we want to return.

So for example, looking at the shipping rates table, if the net total is under 25, we return 1.25.

If the net total is between 25 and 34, we return 2.25 and so on.

The net total range is column 1 and the shipping rates are column 2. We want to return the shipping rates, so type 2 in the 'col index num' field.

Click OK.

Try adjusting the item prices or number of items and see what happens to the shipping rate.

Types of Data

There are several different types of data you will come across while using Excel. These data can be numeric such as whole numbers called integers (eg 10), numbers with decimal points (eg 29.93), currencies (eg £4.67 or $43.76), as well as date and time, text and so on.

Going back to our scoring spreadsheet, we need another column for the average scores.

Insert a new column and type the heading 'Average' as shown below.

D2	▼ ⋮	✕ ✓ ƒx	=E2/D2

◢	A	B 22-Apr	C 29-Apr	D Played	E Total	F Average
1						
2	Barbara	21	19	2	40	=E2/D2
3	Ann	10	21	2	31	
4	Flo	7	7	2	14	
5	Rose	9	12	2	21	
6	Emily		0	1	0	
7	Josie	21	21	2	42	
8	Lin			0	0	
9	Joan	19		1	19	
10	Eva	21	14	2	35	

We are going to work out the average scores over the number of games the players have played. In the Cell F2 enter the formula

```
Average = Total Score / Total number of Games Played
```

The total score is in E2 and the total number of games played is in D2.

So we enter into F2:

```
= E2 / D2
```

Use the forward slash for divide: **/**

Replicate the formula down the column as we did previously in the exercise.

Now the number format isn't as accurate as we want it. We need to tell Excel that the data in this column is a number, accurate to two decimal places.

Highlight the cells you want to apply the number format to, as shown below.

▲	A	B 22-Apr	C 29-Apr	D Played	E Total	F Average
1						
2	Barbara	21	19	2	40	20
3	Ann	10	21	2	31	15.5
4	Flo	7	7	2	14	7
5	Rose	9	12	2	21	10.5
6	Emily		0	1	0	0
7	Josie	21	21	2	42	21
8	Lin			0	0	0
9	Joan	19		1	19	19
10	Eva	21	14	2	35	17.5

On the home ribbon go up to number format (it will currently say 'general' in box). Click the little arrow next to it.

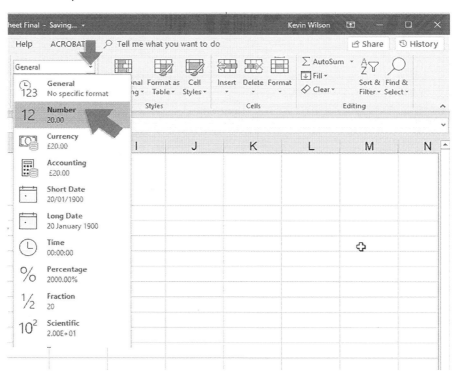

From the drop down menu click number. This will format all the selected cells as a number with 2 decimal places.

It would be the same for recording the fees paid by the players. Insert another column and call it 'fee'. Say the fees are 4.50. When we enter 4.5 into the cell, Excel thinks it's just a number, so we need to tell Excel that it is currency.

Select all the data in the fee column. You don't need to include the heading row.

	B	C	D	E	F	G
	22-Apr	29-Apr	Played	Total	Average	Fee
2	21	19	2	40	20.00	4.5
3	10	21	2	31	15.50	4.5
4	7	7	2	14	7.00	4.5
5	9	12	2	21	10.50	4.5
6		0	1	0	0.00	4.5
7	21	21	2	42	21.00	4.5
8			0	0	0.00	4.5
9	19		1	19	19.00	4.5
10	21	14	2	35	17.50	4.5

On the home ribbon go up to number format (it will currently say 'general' in box). Click the little arrow next to it.

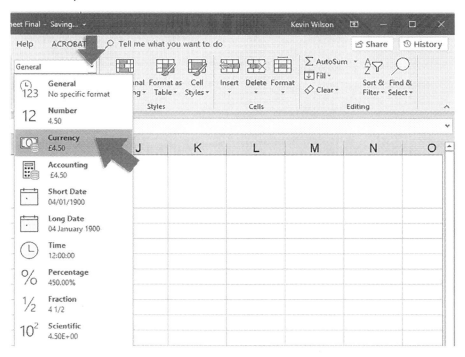

From the drop down menu click currency. This will format all the numbers as a currency.

Cell Referencing

In Excel, there are two types of cell referencing to think about when copying formulas to other parts of your spreadsheet. Do you want the formula to reference the same cells regardless of where you paste it? Or do you want the cells referenced in the copied formula, to change relative to their new position? You might use absolute cell referencing when referencing a look up table of values, and relative referencing when you want to total up a column or row.

Relative

Relative cell referencing means that as a formula or function is copied and pasted somewhere else in your spreadsheet, the cell references in the formula or function change to reflect the function's new location.

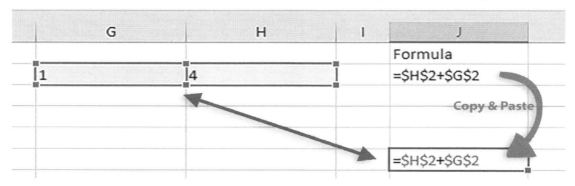

Absolute

Absolute cell referencing means that as a formula or function is copied and pasted somewhere else in your spreadsheet, the cell references in the formula or function do not change, they stay fixed on a specific cell.

You indicate an absolute cell reference using a dollar sign ($).

Where you put the dollar sign will indicate which row or column is to remain absolute - meaning it doesn't change when you copy the formula.

A1	Column & Row do not change when formula is copied to another cell
A$1	Row does not change, but column will change when formula is copied
$A1	Column does not change, but row will change when formula is copied

All you need to remember is to put the dollar sign before the row or column reference you want to remain the same regardless of where you copy and paste the formula.

Adding Charts

There are many different types of charts to choose from, here are a few examples of some common ones.

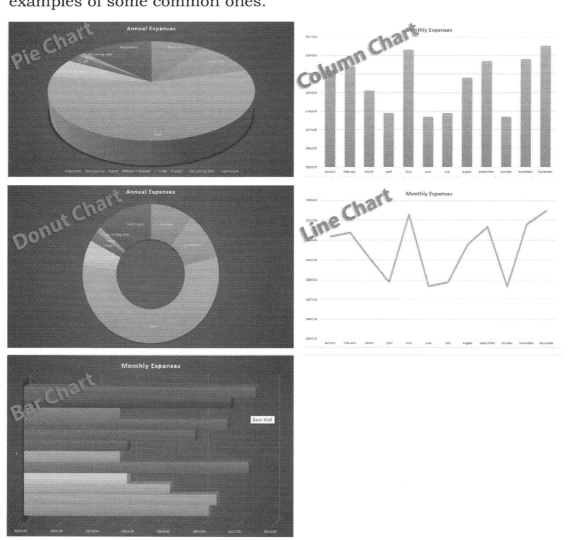

Column and bar charts compare values with each other, line charts show trends over time, donut and pie charts represent proportions of a whole or a percentage.

You will need to use the correct chart for the data you want to represent.

The easiest way to add a chart is to select from your spreadsheet, a column you want for the X-Axis and a column you want for the Y-Axis.

I am going to make a chart on the total scores.

First select all the names in the first column. This will be the X-Axis on the chart.

10R x 1C	▼	⋮	✕	✓	*fx*		

◢	A	B	C	D	E	F	G
1		22-Apr	29-Apr	Played	Total	Average	Fee
2	Barbara	21	19	2	40	20.00	£9.00
3	Ann	10	21	2	31	15.50	£9.00
4	Flo	7	7	2	14	7.00	£9.00
5	Rose	9	12	2	21	10.50	£9.00
6	Emily		0	1	0	0.00	£9.00
7	Josie	21	21	2	42	21.00	£9.00
8	Lin			0	0	#DIV/0!	£9.00
9	Joan	19		1	19	19.00	£9.00
10	Eva	21	14	2	35	17.50	£9.00

Now hold down the control key (ctrl) on your keyboard. This allows you to multi-select.

While holding down control, select the data in the total column with your mouse.

This will be the Y-Axis on the chart. Note the data in the names column is still highlighted.

E1	▼	⋮	✕	✓	*fx*	Total	

◢	A	B	C	D	E	F	G
1		22-Apr	29-Apr	Played	Total	Average	Fee
2	Barbara	21	19	2	40	20.00	£9.00
3	Ann	10	21	2	31	15.50	£9.00
4	Flo	7	7	2	14	7.00	£9.00
5	Rose	9	12	2	21	10.50	£9.00
6	Emily		0	1	0	0.00	£9.00
7	Josie	21	21	2	42	21.00	£9.00
8	Lin			0	0	#DIV/0!	£9.00
9	Joan	19		1	19	19.00	£9.00
10	Eva	21	14	2	35	17.50	£9.00

Release the control key and go to the insert ribbon.

In the centre of the ribbon, you will find some different types of charts – line charts, column charts, pie charts.

I am going for a nice 3D column chart. Click the 3D column chart shown below to select it.

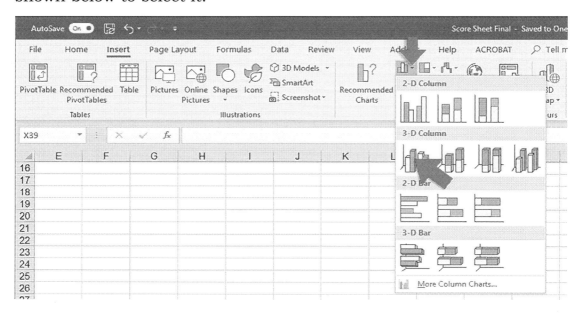

Excel will paste your chart into your spreadsheet.

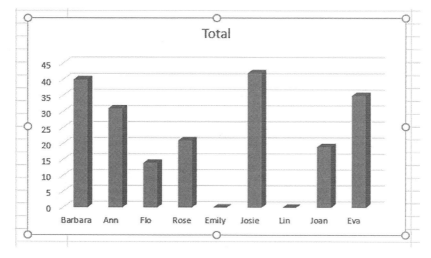

You are automatically taken to the design ribbon where you can select a style to auto-format the chart for you.

Select a style from the options that looks good. To see more styles, click the small arrow to the bottom right of the chart styles box.

I'm going for a nice shaded effect that matches the shading on my table.

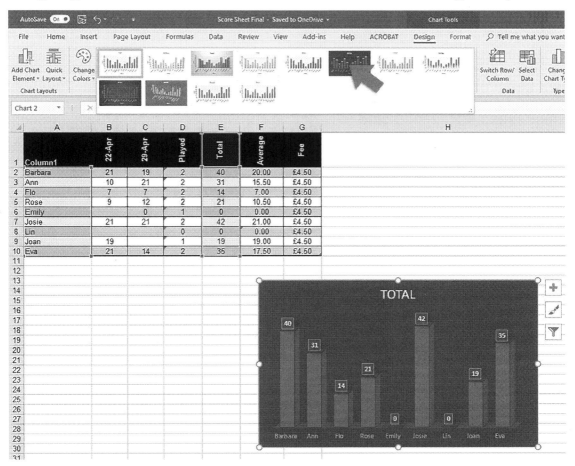

Formatting Charts

You can format and customise the individual chart elements, such as the axis, axis titles, chart title, data labels, gridlines and the legend.

Chart Titles

Excel will automatically give your chart a title, but more often than not, the title isn't very explanatory.

Click on the automatically generated title on your chart, delete the text then type in your own title, 'Final Scores'.

Chart Elements

Charts are made up of elements. These could be axes, titles, gridlines, data and so on. To edit the chart elements, click on your chart to select it.

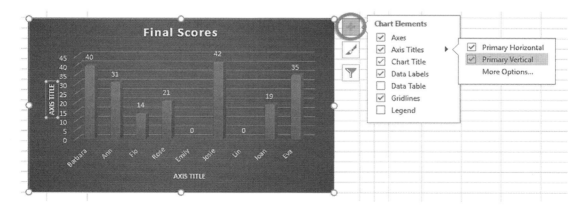

You'll see three icons appear down the right hand edge of the chart. Click on the top one to reveal the slide out menu. From here, you can add axis titles, chart titles, labels, gridlines and a legend, by clicking the tick boxes next to the elements in the list.

Axis Titles

On some charts, Excel might not have added any axis titles. If this is the case, click your chart then click the chart elements icon, circled below.

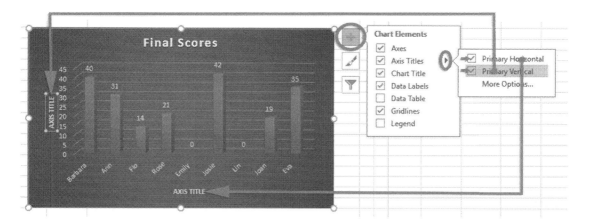

In the slide out menu, click the small right arrow next to 'axis titles'. From the slide out, click both 'primary horizontal' and 'primary vertical', for both X and Y axis on your chart.

To change the text in the axis titles, click on the title, delete the text and type in your titles. In this example, the horizontal axis is 'player name' and the vertical axis is 'final score'.

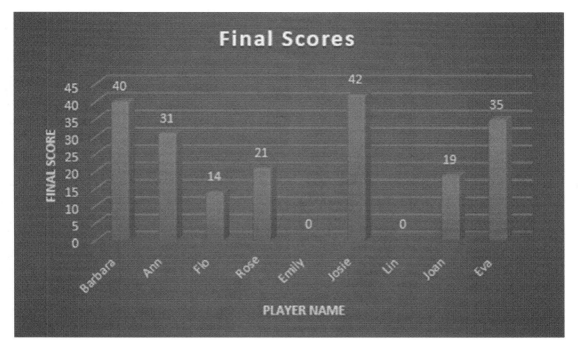

Customising Charts

There are shortcuts to changing elements of your chart, but to give you the most control over the changes, we'll do it this way.

Right click on a blank space on your chart and from the popup menu, click 'format chart area'.

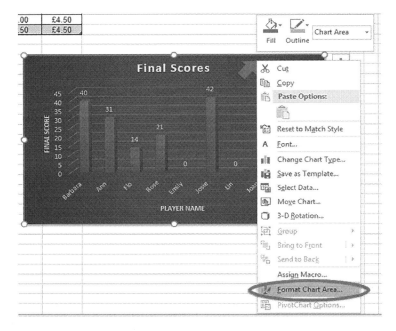

In the side panel that appears, you have a number of options.

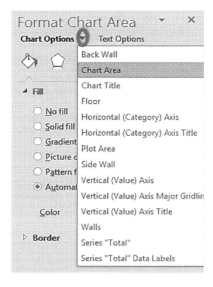

Click the small down arrow next to 'chart options' to open the drop down menu.

Here you can select the element of the chart you want to customise (chart colour, labels, and so on).

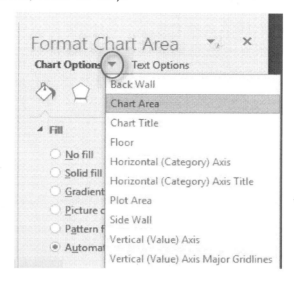

Each option on the menu will change a specific part of your chart. In the illustration below, you can see each part of the chart corresponds to an option on the menu.

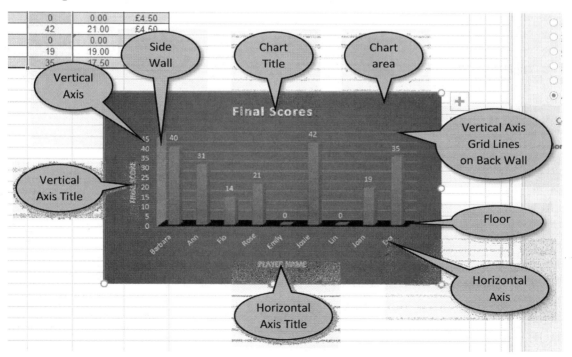

Chart title, horizontal axis, vertical axis, and so on. If you want to change the chart area colour, select 'chart area', if you want to change the axis titles, select axis title from the menu, and so on.

Change Background to Solid Colour

To change the background colour, right click on a blank space on your chart and from the popup menu, click 'format chart area'.

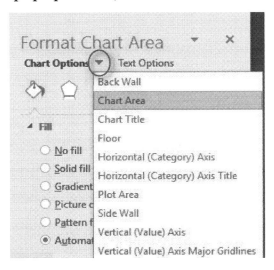

In this example, we want to change the background colour. The background is called the 'chart area', so make sure 'chart area' is selected.

To change to a solid colour, expand the fill section by clicking on the small down arrow next to fill. Click 'solid fill', then click the down arrow next to the paint pot, and select a colour.

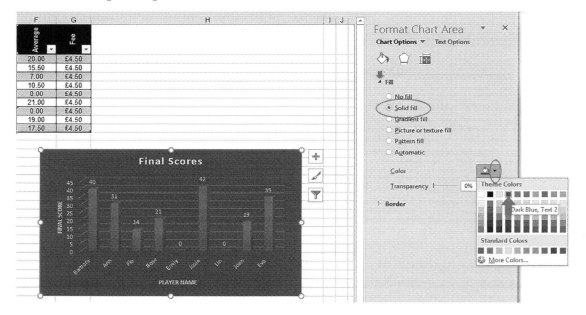

Change Background to Gradient Colour

You can also apply a gradient colour, meaning one colour blends into another over the surface of your chart.

To do this, right click on your chart, click 'format chart'. From the chart options make sure 'chart area' is selected as in the previous section, except from the fill options, click 'gradient fill'.

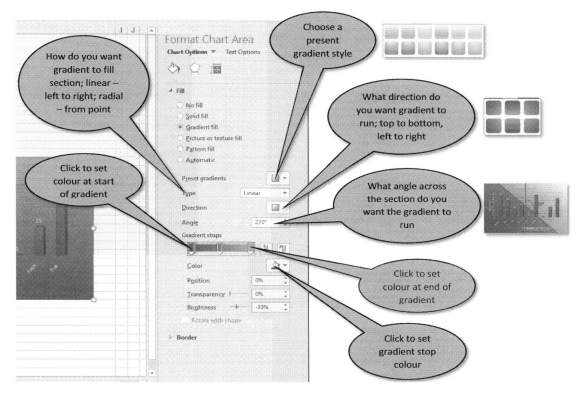

You can customise your gradient. Take a closer look at the bottom section of the gradient settings. You can choose from several gradient presets. Linear gradients run left to right or top to bottom. Radial gradients radiate out from a point on the chart.

You can select the type of gradient from the 'type' drop down field.

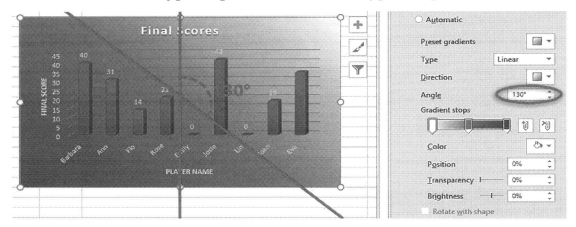

You can also set the angle at which the gradient runs. This only applies to linear gradients and sets the angle at which the colour begins to change. As you can see in the example above, the angle is set to 130° which means 130° from the vertical axis shown in red.

Each stop on the gradient bar represents a colour. You can change these colours by clicking on the stop, then selecting the paint pot. From the popup dialog box, click a colour.

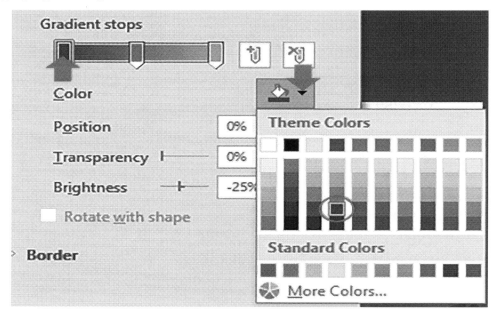

For each of the stops, you can change the position of the gradient (where the colour blends), as well as the brightness and transparency of the colour gradient.

Change Chart Type

To change your chart type, eg from a column chart to a bar chart, click on your chart and select the design ribbon. From the design ribbon, click 'change chart type'.

From the popup dialog box, look down the left hand side for the types of chart you want (pie, bar, line, etc), and select one.

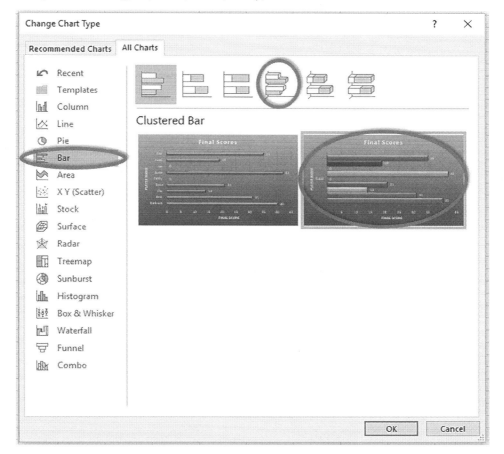

From the right hand pane, select the style of chart you want.

For this example, I am going to choose a nice colourful bar chart.

Move and Resize Charts

To resize, click on a blank section of your chart. You'll notice some small white dots appear around the chart. These are called resize handles. Drag the resize handles across your page to the size you want the chart.

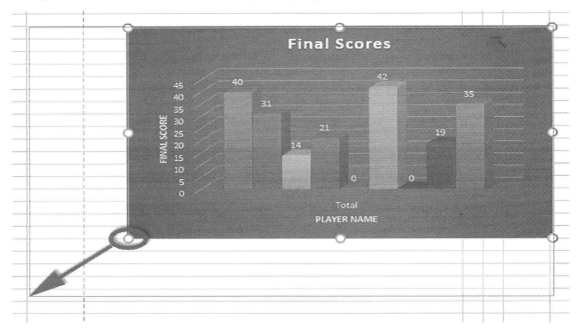

To move your chart into position, click in a blank section of your chart, then drag it with your mouse into a new position.

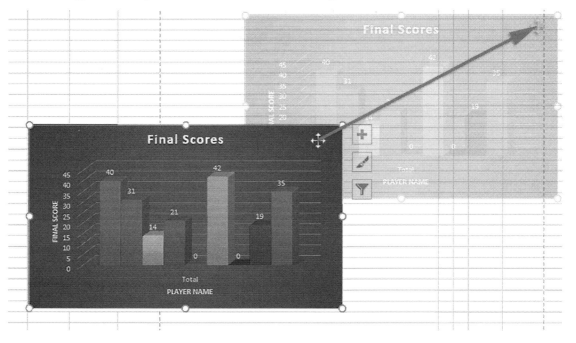

Data Analysis with Goal Seek

Goal seek allows you start with the desired result, the goal in other words, and calculates the value required to give you that result.

For this example, use the **goal seek** worksheet in the **Data Analysis Starter.xlsx** workbook.

Say we want to take out a loan of £10,000. This particular bank has an interest rate of 3.3%. We're paying the loan off over 60 months with a payment of £181.02. We can afford to pay off £200 per month. We can use goal seek to find out how many months we'll be paying the loan off.

First click the monthly payment (cell C4), because this is what we want to change. From the data ribbon, click 'what-if analysis'. From the drop down menu, click 'goal seek'.

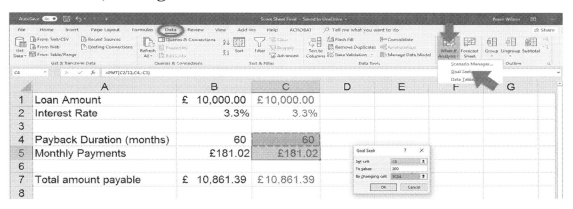

On the dialog box that appears, click in 'to value' and enter 200. This is our target amount or goal.

Now we want to achieve this goal by changing the payback duration, so click in 'by changing cell' on the dialog box, then click the cell with the number of months (C4 in this case).

Click OK. We have an answer... It would take 54 months at £200 a month.

	A	B	C	D	E
1	Loan Amount	£ 10,000.00	£10,000.00		
2	Interest Rate	3.3%	3.3%		
3					
4	Payback Duration (months)	60	54		
5	Monthly Payments	£181.02	£200.00		
6					
7	Total amount payable	£ 10,861.39	£10,772.61		

Goal Seek Status   ?   ×
Goal Seeking with Cell C5 found a solution.
Target value: 200
Current value: £200.00
Step   Pause   OK   Cancel

Data Analysis with Scenario Manager

When creating spreadsheets, you will probably want to explore "what-if" scenarios and see how different values effect results. Say we were running a small bookstore. We bought in some books and we want to see what our sales revenue and profit will be for different prices to help us price our books.

For this example, use the **scenario manager** worksheet in the **Data Analysis Starter.xlsx** workbook.

Creating Scenarios

To add a scenario, go to your data ribbon and click 'what-if analysis'. From the drop down menu, select 'scenario manager'.

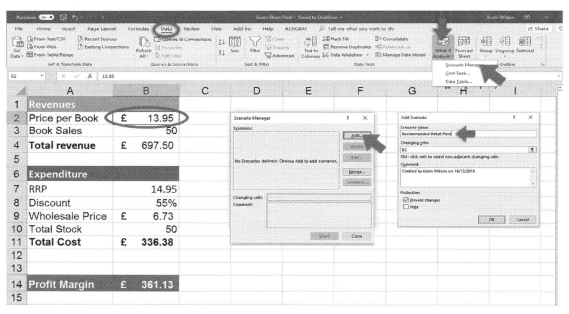

From the dialog box that appears, click add. Then from the 'add scenario' dialog box, type in a meaningful name in the field 'scenario name'.

Click in the 'changing cells' field underneath, then click the cell or cells you want to change. In this case we want to change the price per book in cell B2. So click B2.

Click OK.

Repeat the process and create scenarios for 'Sale Price' at £10.95, and 'Give Away' price at £8.99

Now in the scenario manager dialog box, you'll have three scenarios you can click on, and instantly see the results.

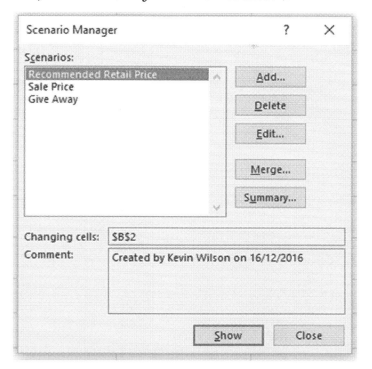

Click on one of the scenarios then click show.

Recommended Retail Price		
Revenues		
Price per Book	£	14.95
Book Sales		50
Total revenue	£	747.50
Expenditure		
RRP		14.95
Discount		55%
Wholesale Price	£	6.73
Total Stock		50
Total Cost	£	336.38
Profit Margin	£	411.13

Sale Price		
Revenues		
Price per Book	£	10.95
Book Sales		50
Total revenue	£	547.50
Expenditure		
RRP		14.95
Discount		55%
Wholesale Price	£	6.73
Total Stock		50
Total Cost	£	336.38
Profit Margin	£	211.13

Give Away Price		
Revenues		
Price per Book	£	8.99
Book Sales		50
Total revenue	£	449.50
Expenditure		
RRP		14.95
Discount		55%
Wholesale Price	£	6.73
Total Stock		50
Total Cost	£	336.38
Profit Margin	£	113.13

If you need to edit any of the scenarios, just click on the name in the scenario list and click edit. You'll be able to go through the add scenario process again and amend the values.

Summary Reports

You can also generate quick reports of your scenarios. To do this, go to your scenario manager.

Data Ribbon -> What-If Analysis -> Scenario Manager

From the scenario manager dialog box, click 'summary'.

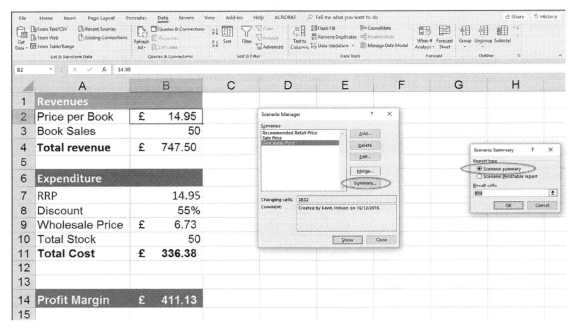

On the scenario summary dialog box, click 'scenario summary', to produce a report.

For the 'result cells', this is the cell or cells we're looking at when we're changing the values in the scenarios.

We want to show how changing the price per book affects profit margin. So here, select B14 because this is where the value for profit margin is.

If we wanted to show how changing the price per book affects total revenue, we'd select the total revenue value in B4.

Click OK.

Here you can see Excel has created a new worksheet with our report on.

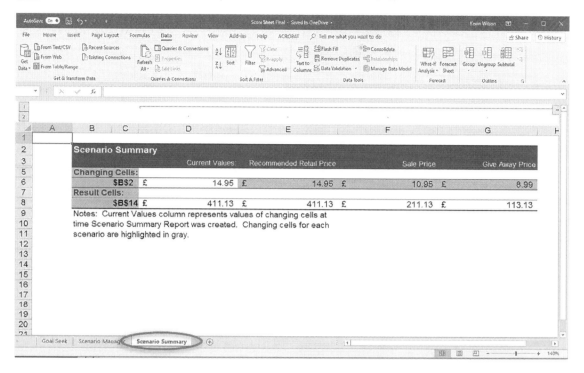

If you look at the report, some labels aren't really that clear, 'changing cells' or 'result cells' don't really tell us much. Good practice is to change these to more meaningful names.

To do this, just delete the text in the cells you want to rename then type in your own, as shown below.

Scenario Summary	Current Values:	Recommended Retail Price	Sale Price	Give Away Price
Scenarios	£ 14.95	£ 14.95	£ 10.95	£ 8.99
Profit Margins	£ 411.13	£ 411.13	£ 211.13	£ 113.13

Notes: Current Values column represents values of changing cells at time Scenario Summary Report was created. Changing cells for each scenario are highlighted in gray.

This now makes a bit more sense.

Creating Pivot Tables

A pivot table is a data summarisation tool and can automatically sort, count, total or average the data stored in one table or worksheet and display the results in a new table or worksheet. Reports can then be produced to present the data.

With a pivot table you can quickly pivot data, meaning you reorganise or summarise the data. Pivoting data can help you answer different scenarios, for example, best selling products, sales channels and so on.

For this example, use the **pivot table data** worksheet in the **Data Analysis Starter.xlsx** workbook.

First click in any cell in the data table. This is to indicate to Excel what table of data it should use to create the pivot table.

From the insert ribbon, click 'pivot table'. Make sure Excel has selected the correct range in the 'select a table or range' field. Excel will indicate the selection with a dashed line around the data.

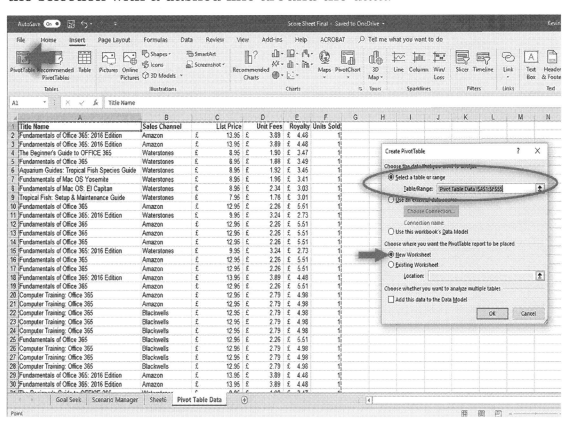

Next, in the dialog box, select 'new worksheet'. Click OK.

You'll see your 'PivotTable Fields' sidebar open on the right hand side.

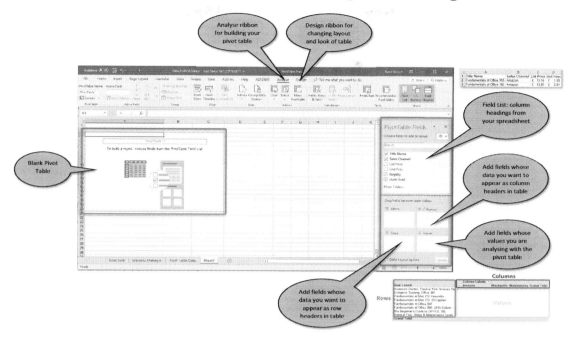

From here we can start building pivot tables. You can add and remove fields. You can drag the fields over to the rows box or the columns box, on the bottom half of the 'PivotTable Fields' sidebar, depending on how you want to analyse your data. Any field you drag to the rows box will appear down the left hand side of the table and anything you drag to the columns box will appear as columns across the top of your table. This makes up the row and column headers of the pivot table.

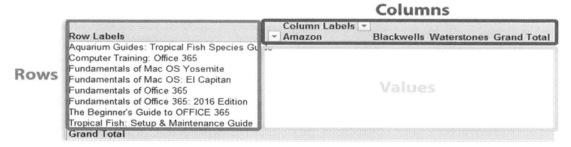

The values box, is the data you want to analyse against the rows and column headers. So, in the example above, our rows are the book titles and the columns are the sales channels.

In the values section, we could add the 'royalty' field to see how much income is generated for each title in each sales channel. Or we could add 'units sold' to the values section to see how many books have sold in each sales channel.

So lets build a pivot table. In this example, we want to find the total income per sales channel.

First add the rows. This will be title name. Either click and drag 'title name' to the 'rows' box, or click the tick next to 'title name'

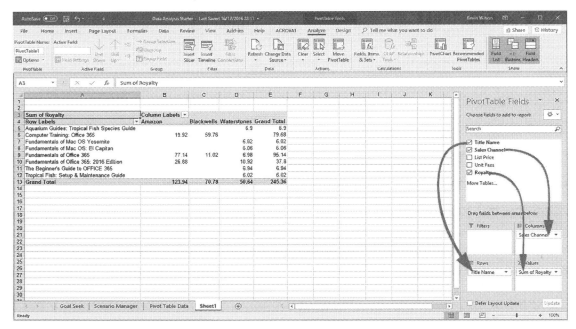

Next we need to add some values. We want the income, in this case income is labelled 'royalty'. So click the tick box next to the 'royalty' field. You can also drag the 'royalty' field over to the 'values' box.

Now we should have a list of books and their total royalties. This is the total income for all sales channels.

Row Labels	Sum of Royalty
Aquarium Guides: Tropical Fish Species Guide	6.9
Computer Training: Office 365	79.68
Fundamentals of Mac OS Yosemite	6.82
Fundamentals of Mac OS: El Capitan	6.06
Fundamentals of Office 365	95.14
Fundamentals of Office 365: 2016 Edition	37.8
The Beginner's Guide to OFFICE 365	6.94
Tropical Fish: Setup & Maintenance Guide	6.02
Grand Total	245.36

The next step is to add the sales channels. We want the royalties to be split into columns, one for each sales channel.

So to do this, click and drag the 'sales channel' field over to the 'columns' box.

Now we can see the royalties for each sales channel - Amazon, Blackwells and Waterstones, as well as grand totals. In this case Amazon generated the highest revenue (£123.94).

| Sum of Royalty | Column Labels | | | |
Row Labels	Amazon	Blackwells	Waterstones	Grand Total
Aquarium Guides: Tropical Fish Species Guide			6.9	6.9
Computer Training: Office 365	19.92	59.76		79.68
Fundamentals of Mac OS Yosemite			6.82	6.82
Fundamentals of Mac OS: El Capitan			6.06	6.06
Fundamentals of Office 365	77.14	11.02	6.98	95.14
Fundamentals of Office 365: 2016 Edition	26.88		10.92	37.8
The Beginner's Guide to OFFICE 365			6.94	6.94
Tropical Fish: Setup & Maintenance Guide			6.02	6.02
Grand Total	123.94	70.78	50.64	245.36

How about the number of books sold? We can answer this question by adding the 'units sold' field.

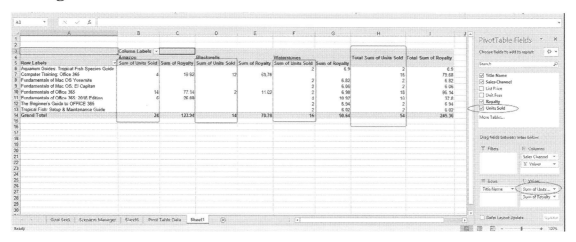

This might be a bit confusing to read. To make the data analysis easier, Excel has a feature called slicers.

Using Slicers

A slicer is essentially a filter, and allows you to filter the data in the pivot table to make things easier to analyse.

In the above example, we can see both units sold and the royalties for each sales channel, all on one table. To make things easier to analyse, we can add a slicer for sales channels that will enable us to select a sales channel, and display a pivot table for only that channel.

This helps break your data down into more concise parts.

To insert a slicer, click any cell in your pivot table, go to the analyse ribbon and click 'insert slicer'.

From the 'insert slicers' panel that opens up, click the field you want to organise the data by. In this example we are organising the data by sales channel, so click 'sales channel'.

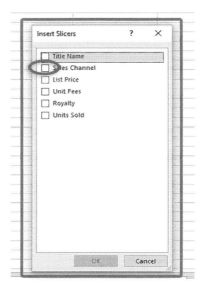

You'll see a slicer pop up with three sales channels, Amazon, Blackwells and Waterstones.

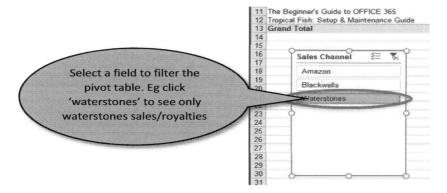

You can select multiple selections in the slicer by holding down the control key while you click.

Now, you'll see your slicer appear on your worksheet.

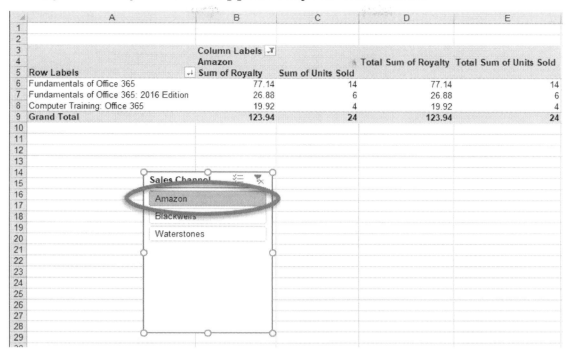

If you select 'amazon' you'll see all sales, etc from the amazon channel. Similarly if you select 'blackwells' or 'waterstones' you'll see sales from those channels.

If you select all of the channels - remember hold down the control key on your keyboard to select multiple options - you'll see sales from all channels.

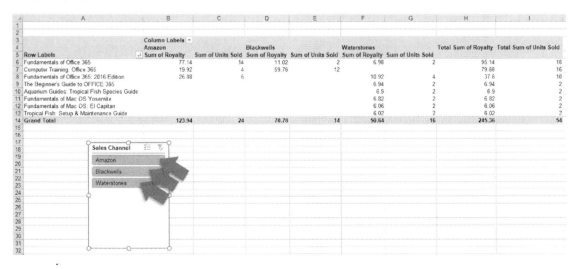

Sorting Pivot Table Data

You can also sort data in these tables in the same way you'd sort any column in your spreadsheet.

Say we wanted to find the best selling book?

I can adjust my pivot table to show total books sold (just need 'title name' and 'units sold' fields).

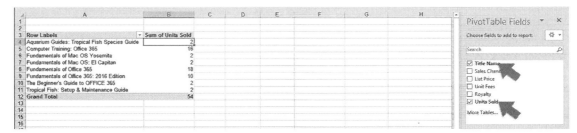

Now click in the 'sum of units sold' field, in the pivot table.

Row Labels	Sum of Units Sold
Aquarium Guides: Tropical Fish Species Guide	2
Computer Training: Office 365	
Fundamentals of Mac OS Yosemite	
Fundamentals of Mac OS: El Capitan	2
Fundamentals of Office 365	18
Fundamentals of Office 365: 2016 Edition	10
The Beginner's Guide to OFFICE 365	2
Tropical Fish: Setup & Maintenance Guide	2
Grand Total	54

Go to your data ribbon and click the 'descending' sort icon.

We can see the best seller is 'Fundamentals of Office 365'.

Row Labels	Sum of Units Sold
Fundamentals of Office 365	18
Computer Training: Office 365	16
Fundamentals of Office 365: 2016 Edition	10
Tropical Fish: Setup & Maintenance Guide	2
The Beginner's Guide to OFFICE 365	2
Fundamentals of Mac OS Yosemite	2
Aquarium Guides: Tropical Fish Species Guide	2
Fundamentals of Mac OS: El Capitan	2
Grand Total	54

Pivot Charts

Pivot charts are pretty much the same thing as regular charts, covered earlier, except they represent data in a pivot table rather than a regular worksheet.

You add your charts in a similar fashion. First click on your pivot table and from the analyse ribbon, click 'pivot chart'.

From the dialog box that appears, select a chart that is most appropriate for the data you are trying to illustrate. You can choose from pie charts, column or bar charts and line charts.

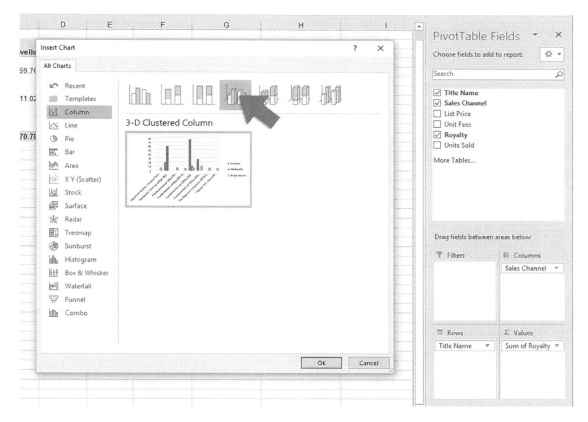

For this example, I'm going to add a nice 3D column chart.

As you can see from the chart, things can be a bit difficult to read on this particular chart. All three sales channels are on the same chart.

It would be nice if we can view them separately. Excel allows you to use slicers, which is essentially a filter.

In this example I am going to filter the chart by sales channel. So from the analyse ribbon, click 'insert slicer'. From the dialog box that appears, select sales channel and click OK.

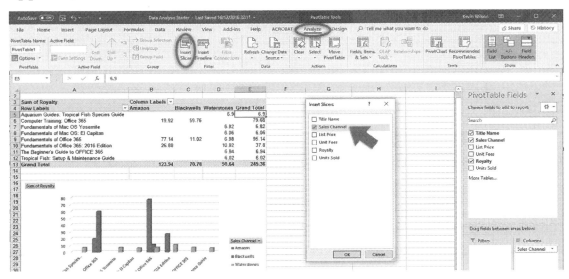

In the popup box that appears, I can select each of my sales channels in turn and take a closer look at the sales data.

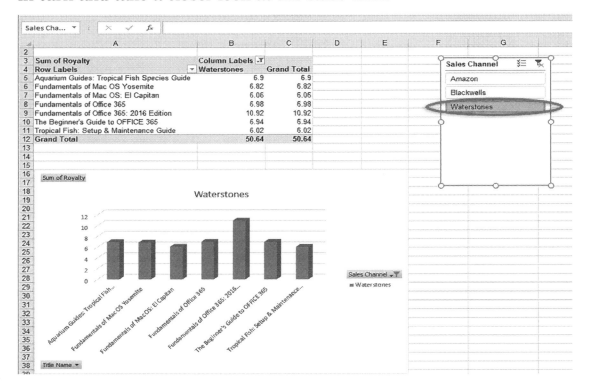

Try experimenting with adding different fields to different boxes on the 'PivotTable Fields' sidebar and see how it affects the pivot table.

You might have something like this...

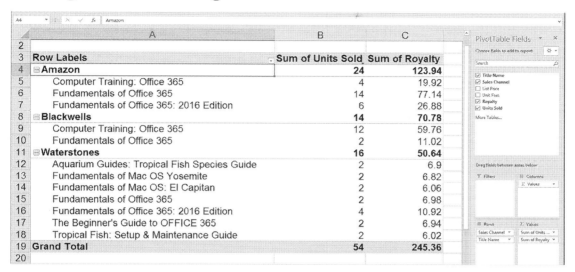

Notice where the fields are on the bottom half of the 'PivotTable Fields' sidebar in relation to the pivot chart.

Give it a try.

Validation Rules

In Excel, you can set a variety of rules to cells to help users enter the correct data.

Lets take a look at an example in the **Data Validation Demo.xlsx** workbook.

By Data Type

Whole numbers are called integers in Excel and do not have any decimal places. In the example, we can add a validation check to the 'number of items' column. It's safe to assume that these will only be whole numbers, don't think anyone will try order half an LED torch light.

Select the cells to apply the validation check to. Go to your data ribbon and click 'data validation'

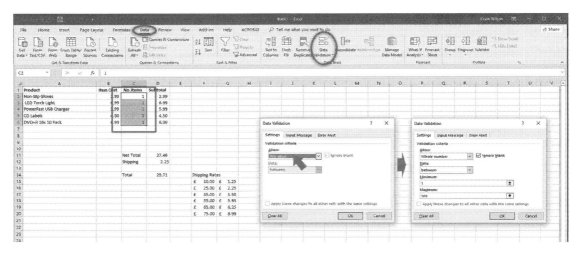

From the dialog box, click the drop down box under 'allow' and select 'whole number', because we only want to allow whole numbers in these cells.

You can also set a criteria for the whole numbers. For example, we could set a range 1 - 500. We could argue that you can't order 0 items on the order form and set a maximum limit of only shipping 500 at a time. So in the data field, select 'between'. Set the minimum value to 1 and the max value to 500.

If there was no maximum limit to the number of items ordered. Instead of selecting 'between' in the data field, you could select 'greater than or equal to' and set the minimum value to 1.

Text Length

You can enforce a specific length of text or numbers with data validation. In our example, we have a field called SKU, this is a unique product code each product in our catalogue has to identify it. In this case, each SKU is exactly 5 digits long and can't be more than 5 or less than 5 digits.

Select the cells you want to apply the validation to, in this example, it's the SKU column.

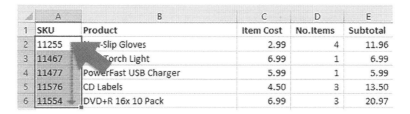

Go to your data ribbon and select 'data validation'.

From the dialog box, in the 'allow' field, select 'text length'.

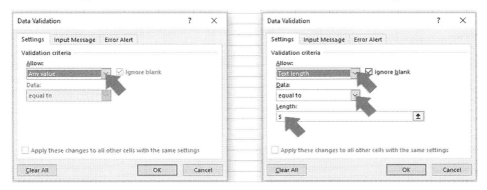

In the 'data' field, select 'equal to', because we want the text length equal to a certain length.

In the 'length' field, select 5. We want the length of the entries to be equal to 5 characters long.

Now when you try type in a number that has more or less than 5 characters, you will get an error message.

Displaying Messages

You can display messages to your users if they input invalid data and messages explaining what data is required.

If we take a look at an example in the **Data Validation Demo.xlsx** workbook

Input Message

Input messages appear, telling the user what data is expected, when the cell is selected.

Going back to our example, remember we added a validation check to the 'number of items' column to accept whole numbers between 1 and 500. We can add an input message to explain this to the user.

To do this, select the cells in the 'number of items' column.

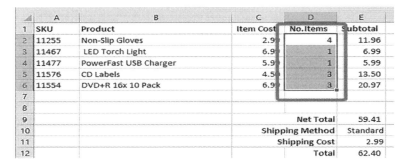

From the data ribbon click 'data validation'.

From the dialog box go to the 'input message' tab.

Check the check box next to 'Show input message when cell is selected', so the message appears when the user clicks on one of the cells.

In the title field enter a title. This could be the name of the column.

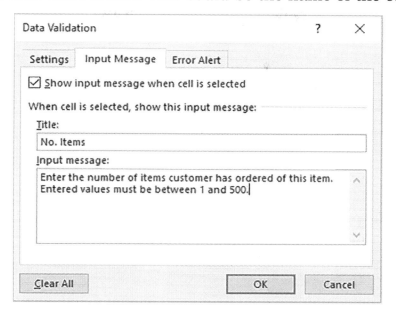

In the 'input message' field, enter the message. This is a brief description of the field and the data that is required from the user.

Click OK when you're done.

When the user clicks on a cell, they'll see the message pop up.

SKU	Product		Item Cost	No.Items	Subtotal	
11255	Non-Slip Gloves		2.99	4	11.96	
11467	LED Torch Light		6.99			
11477	PowerFast USB Charger		5.99			
11576	CD Labels		4.50			
11554	DVD+R 16x 10 Pack		6.99			
				Net Total	59.41	
				Shipping Method	Standard	
				Shipping Cost	2.99	
				Total	62.40	

No. Items
Enter the number of items customer has ordered of this item. Entered values must be between 1 and 500.

Error Messages

If the user enters invalid data, you can alert then using an error message.

If we take a look at an example in the **Data Validation Demo.xlsx** workbook

To do this, select the cells in the 'number of items' column.

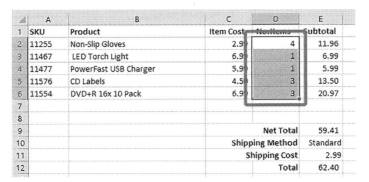

From the data ribbon click 'data validation'.

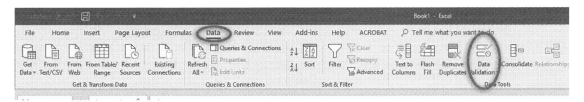

From the dialog box that appears click the 'error alert' tab.

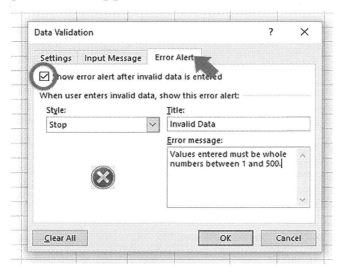

Click the check box next to 'Show error alert after invalid data is entered', so the message appears when the user clicks on one of the cells.

In the title field enter a title. This could be the name of the column.

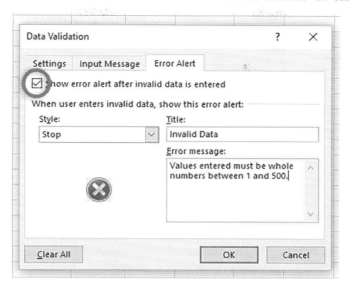

In the 'error message' field, enter the message. This is the message you want to display to the user, type a reminder in here as to what data is expected for that cell.

In the style field. Select the type of error message you want to show. An error, warning or an info box. You have Stop, Warning and Info as shown below.

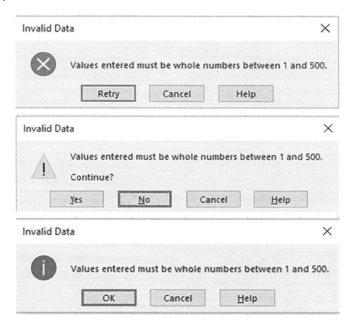

Click OK when you're done. If the user enters invalid data, they'll see the dialog box pop up.

Create a Drop Down List

Drop down lists allow the user to select pre-set options allocated to a particular cell, instead of having to type the data in.

If we take a look at an example in the **Data Validation Demo.xlsx** workbook

To create a drop down list, select the cell you want the drop down list to appear in.

From the Data tab, click the Data Validation.

From the dialog box that appears, in the allow field, click in the drop down, and from the options select 'list'.

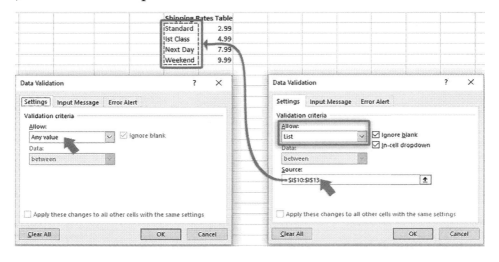

Click in the 'source' field that appears, and select the range of values that you want the user to be able to choose from, in the drop down box we're creating. Click OK when you're done

You'll notice a little down arrow appear next to the cell we selected. Click the arrow to select the desired option and see what happens.

Locking Cells

When your users are using your spreadsheet, they may accidentally wipe out formulas and cells you don't really want them to change.

Excel allows you to lock cells and cell ranges so your users can't change the contents.

If we take a look at an example in the **Data Validation Demo.xlsx** workbook, it would make the spreadsheet more resilient to errors if we locked all the cells with formulas, shipping data, and totals, so the user can't change them.

If you click on 'protect sheet' in the review ribbon, Excel will by default protect all the cells in your spreadsheet. This isn't quite what we want, so we need to tell Excel which cells the user will be able to change.

To do this, select the cells the user is allowed to enter data. In the example, this would be: SKU, Product, Item Cost, No. Items and the shipping option. So highlight these cells.

Right click on the selection and select 'format cells', then go to the 'protection' tab. Click the check box next to 'locked' to remove it. This will unlock the selected cells.

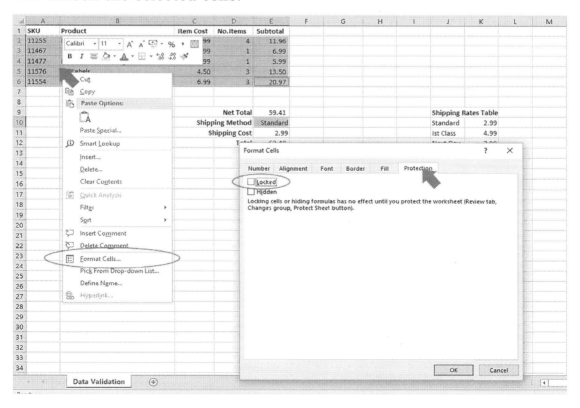

Now go to the review ribbon and select 'protect sheet'.

From the dialog box, you can enter a password to allow users to unlock the sheet temporarily, or leave it blank if not. Below that, you can assign different permissions to the user if you want them to be able to add rows, delete rows or be able to sort. Just click the check boxes next to the options in the list to enable them.

Now, when a user tries to edit a protected cell, they will get an error message.

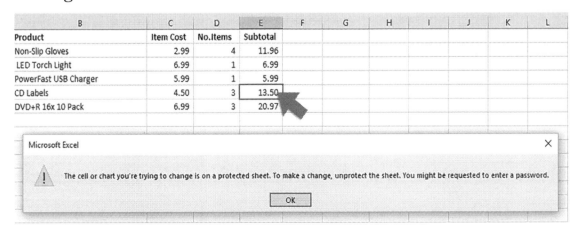

Using Multiple Workbooks

If you have multiple workbooks open at a time, you can easily switch between them on Windows 10. To do this, click the Word icon, on your taskbar.

The workbooks that are currently open will show up as thumbnails. Just click one of the thumbnails to switch to that document.

You can also display the workbooks side by side. Go to your view ribbon and click 'side by side'

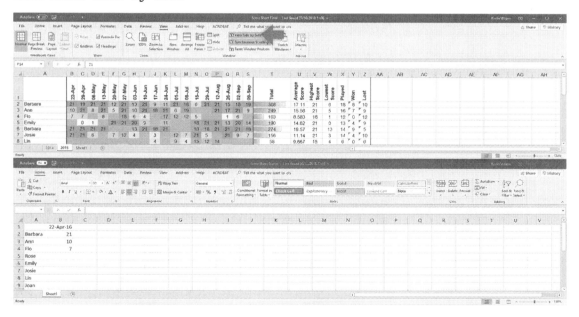

Turn off the synchronous scrolling, otherwise both sheets will scroll at the same time, although this feature can be useful if you are comparing two workbooks.

You can also arrange the windows vertically if that's easier to read. Go to your view ribbon, click 'arrange all'.

From the pop up dialog box select 'vertical'.

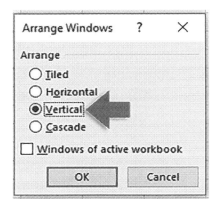

All files open in Excel will be arranged on your screen according to the setting you chose. In this case the two open windows are arranged vertically.

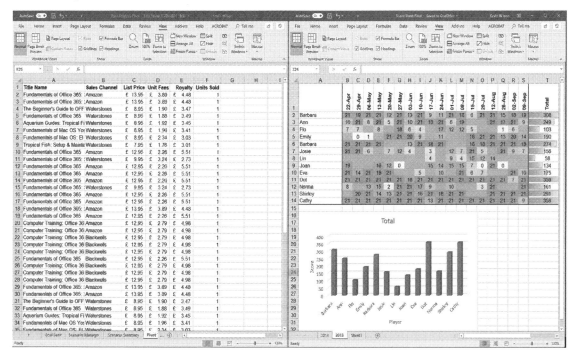

Printing your Spreadsheet

To print your document, click 'file' on the top left hand corner of the screen

From the menu on the left hand side of the screen, select print.

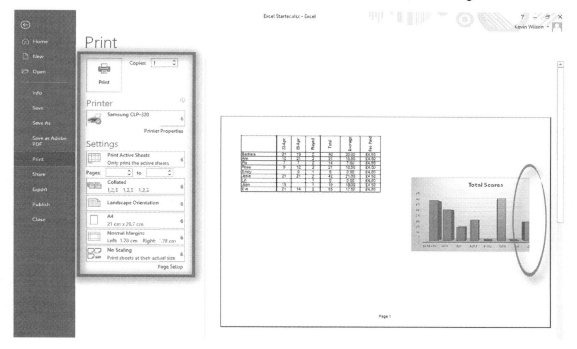

From the settings shown above, you can select the number of copies, the printer you're using, the range of pages you want to print. For example, if you just want to print the first page, last page etc.

You can select landscape or portrait paper orientation - use landscape for printing most spreadsheets.

Select paper size such as letter, legal, A3 or A4.

Margins, you can adjust from here. Select normal, wide margins or narrow margins.

Scaling can be used to make the spreadsheet bigger or smaller to fit your page.

When printing in Excel, keep an eye on the preview on the right hand side of the screen above. Notice how the chart is cut off. Sometimes columns can be cut off too. You can adjust this by going back to your spreadsheet- clicking the back arrow on the very top left of the screen. This will take you back to your spreadsheet.

Excel will have placed dotted lines showing the edge of the page print area. Move the content you want on the page inside this area, either by moving charts by dragging or resizing columns etc.

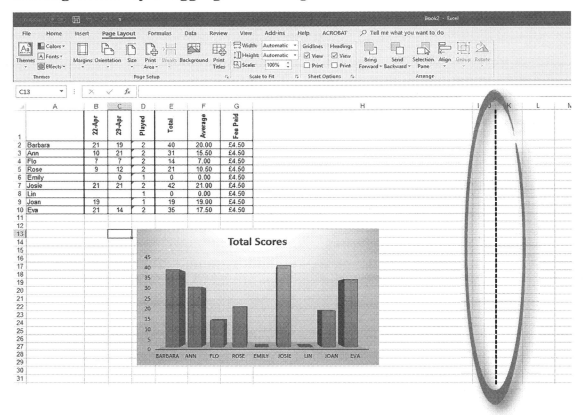

Also check your margins on the page layout ribbon, select narrow.

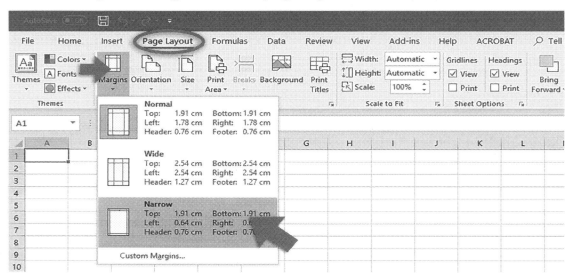

Now go to print your spreadsheet as before. (File -> Print).

Once you are happy with the print preview, print your document.

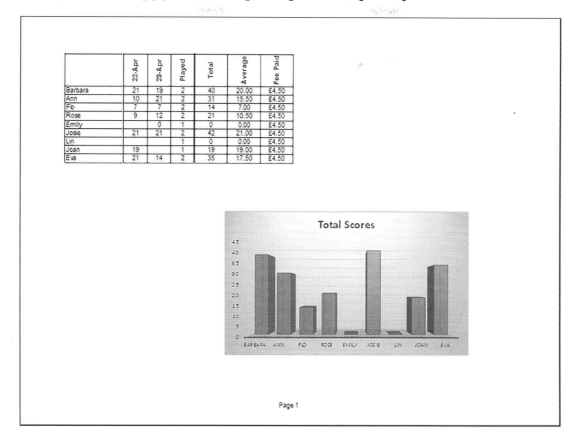

Click the print icon to send the spreadsheet to the printer.

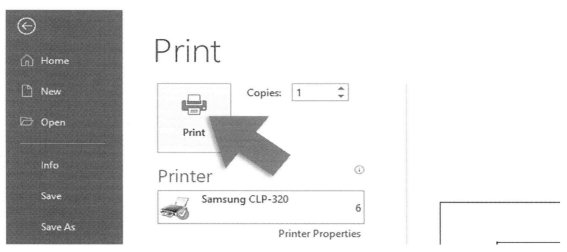

You can make more detailed changes using the 'page setup' settings, in the following sections.

Page Setup

You can use page setup to change how your spreadsheet is displayed on a printed page.

To open the page setup options, click file. Then from the backstage that appears, click 'print'.

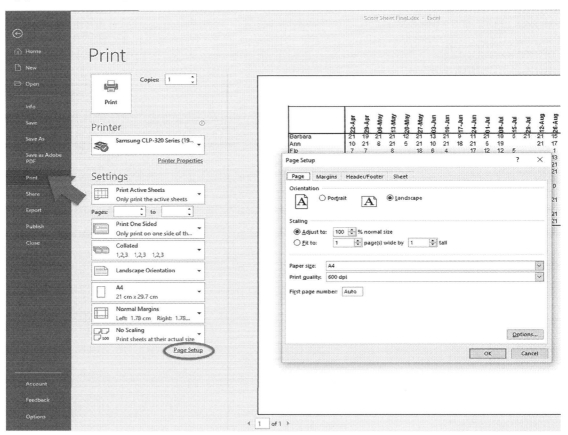

You'll see some basic settings listed down the left of the print window. These are usually the most used settings for changing number of copies printed, single sided or double sided print, orientation - landscape or portrait, paper size - legal or A4, margins and scaling - useful if your spreadsheet just doesn't fit on a page.

To open the full page setup options, click 'page setup' at the bottom of the screen, circled above.

You'll see a dialog box appear with four tabs across the top: page, margins, header/footer and sheet.

Page Options

From the page tab you can set page orientation to portrait or landscape.

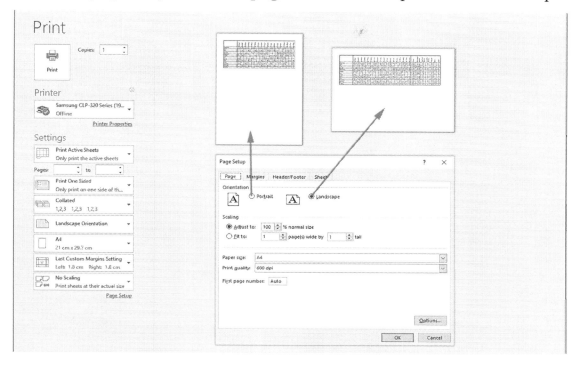

Underneath, you have some options for scaling your spreadsheet. This is useful if you want to shrink your spreadsheet down to fit onto one page. Do this by adjusting the size percentage in the 'adjust to...' field.

If you have quite a large spreadsheet that wont fit on one page, you can scale the spreadsheet across multiple pages. If we look at our example **Score Sheet Final.xlsx** on '2014' worksheet, you'll see that the sheet and the charts appear across 5 pages.

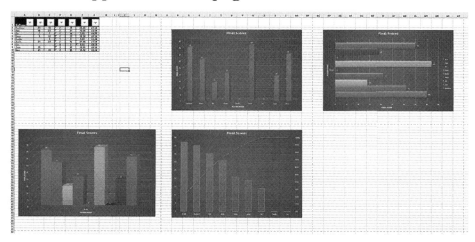

In the scaling section of the page tab, click fit to, then make sure it's set to **1** page wide by **1** page tall.

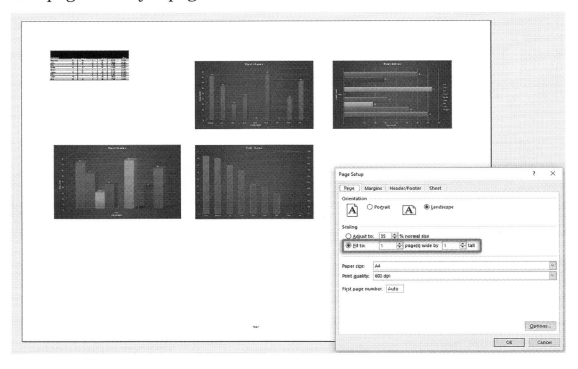

This will fit the spreadsheet to one page.

You can also use the shortcuts on the print screen settings section, as indicated below.

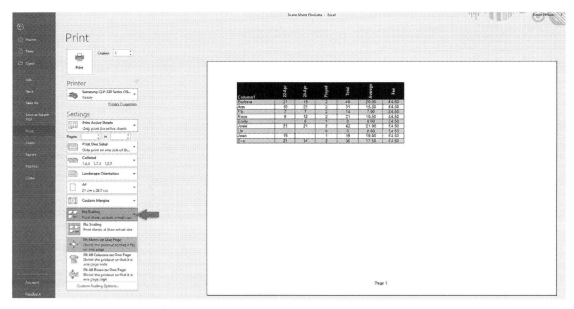

Click 'fit sheet on one page'.

Margins

The margin is the space between the data and the edge of the printed page.

In the illustration below, the top margins are shown in red, the left and right margins are shown in blue and the header/footer margins are shown in green.

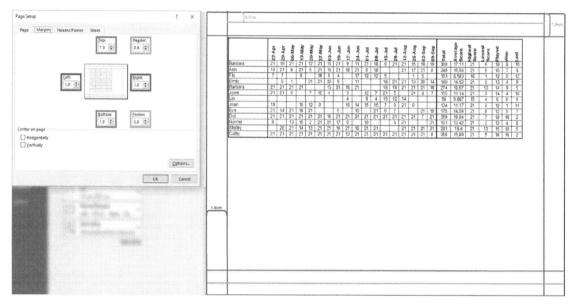

To adjust your margins, go to your page layout ribbon and click 'margins'. From the drop down menu, you can select some presets.

Wide margins give your more space around the edges of your document but you can fit less data on your page.

Narrow margins reduce the space around the edges and allows you to squeeze more onto your page - useful if your spreadsheet just doesn't fit on your page.

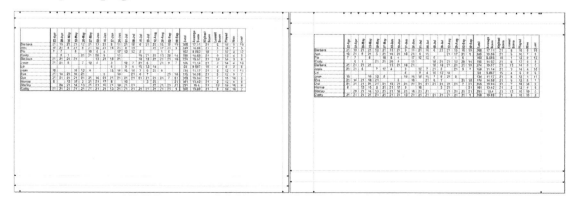

Customising Margins

You can customise your margins to your own specifications. A quick way to do this is to click file, then from the backstage click 'print'.

From the print preview screen, click the 'show margins' icon located on the bottom right of your screen.

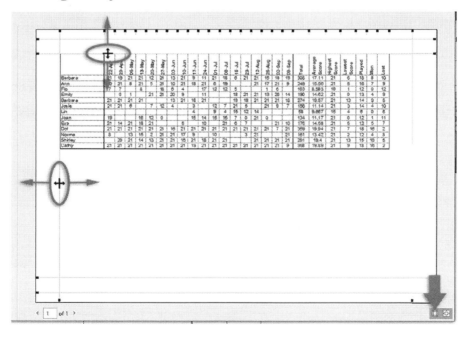

You'll see the margin lines appear on the preview. Click and drag the lines to adjust the margins.

Headers & Footers

Headers and footers appear at the top and bottom of your spreadsheet when it is printed out. You won't see any headers and footers when building your spreadsheet, unless you are in page layout mode.

To quickly edit your headers & footers, click on the 'page layout' icon on the bottom right of your screen. You'll see your spreadsheet on screen divide up into printable pages.

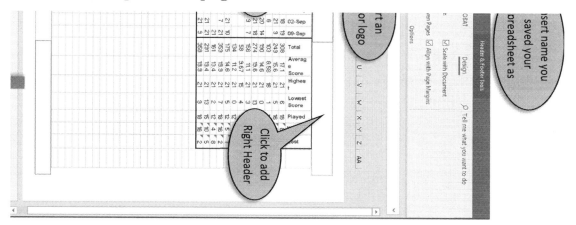

Along the top and bottom, you'll see place holders for your headers & footers. There are three boxes. Click in each of these to add headings.

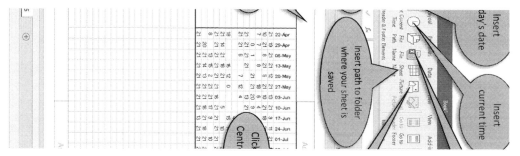

The left box is to add text to the left hand side, the centre box for centred text and the right hand box for right aligned text.

Header		
15/12/2016	League Scores for 2016	&[Page]

To add a header, click in one of these boxes. In this example, I am using the file **score sheet final.xlsx**. I am going to add the date to the left box, the title in the centre box and my initials to the right hand box.

Click in the left hand header box. When you click in one of these boxes, you'll notice a new ribbon appears called 'design'. This ribbon contains all your header and footer tools.

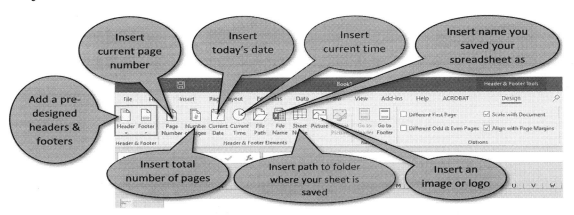

From the design ribbon click 'current date'. This will add today's date to the header box.

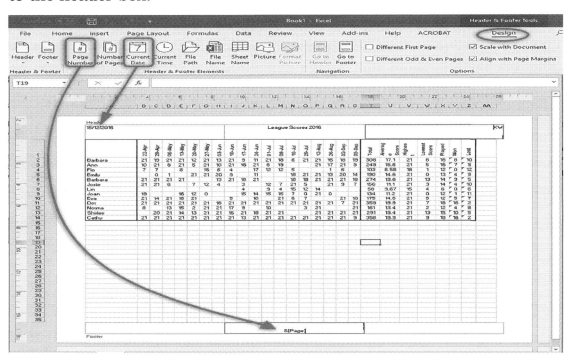

Click the centre box and type 'League Scores 2019' and in the right hand box type your initials. If you want to change the font or text size, you can do this from your home ribbon as normal.

To go to the footer, click in the footer section at the bottom of the page preview. Click the centre box, then from the design ribbon click 'page number.

Page Print Order

Click file, then select print from the backstage. Click 'page setup'. Select the 'sheet' tab.

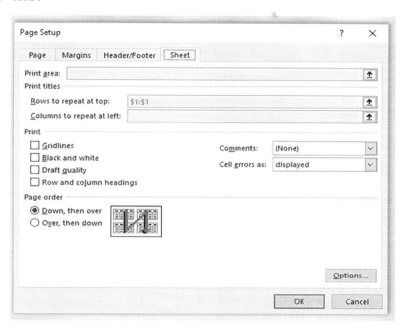

If we take a look at the page order section, this tells Excel in what order to print your spreadsheet if it's larger than one printed page. To explain what this means, if we come out of print preview and take a look at our spreadsheet, you'll notice that Excel has put in some dotted lines.

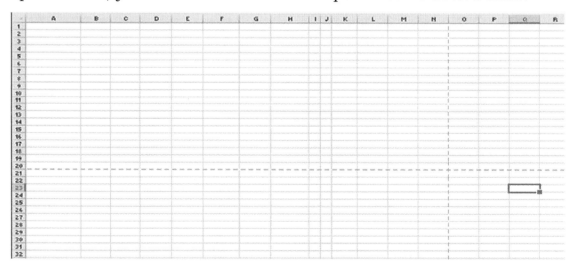

These lines are where Excel has divided your spreadsheet into pages according to your page size and orientation.

Chapter 4: Microsoft Excel

Lets have a look at an example with some data. Open **Score Sheet Final.xlsx** and open the '2014' worksheet.

If you select 'down then over' from the sheet tab on the page setup dialog box, your spreadsheet will print out in this order

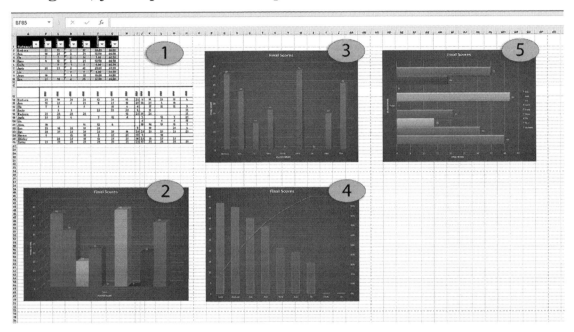

If you select 'over then down', your spreadsheet will print out like this

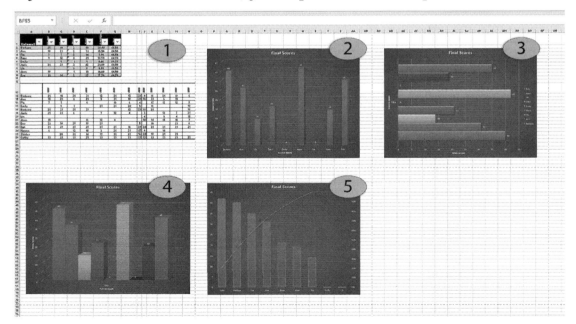

Notice the order pages are printed out.

Print Options

Click file, then select print from the backstage. Click 'page setup'. Select the 'sheet' tab.

Print Row and Column Headers

This prints the row and column reference headers, circled below. Excel doesn't print these by default but should you need to include them in a printout, you can turn them on from the sheet tab.

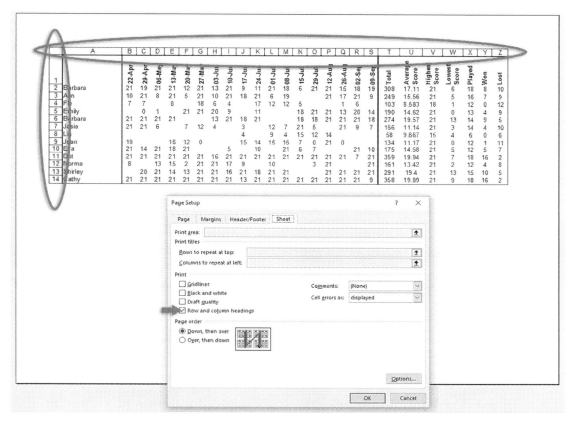

From the sheet tab in the page setup dialog box, go down to the print section and select 'row and column headings'.

Click OK when you're done. Notice the column and row reference headers are visible in the print preview, shown above.

Print Gridlines

This feature prints the gridlines on your spreadsheets regardless if you have added borders when formatting your sheet.

Excel doesn't print these by default but should you need to include them in a printout, you can turn them on from the sheet tab. This feature can be useful for making data clearer in a printout.

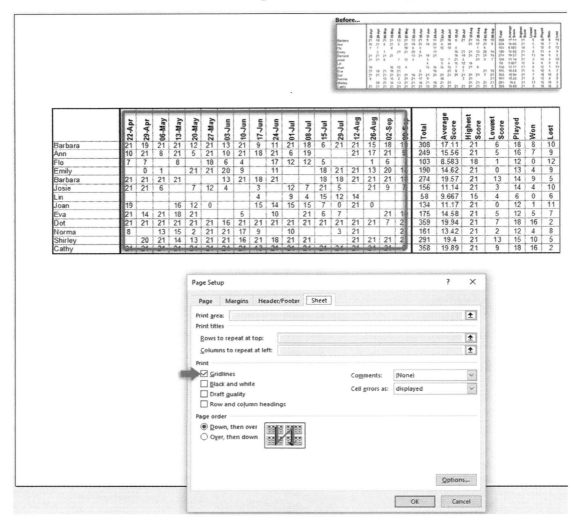

From the sheet tab in the page setup dialog box, go down to the print section and select 'gridlines'.

Click OK when you're done. Notice the gridlines are visible in the print preview as well as the border's we added when formatting our spreadsheet, as shown above.

Print Selection

Print selection allows you to select a specific part of your spreadsheet to print out. You do this by setting a print area.

To set a print area, highlight the area you want to print. In the example **Score Sheet Final.xlsx**, I want to print out the scores and the total, which is the first half of the score table. So highlight A1 to T14, as shown below.

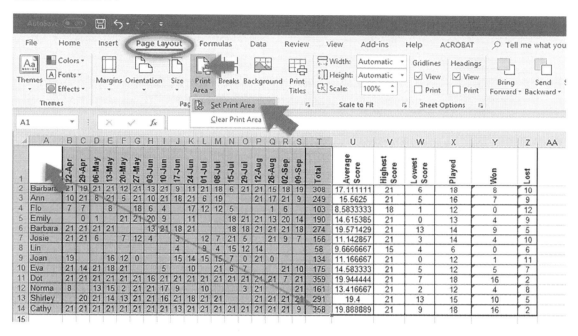

Go to your page layout ribbon and select 'print area'. From the drop down menu, click 'set print area'.

This will tell Excel that you only want to include this area in your printout.

Print Titles

If we take a look at our example bank statement **Statement Example. xlsx,** you'll notice when you go to print preview, it prints out over two pages. If you look at the second page, you'll see Excel has not printed the headings.

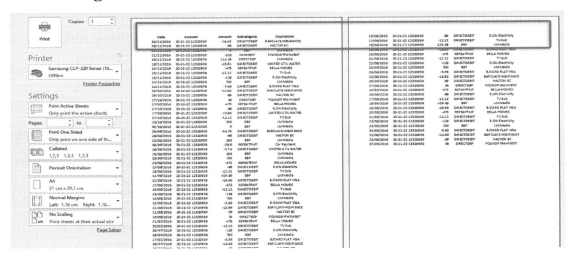

You can mark rows and columns you want to appear on each page using the print titles feature. To do this, go to your page layout ribbon and click 'print titles'.

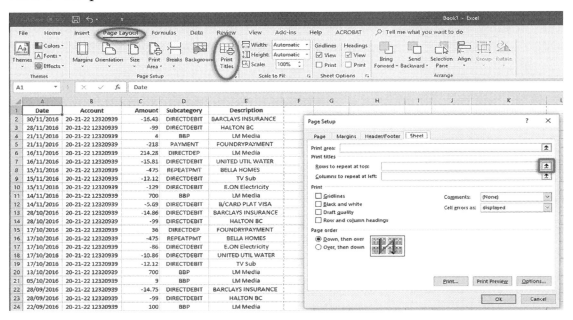

From the dialog box click the small arrow next to 'rows to repeat at top'. We want to repeat the top row on all pages - the column titles.

Now select the top row of the spreadsheet, then click the X on the top right of the small dialog box.

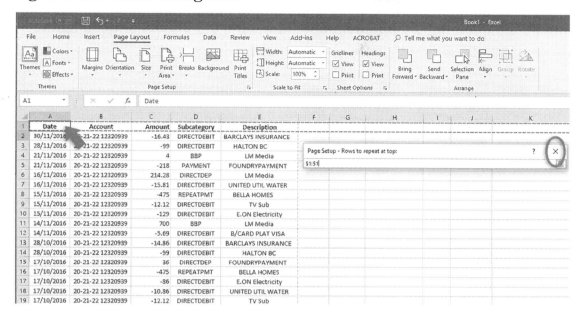

Click OK on dialog box that appears.

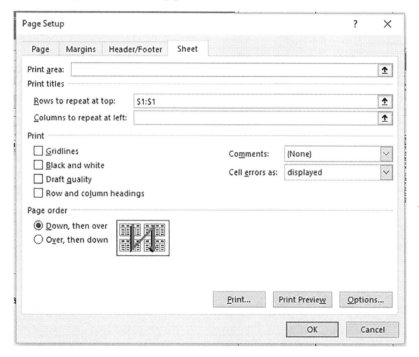

Now, when you go to print preview, you'll see that the top row appears on every page. You can do this with columns too, just select 'columns to repeat at left' from the dialog box instead of 'rows to repeat at top'.

Show & Print Formulas

Sometimes it's useful to be able to view the formulas themselves instead of the result. This helps proof reading and checking to make sure formulas are correct.

To show the formulas, go to your formulas ribbon and click 'show formulas'. To see the whole formula, you might have to adjust the width of the columns.

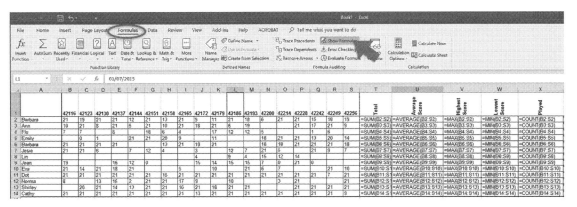

You can also print these formulas if you need to in the normal way. Click file then print.

When you print these formulas, you might need to do some scaling to make them fit onto one page. Use the scaling options at the bottom of the print preview window.

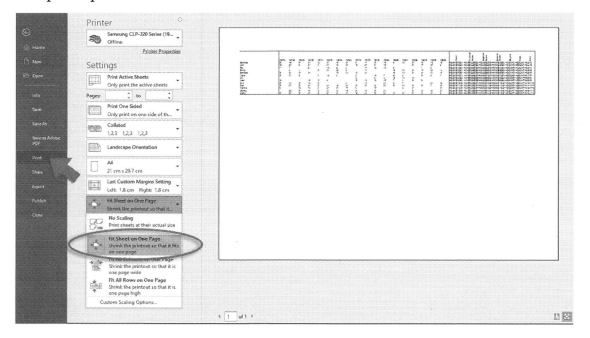

Opening a Saved Workbook

If Excel is already open you can open previously saved workbooks by clicking the FILE menu on the top left of your screen.

From the green bar along the left hand side click 'open', click 'OneDrive - Personal'.

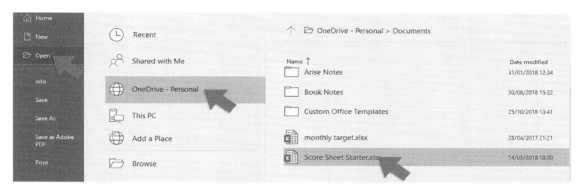

From the list, select the workbook you want to open. The workbook from a previous project was saved as 'excel final.xlsx', so this is the one I am going to open here. Double click the file name to open it.

For convenience, instead of searching through your OneDrive, Excel lists all your most recently opened Excel files. You can view these by selecting 'recent'. Selecting 'workbooks' shows your recently opened spreadsheets, 'folders' shows the folders of the spreadsheets recently opened

Your latest files will be listed first.

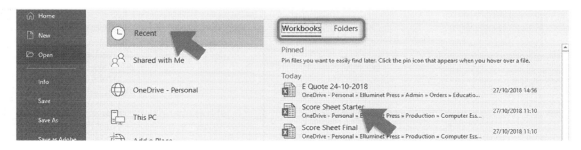

Double click the file name to open it.

Saving Workbooks

To save files, click the small disk icon in the top left hand corner of your screen.

Excel also has an auto save option. This means Excel will automatically save your workbook each time you make a change. To turn this feature on or off, click the 'autosave' icon.

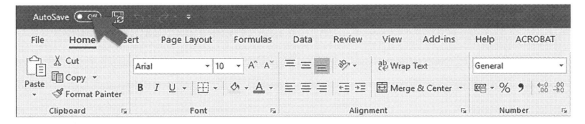

Select your OneDrive - Personal, then select a folder you want to save the file into, eg 'documents'.

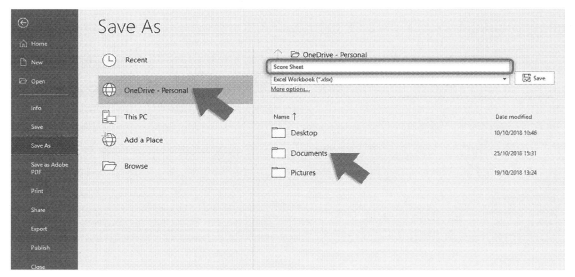

Enter a meaningful name in the text field indicated above by the red arrow.

Click save.

Save as a Different Format

You can save your Excel spreadsheets in different formats depending on what you want to do with the file. You can save as CSV, web pages, and PDFs.

To save files in a different format, eg PDF, click 'file'.

From the backstage, click 'save' or 'save a copy'. Then select OneDrive.

Select where you want to save the file.

Give the file a meaningful name.

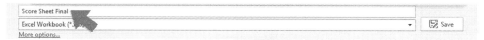

Underneath, select the small down arrow next to the file type field. From the drop down menu, select the file format you want to use.

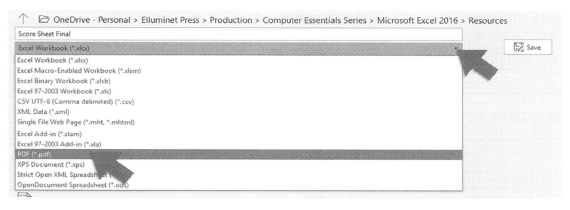

Click 'save' when you're done.

Chapter 5

Microsoft PowerPoint

Microsoft PowerPoint allows you to create multimedia presentations that include animation, narration, images, and videos all from a library of pre designed templates or from a blank canvas.

PowerPoint can be used to create presentations for your up coming sales pitch, perhaps you are giving a lecture on a specific subject, teaching, or feeding back information in a meeting. All these can be enhanced using PowerPoint presentations as a visual aid.

To get your message across, you break it down into slides. Think of each slide as a canvas for the pictures, words, and shapes that will help you build your presentation.

You can create slideshows of family photos and holidays/vacations and send to friends.

You can also print out your presentation slides to give to your audience.

For this chapter, you'll need to download the resources from:

www.elluminetpress.com/office-365-3ed

Getting Started

You can start PowerPoint by searching for it using Cortana's search field on your task bar. Type in 'powerpoint'. Then click 'PowerPoint ' desktop app as highlighted below.

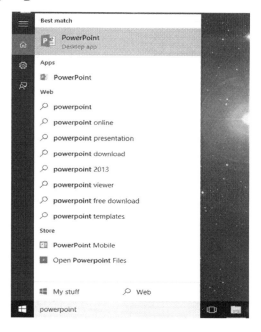

Create a Shortcut

To make things easier, you can pin the PowerPoint icon to your task bar. I find this feature useful. To do this, right click on the PowerPoint icon on your taskbar and click 'pin to taskbar'.

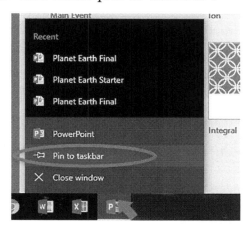

This way, PowerPoint is always on the taskbar whenever you need it.

Chapter 5: Microsoft PowerPoint

Once PowerPoint has started, you'll land on the home screen. On the home screen, you'll see recently used templates along the top, and your most recently saved presentations listed underneath.

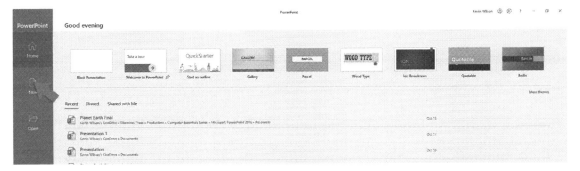

To begin, click 'new' to start. Here you'll find templates and pre-designed themes to help you create your presentation.

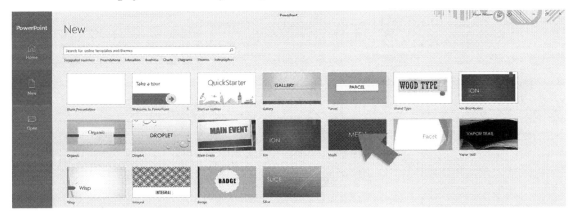

On some templates, you can choose colour schemes and styles for fonts and text. The mesh template has 4 different colour schemes which affect the colour of the text. Click on one and click create.

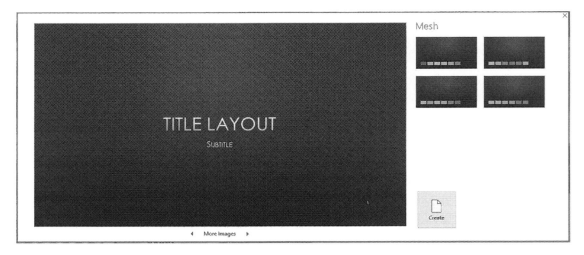

Lets take a look at PowerPoint's main screen. Along the top are your ribbon menu. This is where you'll find all your tools for creating your slides.

Down the left hand side, you'll see a thumbnail list of all your slides in the presentation, in the centre of the screen you'll see the currently selected slide you're working on.

Along the bottom right you'll see icons to add presenter notes and comments. Adjust the view - ie how PowerPoint displays your slides on your screen. You can have normal view, slide sorter view and reading view. The next icon along runs your presentation - use this when presenting to your audience.

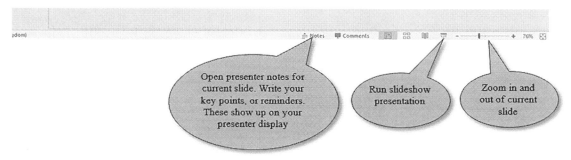

You can also adjust the zoom. This zooms in and out of the current slide. The last icon auto fits the current slide to the same size as the screen.

Speaker notes. These aren't visible to your audience, but will show up on the presenter view while you give your presentation.

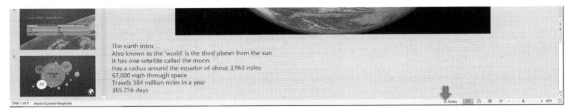

Slide sorter view. Click and drag slides to reorder.

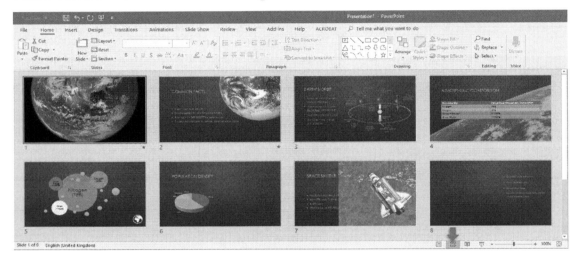

Normal view. Best view for designing your PowerPoint presentations.

The Ribbon

All tools in PowerPoint are organised into a ribbon which is divided into ribbon tabs, each containing a specific set of tools.

The Home Ribbon

All tools to do with text formatting, for example, making text bold, changing fonts, and the most common tools for text alignment, and formatting.

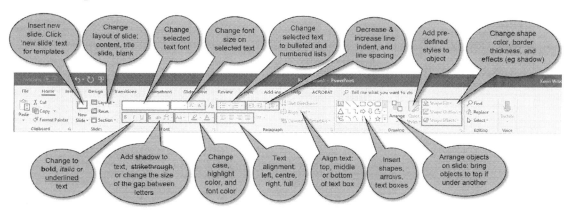

You'll also find your cut, copy & paste functions, as well as shortcuts for adding shapes, and inserting new slides.

The Insert Ribbon

All tools to do with inserting photos, graphics, 3D models, tables, charts, sounds, or movies. You can also insert equations, word art and smart art using this ribbon.

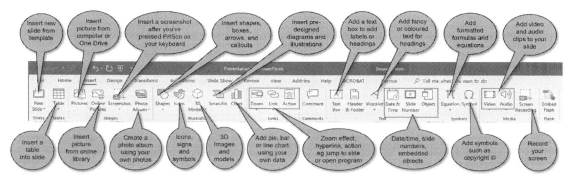

You can create zoom effects to help emphasise an illustration on your slide, as well as screen recordings, and on click actions.

The Design Ribbon

All tools to do with the look of your slide, eg, the slide background.

The Transitions Ribbon

All tools to add effects to show as slides change from one to the next.

The Animations Ribbon

All tools to add slide transitions and adding effects to text boxes, images and headings.

The Slide Show Ribbon

All tools to do with setting up your slide show and running your presentation.

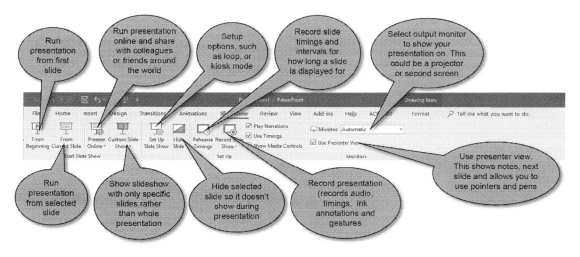

File Backstage

If you click 'File' on the top left of your screen, this will open up what Microsoft call the backstage.

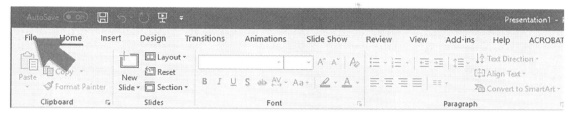

Backstage is where you open or save presentations, print, export or share presentations, as well as options, Microsoft account and preference settings.

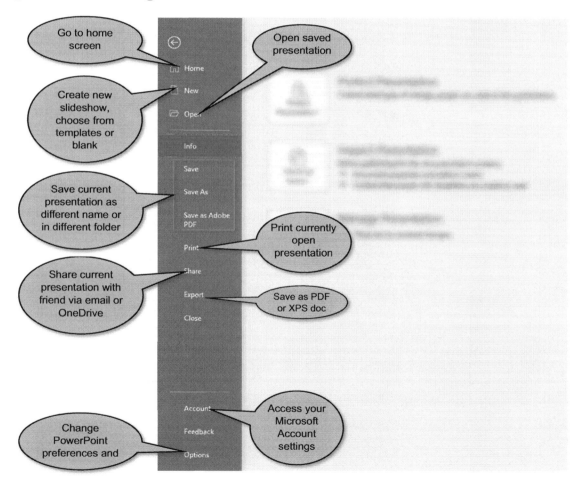

You can also change your Microsoft Account settings, log in and activate your Microsoft Office, change PowerPoint's preferences and so on.

Creating a New Presentation

When you start PowerPoint you'll see the home screen. Here you'll see your most used PowerPoint templates across the top of the screen, underneath that, you'll see a list of your most recently opened presentations.

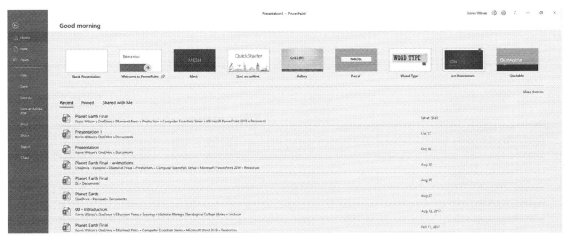

PowerPoint has a wealth of templates and themes for all sorts of different types of presentations. To use the templates, select 'new' from the orange strip along the left hand side of the screen.

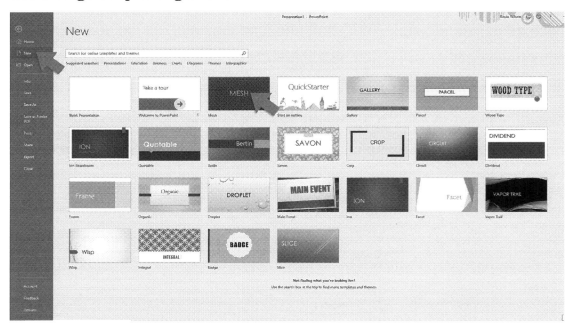

To begin creating our presentation, for this example double click on the 'mesh' template.

This will open up a blank presentation with this template for you to add your content.

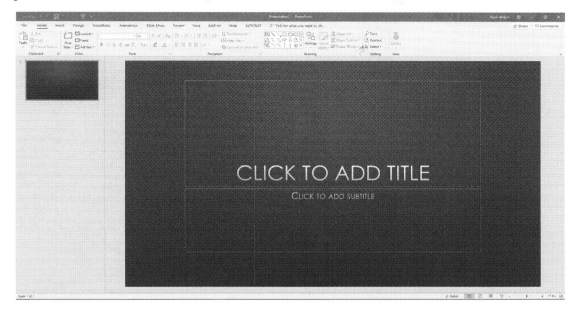

You can search for templates for the presentation you are creating. To do this, use the search field at the top of the screen.

Type in what you're looking for and hit enter.

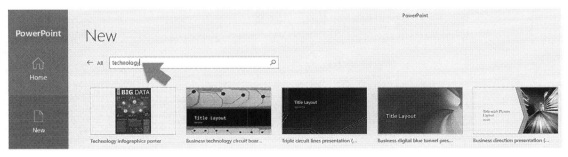

Select a template from the search results.

Designing a Slide

Lets begin by adding the title to our first slide

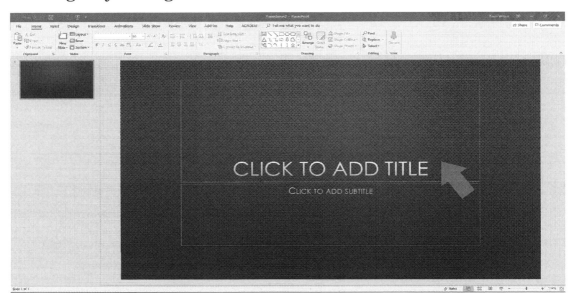

On your slide, click where it says 'click to add title'. This is a place holder for you to enter a title.

Enter the title 'Planet Earth'.

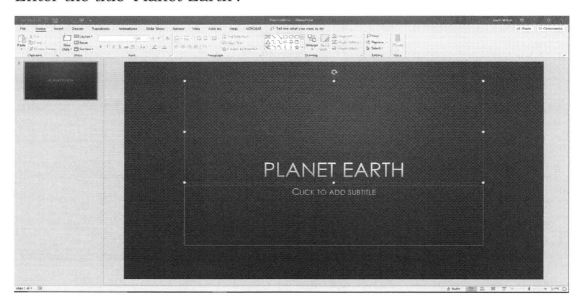

In this example, we won't be adding a subtitle, but you can add one if you want to.

Lets add some images to spice our title slide up a bit.

Adding Images

You can add images or photographs from your computer, for example, photos you have taken. Or you can add images from Office's online library.

From your PC

The easiest way to add an image to your slide, is to first find the image in your pictures library from file explorer. The icon is on your task bar.

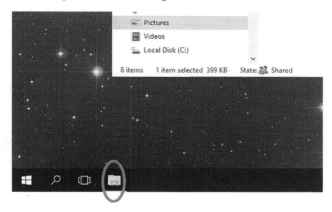

Open up your pictures library, then drag and drop the image onto your open slide, as shown below.

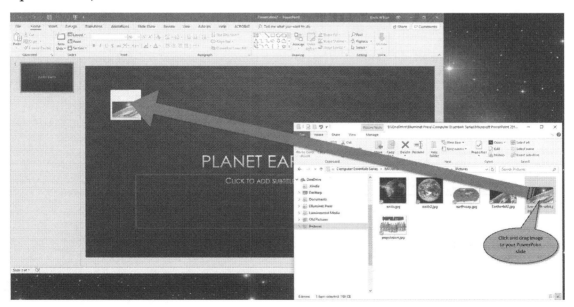

You may need to move your explorer window over to the side if it covers your PowerPoint presentation.

Online Images

You can also add pictures from Office's online library. From your insert ribbon, click 'online pictures'

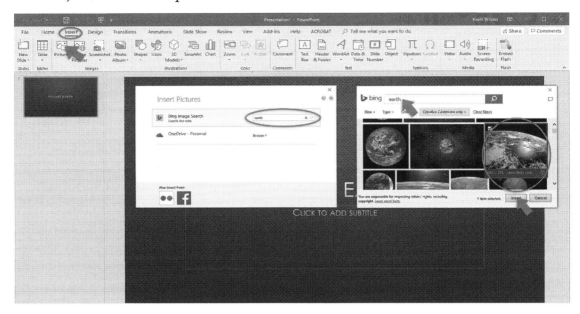

From the dialog box that appears, type your search into the Bing images field and press enter.

From the search results, click the image you want, then click 'insert'.

Now you can place your image and resize it to fit on your slide.

Design Ideas

This is a handy new feature, and appears whenever you insert an image into your slide. PowerPoint will generate some ideas on how to arrange the image you have just inserted into your slide. If you see a design you like, just click on the thumbnail, listed down the right hand side.

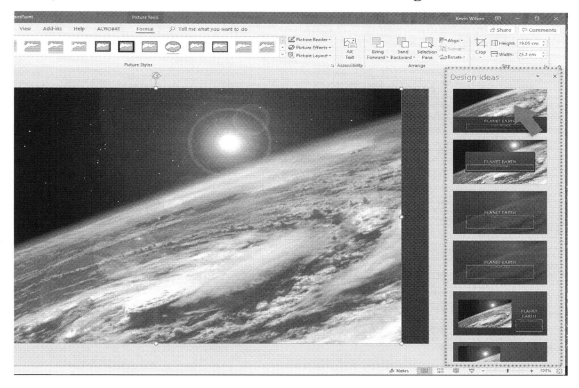

This is a quick way to format and arrange images on your slides.

If you don't choose any of the design ideas, you can arrange the image on the slide yourself.

Resizing Images

If you click on your image, you will notice a border surrounding it.

In each corner and along the sides you will notice little white dots.

These are resize handles. You can click and drag these to resize your image.

To resize the image, click and drag the resize handles until the image is the size you want.

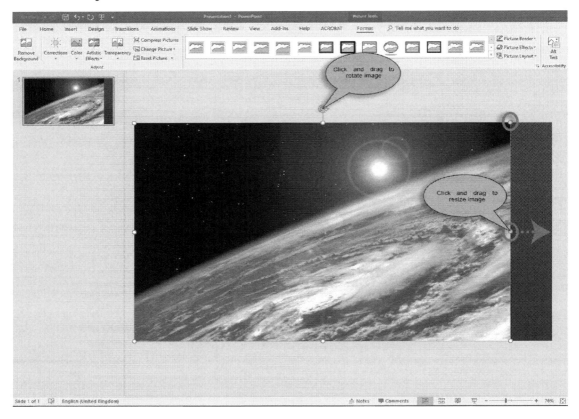

Image Arrangement

You will notice that when you have resized the image, it covers the title. This is because PowerPoint constructs slides using layers. So the title "Planet Earth" will be on one layer, and the image will be on another layer. Now, because the image was inserted after the title, the image layer is on top of the title layer. We want the title layer on top.

We can adjust this by changing the arrangement.

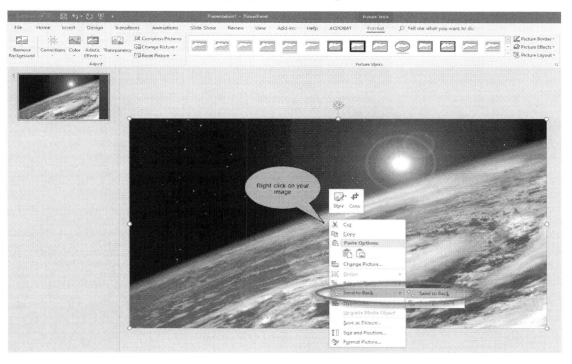

We want to put the image behind the title, so it's in the background on the slide. To do this, right click on your image and from the pop up menu, select 'send to back'.

You will see the image drop behind the text layer.

This is useful if you have a lot of images and text that you need to lay out on your slide.

You can now type the title 'Planet Earth' in the text box, and drag it to the desired position on the slide.

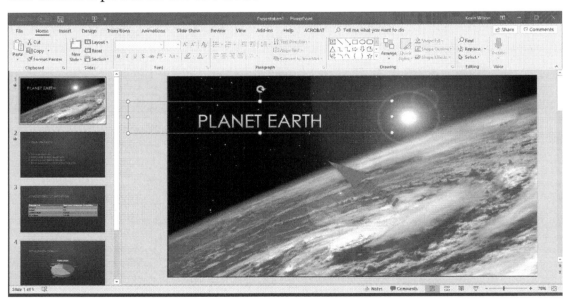

In my example, I'm going to put the title in the top left of the slide against the black. To drag the title text box, when you click on it, you'll see a box appear around the title text box. Click and drag the dotted line surrounding the title, to move your image.

Adding Objects

PowerPoint has a large library of objects you can add to your slides. There are speech bubbles, circles, squares, lines, arrows, stars and a whole lot more to choose from.

Shapes

To insert shapes, go to your insert ribbon and click 'shapes'. From the drop down menu you'll see a whole variety of shapes you can insert.

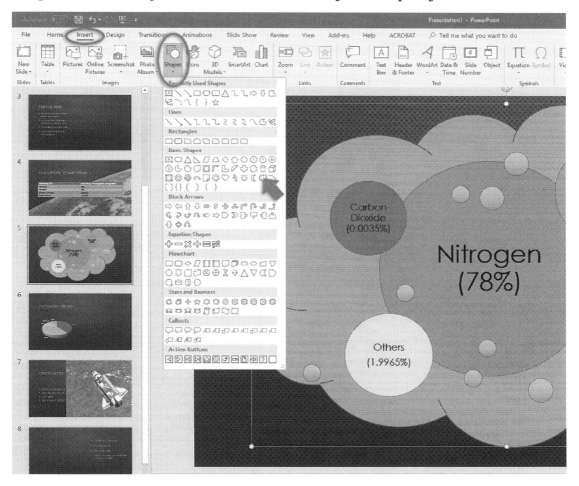

For this example, I am going to add a cloud shape to the atmosphere slide in my presentation. A cloud could represent the air, as this slide is illustrating. Inside the cloud or the air we could show the different gases.

So use the shapes to compliment and illustrate your slides.

You can change the fill colour of the shape and the outline. To change the fill colour, click on the shape and select your format ribbon. Click 'shape fill' and from the drop down, select a colour.

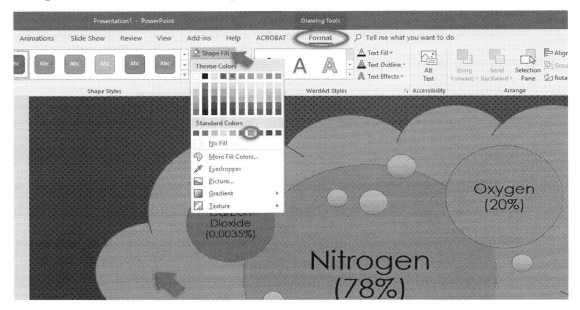

You can change the border of your shape in a similar fashion. Click your shape and from the format ribbon, select 'shape outline'.

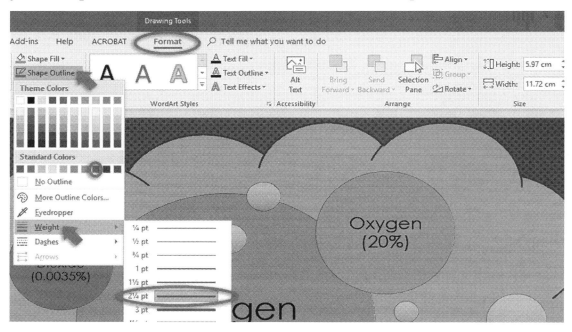

From the drop down, select a colour. Then go further down the menu and select 'weight'. This is the thickness of the border. From the slide out select a border thickness.

Icons

Icons make nice little decorations and illustrations for your slides. You can use them as logos, or to illustrate a point.

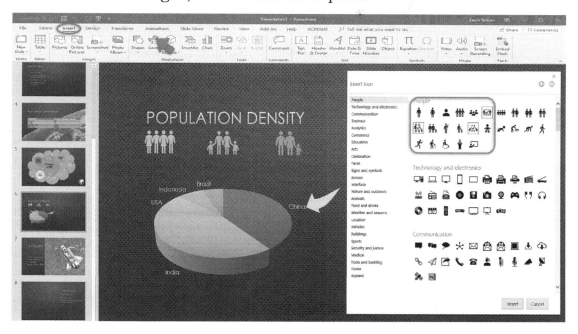

Here I'm using an arrow to point to China for having the largest population, and adding some icons of people to illustrate population.

You can change the colours of your icons. To do this, click on an icon on your slide, then from the format ribbon, select 'graphics fill'.

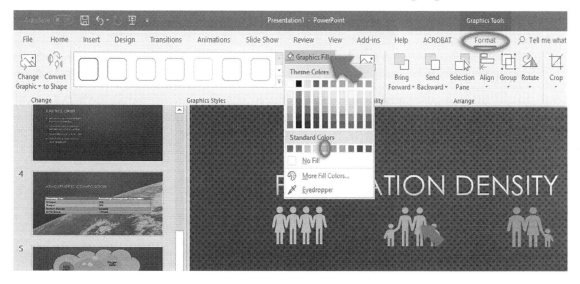

Select a colour from the drop down menu.

SmartArt

SmartArt allows you to create info graphics, charts and so on. There are a lot of different types of pre-designed templates to choose from.

First, insert a new slide, or select the slide you want the SmartArt to appear. To insert SmartArt, go to your insert ribbon and click 'SmartArt'.

From the dialog box that appears, select a design. In this example, I am trying to illustrate the composition of gasses in the atmosphere, so I'm going to choose the circle design below that looks like gas molecules.

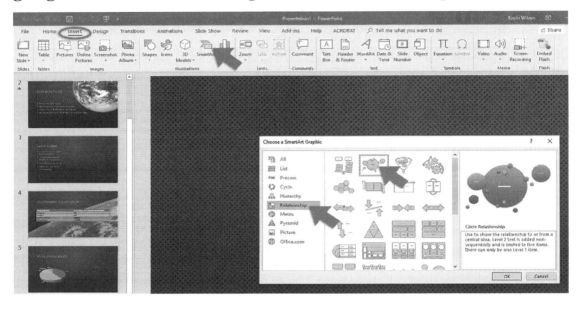

To edit the information, click in the text fields and enter your own data.

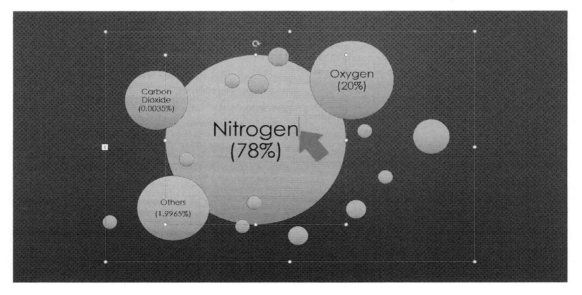

You can also change the design of the graphic. For example, change the layout, colour, add some shadows?

Lets change the colour of the 'other gasses' circle. To do this, click on the circle

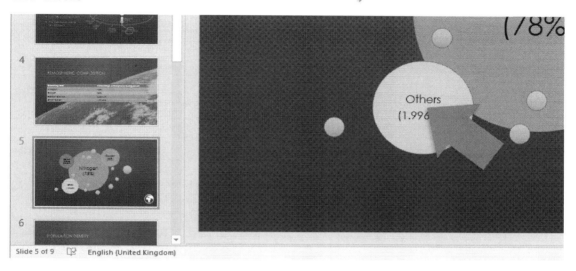

Select the format ribbon under 'smartart tools'.

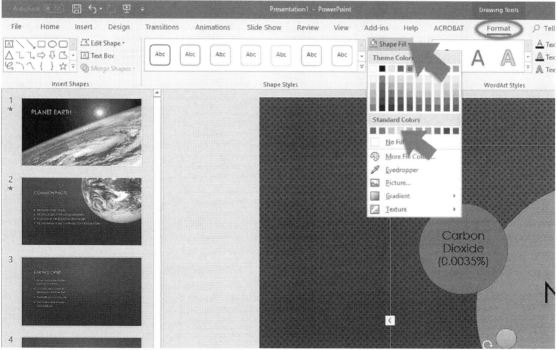

From the format ribbon, click 'shape fill'. Select a colour from the drop down menu. I'm going to colour this one yellow.

Try changing the colours of the other circles.

How about some shadows to separate the circles from each other and add a bit of depth to the graphic.

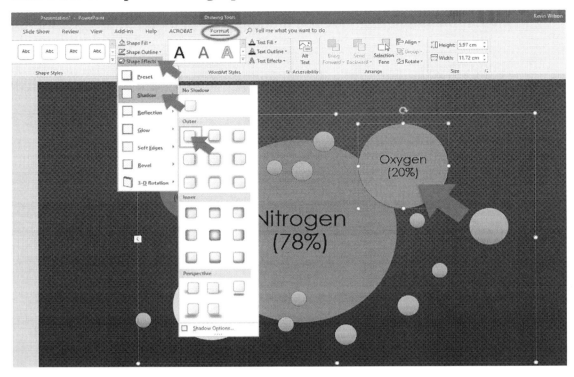

Do the same on some of the other circles. Try some of the other effects too. What about a glow?

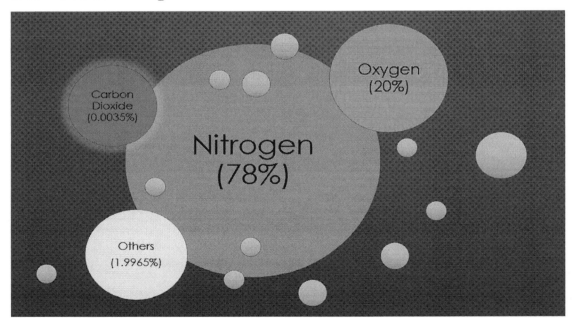

Experiment.

There are also some pre set styles that you can use to format your SmartArt graphic.

To do this, click on your SmartArt graphic on the slide.

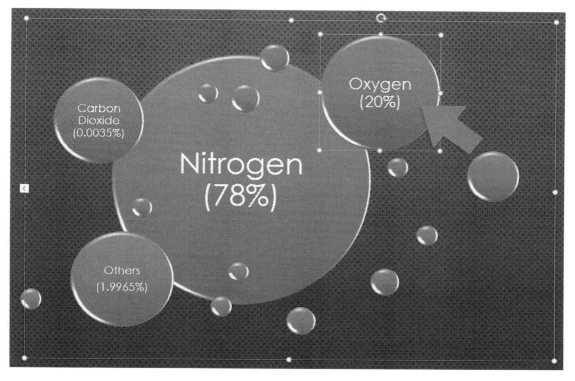

Select the 'design' ribbon under 'SmartArt tools. In the centre of your ribbon, you'll see some styles. Click on one of the icons to select the style.

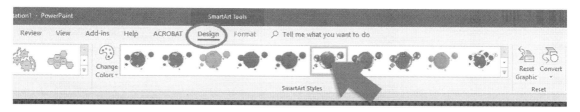

Try different ones to see what effect they have on the SmartArt graphic on your slide.

Adding a New Slide

To continue building our presentation we need additional slides to show our information.

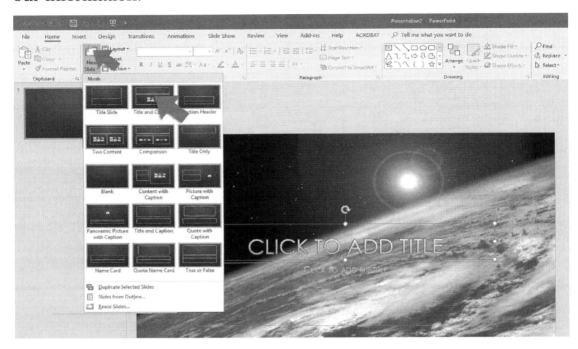

To add a new slide, go to your home ribbon and click on icon 'New Slide'. Make sure you click on the text to reveal the drop down menu.

From the drop down menu, select 'title and content' because we want a title on the slide but also we want to add some information in bullet points.

To add your text and titles, just click in the text boxes and start typing your information as shown below.

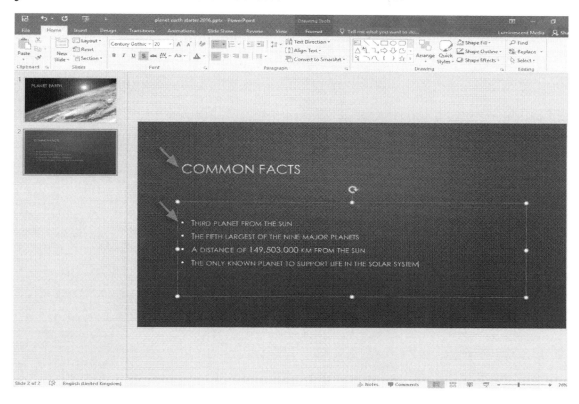

You can make text bigger by selecting it. Drag and highlight the text. From your home ribbon select the increase font size icon.

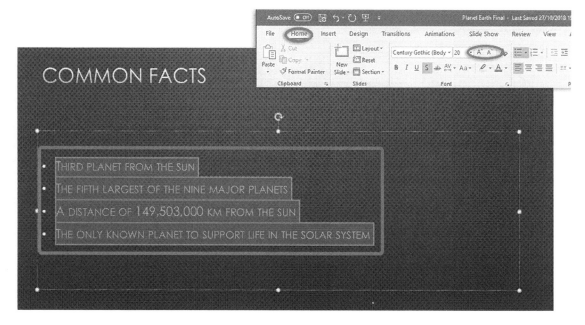

Slide Masters

Slide masters allow you to create layouts and templates that are common to all your slides, so you don't have to make those changes to each slide.

Say you are creating a presentation and want a company logo on the bottom, you can add it to your slide master and the logo will appear on every slide you create.

To edit your slide masters, go to your view ribbon and click 'slide master'.

The larger slide listed down the left hand side is your master for all slides. The smaller ones are masters for individual slide templates such as 'title slides' or 'title and content' slides. These appear in the 'new slide' drop down menu. You can split them up so you can create templates for specific slides.

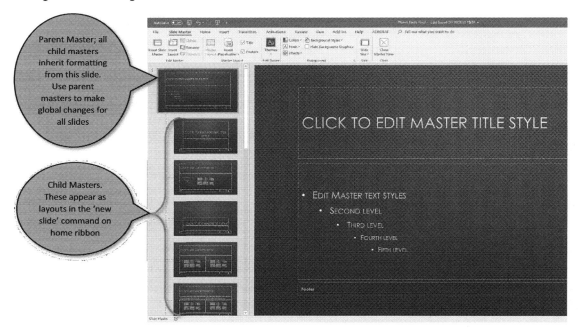

This way, you can have consistent layouts for all your title slides and all your content slides, without having to change the size of the title or position of text or the font every time you insert a new slide.

In this simple example, I am going to add the company logo to the bottom right of every slide. To do this, click on the larger master slide in the list on the left hand side.

Open your file explorer and navigate to your pictures folder, or the folder where the picture you want is saved. Click and drag your image onto the master slide.

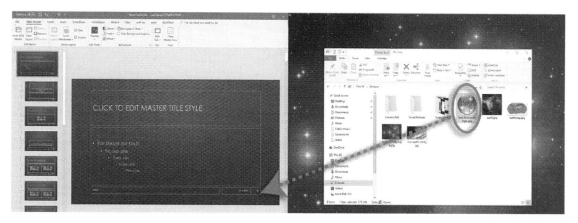

You may need to resize your picture and position it in the correct place.

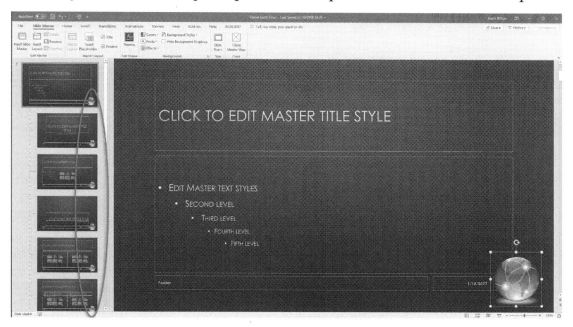

Notice, when you add the logo to the larger slide, it appears on the smaller slides too. This is because the smaller slides inherit their formatting from the larger slide (the larger slide being the parent master slide).

When you're finished click 'close master view'.

Adding Notes

You can add speakers notes to your slides. These notes appear on the presenter view when running your presentation. They can also appear on printed handouts.

First reveal the notes pane. The notes pane is located at the bottom of your screen, but is usually hidden by default. To reveal the pane, click on the dividing line just above the scroll bar, illustrated below with the red arrow. You'll notice your mouse cursor change to a double headed arrow.

Then drag your mouse upwards to reveal the notes pane. You can add speakers notes, bullet points to help you when you're presenting.

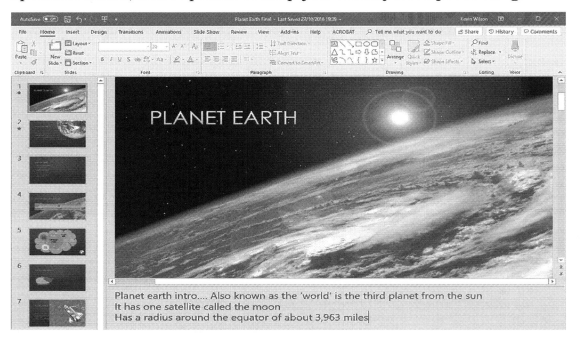

These notes will appear on your presenter view, when you run your presentation.

You can also include your notes in printed slide handouts. Go to FILE, then select print. Change the option, circled below, to 'Notes Pages'.

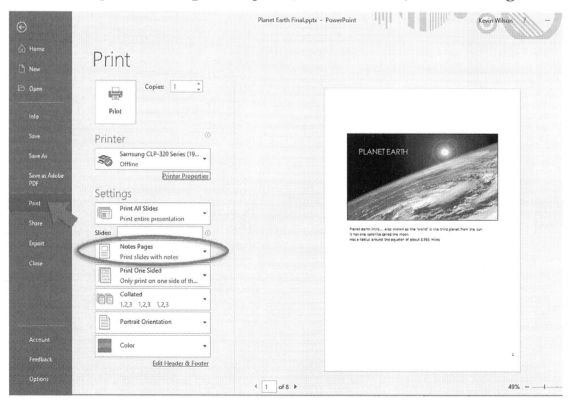

Changing the Slide Order

You can easily change the order or the slides in your presentation. To do this, on the left hand side of your screen, click and drag the slide thumbnails.

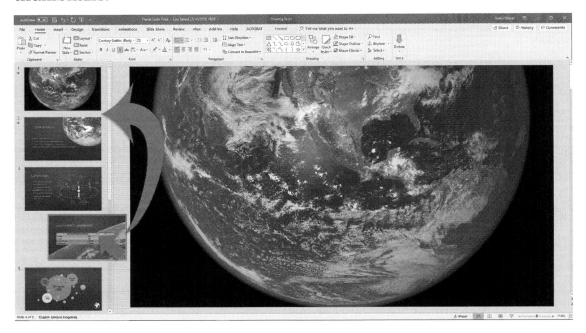

You'll see the other slides shift out the way. Drop the slide into the position you want.

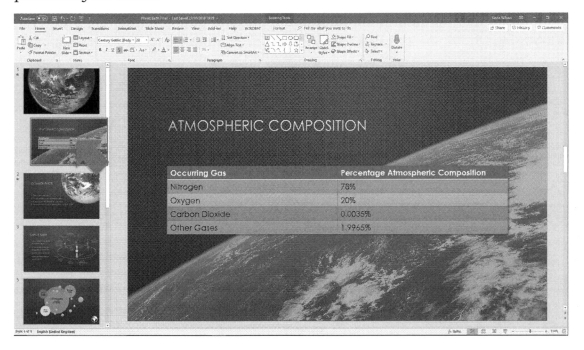

Insert a Table

We are going to add a table to a new slide. In this example I have added a new slide with 'title and content'. You can also add a table from the insert ribbon.

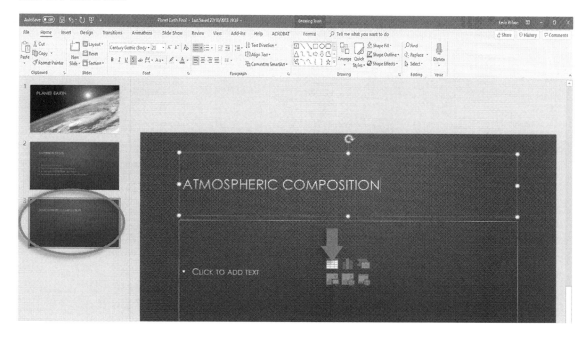

To add a table to this slide, just click the table icon from the template as indicated above. In the dialog box that appears, enter the number of columns and rows. This table is going to have 2 columns.

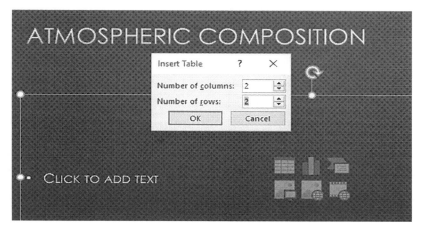

Once you have done that, enter the data into your table. Press the tab key to move between cells of the table. Don't worry about the number of rows, a new row will be inserted at the end of each row when entering your data - just press tab.

You can also insert a table directly. To do this, go to your insert ribbon and click 'table'.

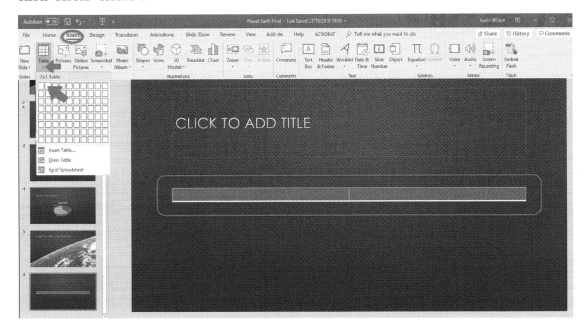

You can move or resize the table. If you click on the table, you'll notice an outline appear around the table with small dots around the edges. These are called resize handles and you can click and drag them to resize your table.

If you click on the edge line of the table and drag your mouse, you can move your table to the desired position on your slide.

Formatting Tables

To do basic formatting, select the table with your mouse and click your design ribbon.

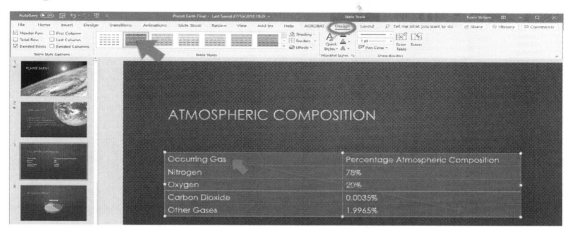

From here you can add some borders, change the shading or add an effect.

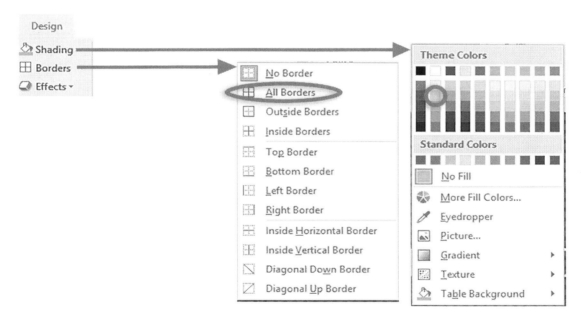

Click 'shading' and add a background colour to the cells. Since the slide is mostly grey, I'm going to choose a lighter grey to compliment the slide colour.

Then click borders, and select 'all borders' to put a border around all cells. You can also select individual cells or groups of cells and add borders to those to emphasise different parts of the table.

You can adjust the border thickness using the 'draw borders' section of the design ribbon. Click the drop down circled below and from the menu, select a thickness.

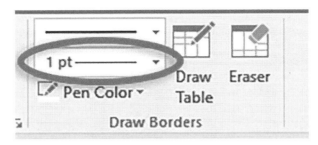

Finally click 'effects'. Select the type of effect you want (shadow or reflection effects work well). In the example, I am going to add a reflection effect to the table. Go down to 'reflection' and from the slide out, select the type of reflection effect.

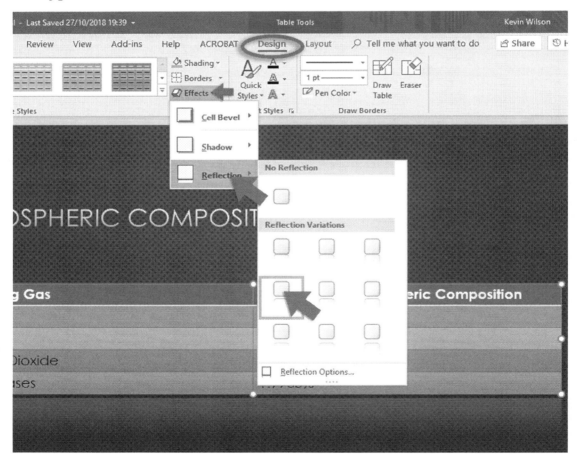

Try experiment with some of the other borders, shadings and effects using these controls.

Table Themes

You can format your table using PowerPoint's pre-designed themes. This makes formatting your table quick and easy.

Click on the table then select the Design ribbon.

Along the centre of the Design ribbon you will see a number of pre sets. Click the small down arrow at the bottom right to expand the selections, circled above.

Click on a design to apply it to the table.

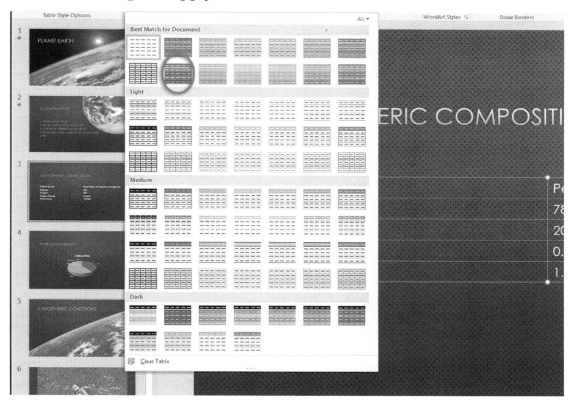

You can experiment with the designs by clicking on these and see how they look.

PowerPoint will automatically format the table using the colours and shadings in the themes.

Add a Chart

We are going to add a chart to a new slide. In this example I have added a new slide with 'title and content'

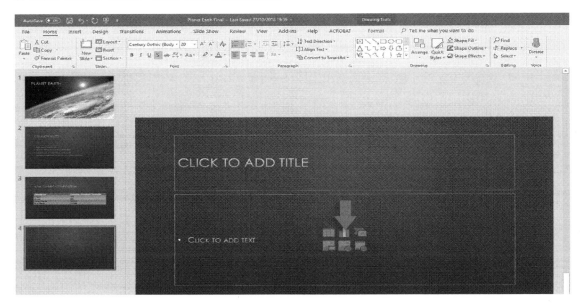

On the slide template, click the chart icon shown above. From the dialog box that appears, select the type of chart you want. In this example, I am going to use a nice 3D pie chart.

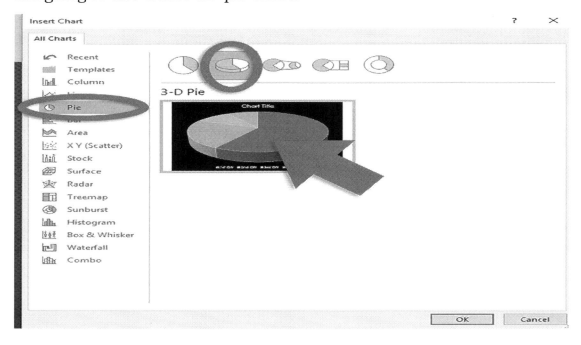

Click OK when you are done.

You'll see a spreadsheet like table open up where you can add some data. Enter the data in table shown below.

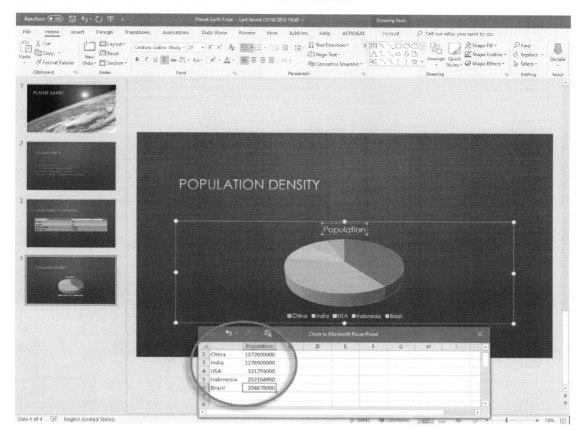

As you enter your data, you'll notice PowerPoint begins to construct your chart.

Remember when constructing your charts, **Column A** is the **X axis** on your chart, **Column B** is the **Y axis**.

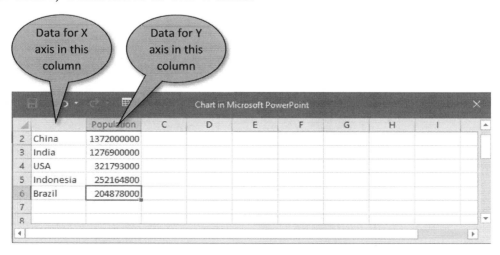

Formatting Charts

PowerPoint has a few chart formatting tools to take note of. First click on your chart to select it, you'll notice two new ribbons appear: design and format.

Lets have a look at the design ribbon. Note that there are actually two design ribbons. Make sure you select the ribbon under 'chart tools'.

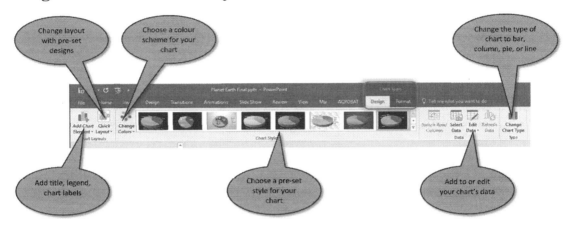

From here, you can do most of your basic chart formatting such as adding titles, editing your chart data and apply chart styles to make your charts look more visually appealing.

Chart Titles

To a chart title, click on your chart and select the design ribbon. From the design ribbon, click 'add chart element'. Go down to 'chart title' and from the slide out click 'above chart'.

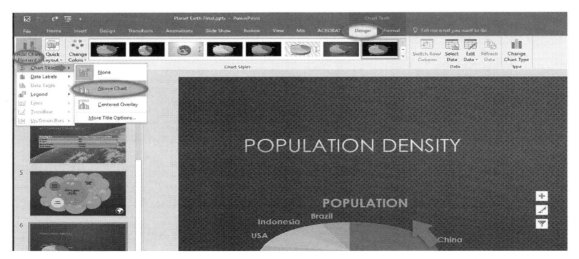

Data Labels

Data labels are the labels that describe what the elements of the chart represent. You can either label each element of the chart or use a chart legend.

Click on your chart.

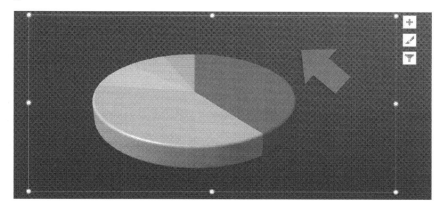

Select 'add chart element' from the design ribbon. From the drop down menu, go down to 'data labels' and from the slide out, click 'data callout' or 'outside end'.

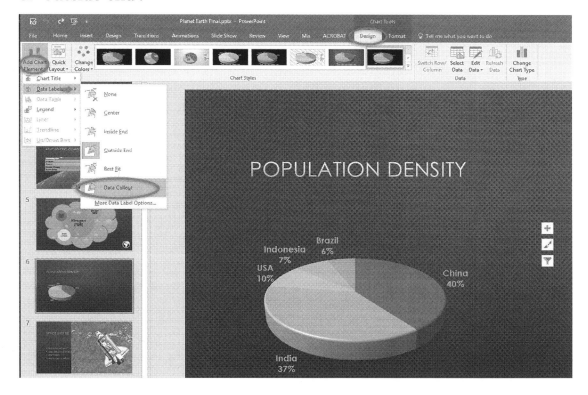

This tells PowerPoint where to position your labels.

Chart Legends

Chart legends are good for explaining what the different parts of your chart represent.

To add a legend to your chart, click on your chart and select your design ribbon, then click 'add chart element'.

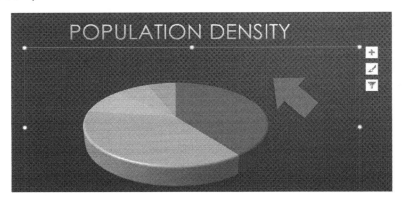

From the drop down menu, go down to 'legend' and from the slide out, click on the position you want the legend.

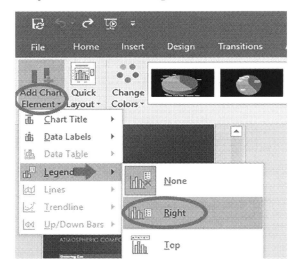

On the right is usually a good place.

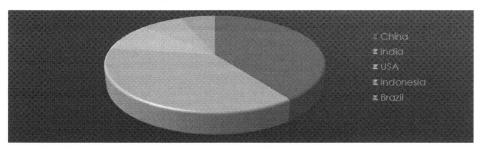

Edit Chart Data

To edit your chart data, click on your chart to select it.

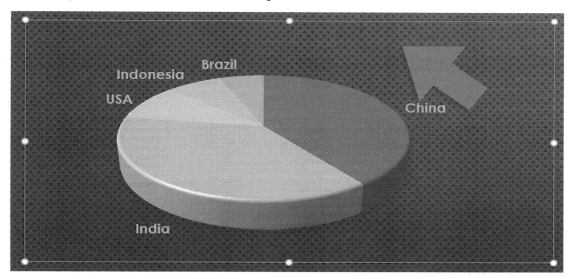

Select your design ribbon under 'chart tools'. Click on 'edit data'. If you get a drop down menu, select 'edit data' again.

You'll see a spreadsheet like window open up with the data used to generate your chart.

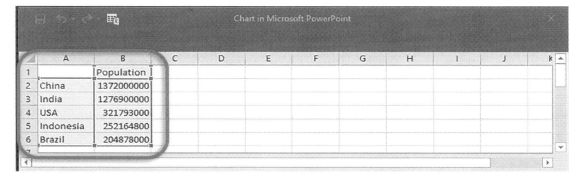

You can edit the data or add to the data from here and PowerPoint will automatically update your chart accordingly.

Chart Styles

You can style your charts pretty quickly using the style options on your design ribbon.

First, click your chart to select it.

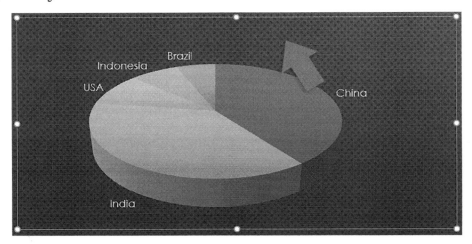

Go to the 'design' ribbon under 'chart tools'. On the centre of your design ribbon, you'll see some chart styles. Click on one of the thumbnail icons to apply a style to your chart.

PowerPoint will apply the style to your chart.

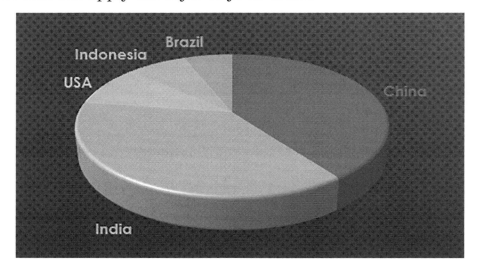

Chart Colour Schemes

You can also change the colour schemes (the colours used to represent the different data in your chart).

Sometimes the colours aren't as clear, so having the ability to choose different colour schemes helps with clarity and makes your chart stand out a bit more on your slide.

To do this, click on your chart to select it.

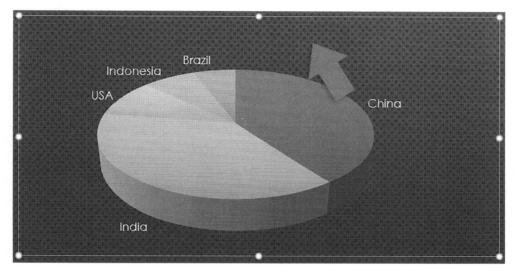

From the design ribbon under 'chart tools', click 'change colors'.

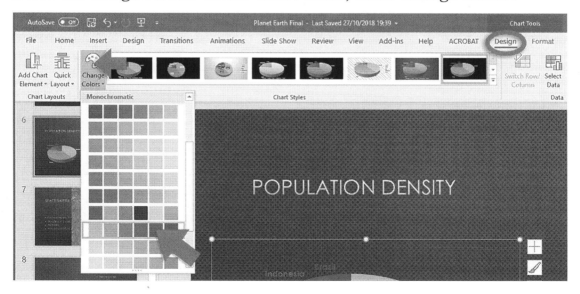

From the drop down menu, select a colour scheme that shows up your chart clearly and matches the colours of your slide.

Adjusting Images

Sometimes it helps to make some minor adjustments to your photographs or images to make them blend into your slide a little better. You can change the brightness, contrast and colours of the images. You can do all this by experimenting with the adjustments on the format ribbon.

For example. If we add another slide with the photograph of planet earth, the photo has a black background. We can make a few adjustments to this image to make it blend into the slide a little better.

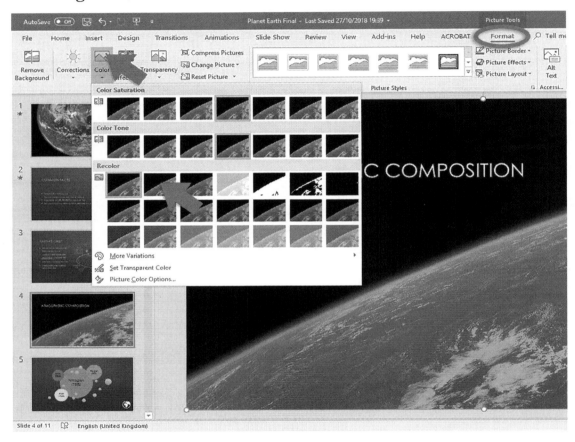

Click on the image on the slide and then click the format ribbon. On the format ribbon go to the adjustment section on the left hand side.

From the drop down menu, you can select 'color' if you want to change the colour blending of the image, eg select a grey tint to match the background theme of the slide.

You can also do the same for other corrections such as brightness and contrast. Do this by selecting 'corrections' from the format ribbon instead of 'color'.

Removing Image Backgrounds

This works best on images that don't have complex or crowded backgrounds.

Instead of seeing the black background from the image, it would be better to use the slide background itself, rather than covering it up.

To remove the background, make sure your image is selected and click 'remove background' from the format ribbon.

This will highlight all the bits PowerPoint is going to remove from the image in dark purple. You will also notice a box surrounding the area.

Resize this box by clicking and dragging the resize handles until the box surrounds the area of the image you want to keep as shown above. In this case, around the earth.

Once you have done this click 'keep changes'.

Notice you can now see the slide background instead of the black background on the image.

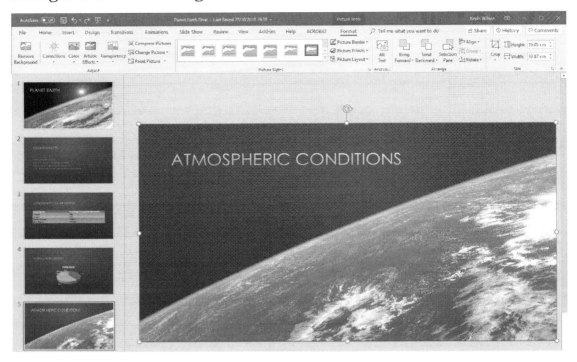

If your image is a bit more complex and doesn't have a solid background, such as this one of the shuttle, we'll need to tweak the purple mask a bit. After we align the mask box around the shuttle, if you look closely, you'll see that the purple mask has spilled over onto the edges of the wings.

You can mark these areas of the image you don't want PowerPoint to mask out. To do this, click 'mask areas to keep'.

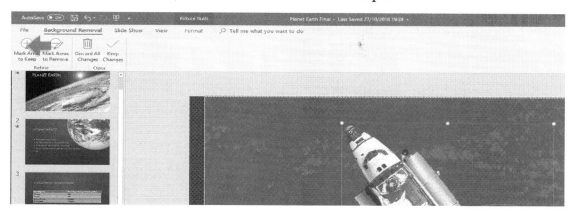

On your image, draw a line across the bit of the image you want to keep. In this case, the edges of the wings. Shown below.

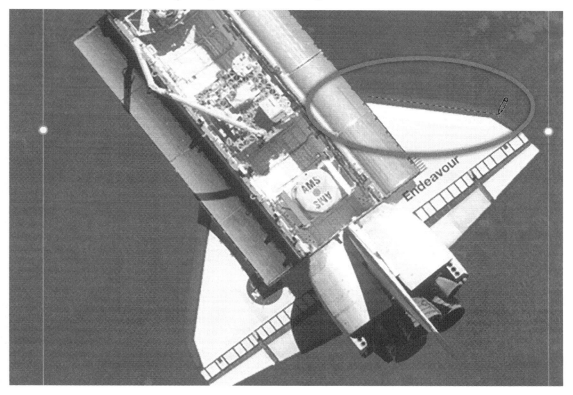

Once you've done that, you'll see the purple mask disappear from the edges of the wings.

Remember, anything highlighted in purple will be removed.

Click 'keep changes', when you're finished.

Slide Transitions

A slide transition is an animation or effect that is displayed when you move from one slide to the next.

To add transitions to PowerPoint slides, click the slide you want to add the transition to, then go to the transitions ribbon.

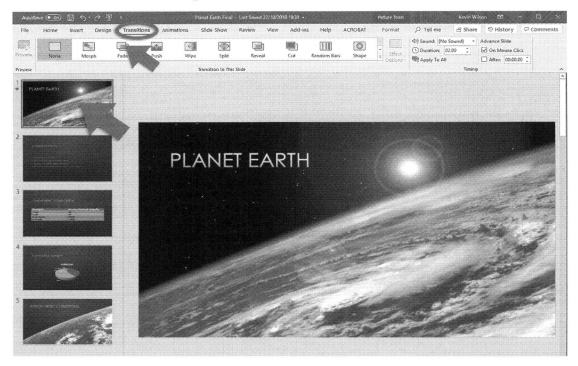

From the transitions ribbon, you can select from several pre set transitions. If you click on a transition, for example 'fade', this will apply the transition to the selected slide.

You can change the duration of the transition. The current duration is 0.7 seconds. If you want a slower transition, increase the duration. Try 1 or 2 seconds.

You can tell PowerPoint to wait for a mouse click to transition to the next slide, or you can make PowerPoint transition to the next slide after a set time. On the far right of your transitions ribbon, use 'on mouse click' to transition to next slide when you click the mouse, or un-check 'on mouse click' box and adjust the timer where it says 'after' with the length of time to display the slide.

To apply the transition to the whole presentation, click 'apply to all' on the right hand side of the ribbon.

Morph Transitions

The morph transition allows you to animate objects from one slide to the other. You can use text, shapes, pictures, charts, WordArt, and SmartArt.

To use the morph transition, you'll need two slides with at least one object appearing on both. The best way to achieve this is to create one slide with all the objects in the start position, then duplicate the slide and move the objects into the finish position. First slide morphs into second slide.

Create a new slide. In this example, I'm going to add the three planets, venus, earth and mars. This is the slide with all the objects in the start position of the morph animation.

Now, duplicate the slide. This slide has all the objects in the end position.

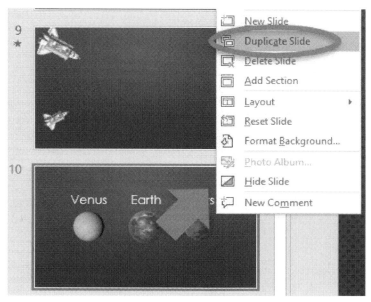

On the duplicate slide, move and resize the objects into the end position. You can also add more objects. I'm going to add a text box to show the stats for planet earth

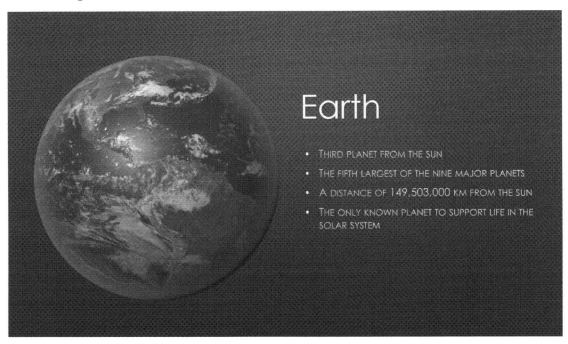

On the transitions ribbon, select morph.

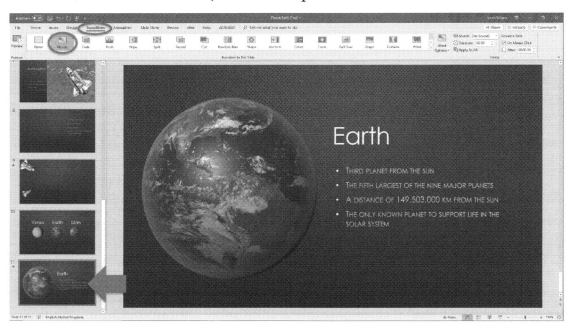

Watch the two slides transition into each other. Click 'preview' on the left hand side of the transition ribbon to see the morph.

Animations

You can add animations to slides to move text boxes, make bullet points appear, animate shapes and so on. This can help to make your presentation flow so objects and text appear at the right time while you're presenting. Animation effects can also help to emphasise certain points.

Effects

Looking at the slide below, say you wanted each bullet point to appear one at a time, instead of all at once.

You can do this by adding an animation to the text box. Click into the text box and select your animations ribbon.

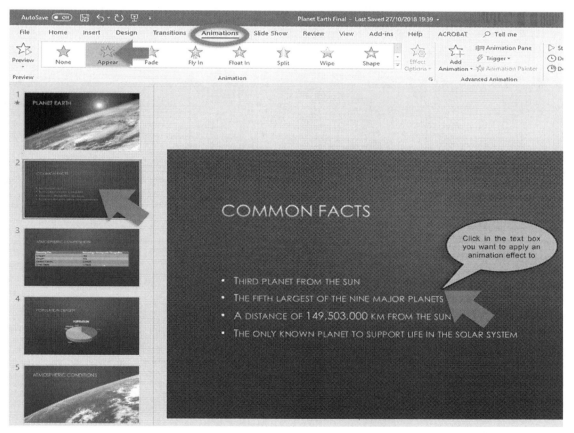

For this example, I am going to add a fade effect. To do this, select 'fade' from the animation pre sets circled above.

Try one of the other effects and see what happens. You can apply an effect, in the same way, to any object, photo, textbox, heading or logo.

Motion Paths

A motion path is an animation effect that allows you to move an object such as a photo, shape or text box across the screen.

To create a motion path, first click on the object you want to animate. For simplicity's sake, I'm going to use a circle. Go to your animations ribbon, click 'add animation' and select 'lines' from the motion path section of the drop down menu.

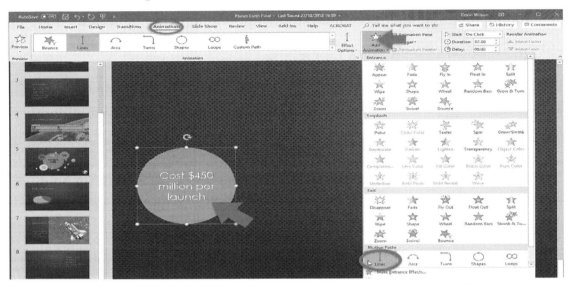

Now, if you look really closely, you'll see two very small dots on the light blue circles. One dot is green, this is the starting point. The other dot is red, this is the end point.

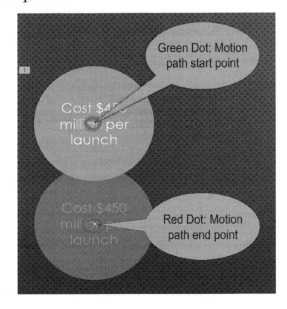

To create a motion path, you need to drag the green dot to the point you want the object to start at, then drag the red dot to the point you want the object to end up.

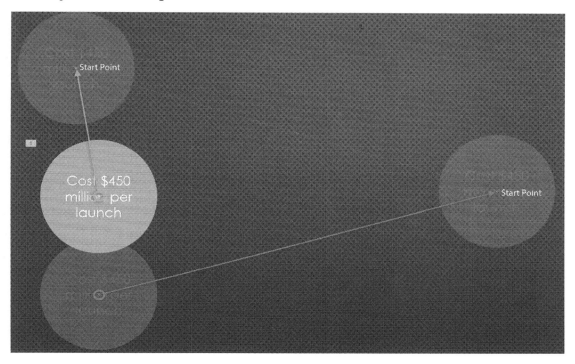

If you click 'preview' on the top left of your animations ribbon, you'll see the circle move left to right across the screen.

You can apply this effect to any object, textbox, photo or heading. You can also use different paths: arcs, turns or loops, and manipulate them in the same way, by moving the start and end points. Try an arc, to move the path, drag the resize handles on the box around the arc path.

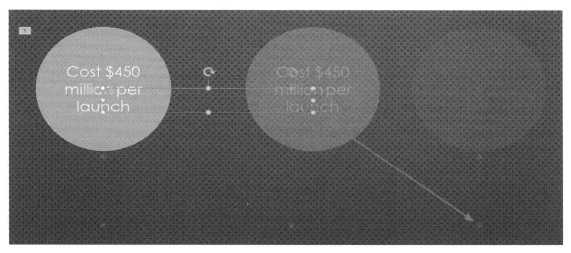

So you end up with something like this... you can see the motion path arc down then back up in a 'U' shape.

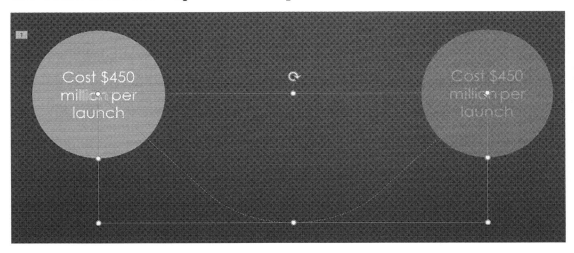

If the resize box disappears, click back on the motion path.

Custom Motion Paths

You can also draw your own paths if you prefer. Click on the object you want to animate. Go to your animations ribbon, click 'add animation'. From the drop down menu, go right down to the bottom and click 'custom path'.

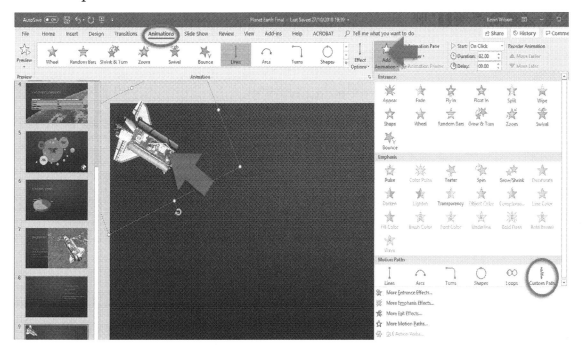

Now draw the path on the slide with your mouse. Highlighted below in red.

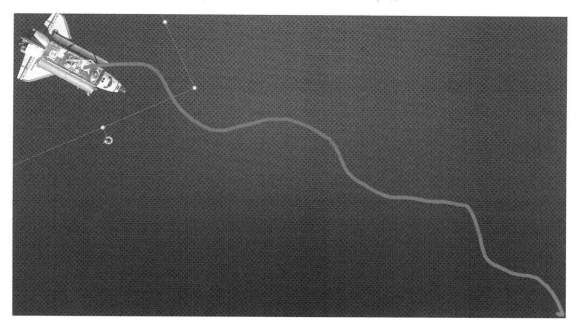

Double click on the position on the slide you want the object to end on.

Now, when you preview your slide, you'll see the ship fly to the bottom right corner.

If you double click on the path you have just drawn, you can make some adjustments to the speed and the timing.

Effects & Timings

You can adjust the timings. Set a 'smooth start' means the shape will start to move slowly then accelerate to full speed as it moves across the screen. Similarly 'smooth end' means the shape will gradually slow down as it nears the end of the motion path, rather than stopping suddenly.

'Bounce end' allows you to add a bounce effect to the shape when it gets to the end of the motion path - you can get the shape to bounce in a similar way to a ball bouncing on a hard surface.

Change these by entering the number of seconds into the boxes in the effect tab.

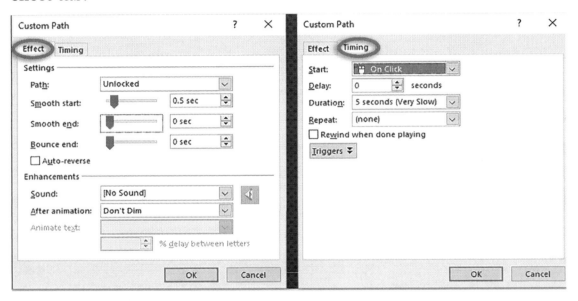

On the timing tab, you can set the trigger that starts the shape moving. Change this in the 'start' field. On mouse click is usually best to start your animation if you are presenting to an audience.

You can also set a delay before the animation begins with the 'delay' field, enter the number of seconds.

You can change the duration of the animation using the 'duration' field. This slows down or speeds up the animation on your shape.

You can set the animation to repeat a set number of times or until you click the mouse again, using the 'repeat' field.

Animation Pane

With the animation pane you can view and manage all of the animations that are on the current slide. From here you can adjust timings and the order of your animations.

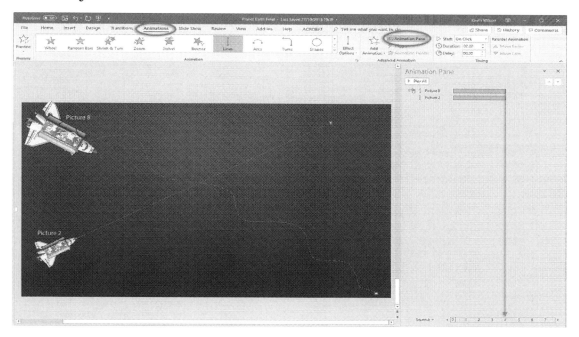

In this slide, we have two images, note their names: 'Picture 8' and 'Picture 2' as listed in the animation pane. Next to the object names in the animation pane, you'll see a blue bar. This is a timing bar and indicates how long the animation on that particular object is. The left hand side of the bar indicates the start while the right hand side of the bar indicates the end of the animation. You'll see a meter right at the bottom of the animation pane showing the number of seconds.

By default, PowerPoint will play the animations one at a time as listed in the animation pane. So for example, in the slide above, the animation on 'picture 8' will play, then when that animation is finished, the animation on 'picture 2' will start.

You can change the length of the animation by dragging the right hand edge line of the blue bar to the right, in the animation pane. You'll see the number of seconds on the end increase.

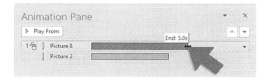

You can get the animations on the objects to start at the same time. On the animations pane, the first object in the list has a small mouse icon next to it, this means that the animation on that object will start when the user clicks the mouse.

Right click on the second object in the list and from the drop down menu, click 'start with previous'.

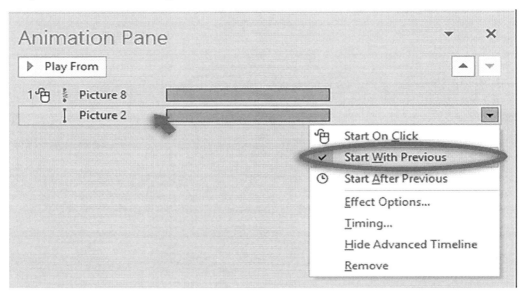

Now both animations will start at the same time. If you wanted 'picture 2' to start a bit after 'picture 8', drag the left hand edge of the blue bar next to 'picture 2', to the right. You'll see some seconds. This is the amount of time before the animation on this object starts. In this example, 'picture 2' will start 1.6 seconds after the user clicks the mouse.

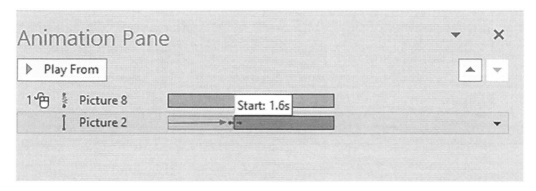

Picture 8 will start as soon as the user clicks the mouse.

This is useful if you have a sequence of objects that need to appear at different times during the slide animation.

Adding Video

You can add videos from your computer and videos from an online video sharing source such as YouTube.

Add Video on your PC to a New Slide

To add a video to a new slide, click 'new slide' from your home ribbon. From the drop down menu, click 'content with caption.

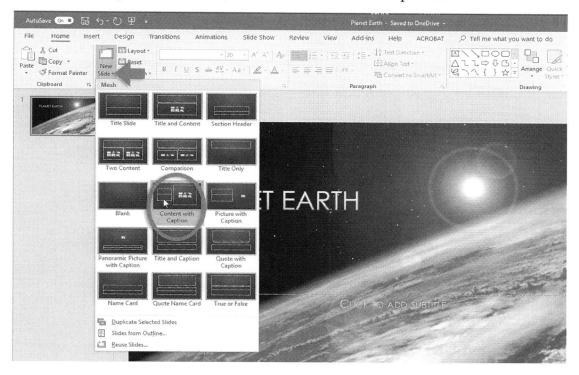

On the new slide, click the 'insert video' icon

Select 'from a file', then from the popup dialog box, navigate to the folder on your computer where your video is saved. In this example, the video is in the 'videos' folder.

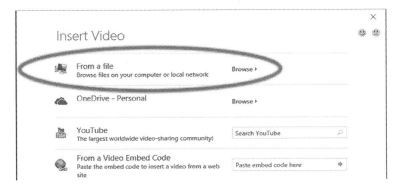

Double click on the video you want to add.

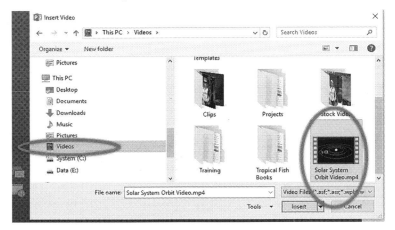

Add a title and some bullet points to your slide and here we go.

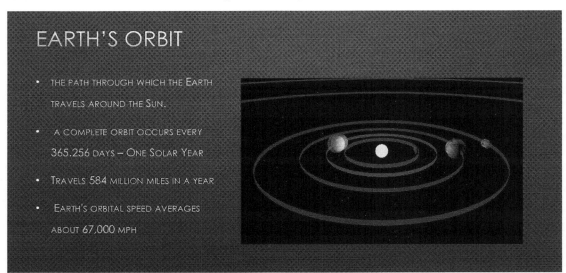

Add video from your PC to an Existing slide

If you already have a slide that you would like to add video to, go to your insert ribbon and click 'video'.

From the drop down click 'video from my pc'. Select 'online video' if you are linking to a YouTube video.

From the dialog box, double click the video you want to insert.

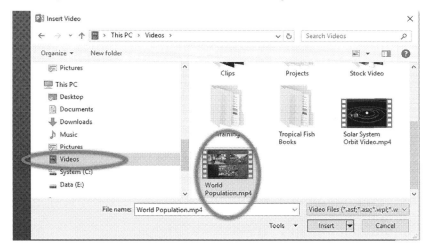

You may need to resize your video, if you don't want it to fill the screen. You can do this by clicking and dragging the resize handles on the edges of the video.

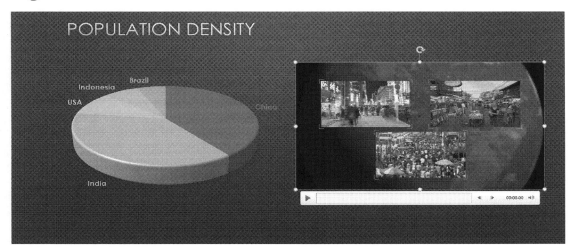

Trimming Videos

You can trim videos to start in exactly the right place. You can't do this with online videos yet, but you can trim any that have been downloaded to your computer.

Click on your video and from the playback ribbon, click 'trim video'.

From the popup dialog box, drag the start point towards the right (indicated in red, above), to the point where you want the video to start. You'll see a preview of the video at the top of the dialog box.

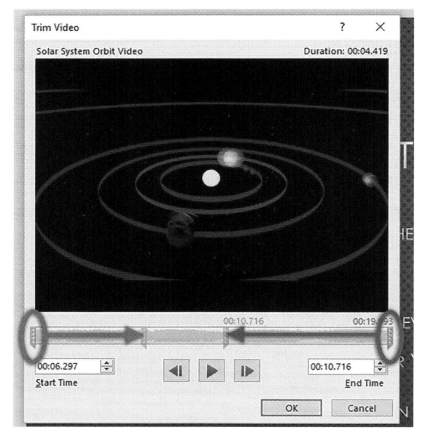

Do the same with the end point. Drag the end point to the left (indicated in blue, above), to the point you want the video to stop.

Click OK when you're done.

Online

You can link to YouTube videos from your slide. Insert a blank slide, then from your insert ribbon click 'video'. From the drop down menu select 'online video'.

From the popup dialog box, go down to YouTube, and in the search field type in what you're looking for. In this example, I'm looking for a video to go on my space shuttle page, so I typed 'space shuttle launch'.

Double click on the video thumbnail in the search results to add the video to your PowerPoint slide. You might need to resize your video and move it into position on your slide. Add some information about it too.

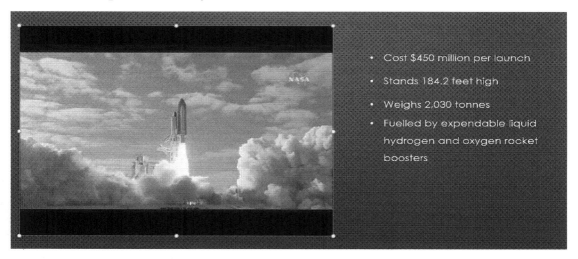

Adding Sound

You can add audio files that contain music or voice as well as record your own audio.

Recording Audio

To record audio, the first thing you should do is invest in a good microphone, especially if you intend to use your recordings as voice overs or links in a recorded presentation. This will vastly improve the quality.

The mic pictured below is a fairly inexpensive option.

This type of microphone will plug directly into a USB port on your computer or laptop with little or no configuration, which makes it ideal for PowerPoint presentations.

This comes in handy for recording narrations and presentations. We'll cover this a bit later.

Audio from your PC

If you already have a slide that you would like to add audio to, go to your insert ribbon and click 'audio'. From the drop down click 'audio on my pc'.

From the dialog box that appears, browse to the audio file you want to insert. In this example, my audio is stored in my music folder.

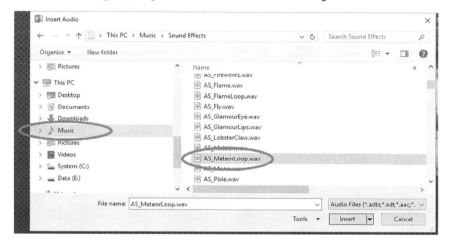

Your audio will show up as an icon on your slide.

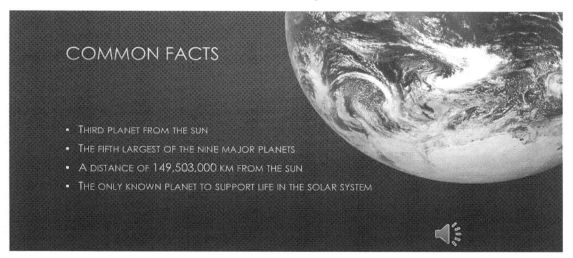

By default, you'll need to click the icon when showing your presentation to start the audio.

To change the audio settings, click on the audio icon on the slide

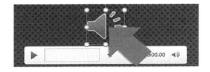

Select the 'playback' ribbon under 'audio tools'.

From here you can listen to a preview, trim the audio clip so it starts and ends in specific parts of the track.

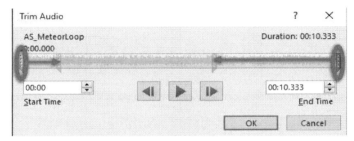

You can add a fade in effect, so the audio fades in at the beginning and fades out to silent at the end, using the 'fade duration' options.

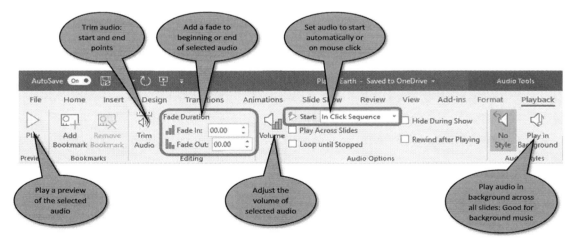

You can change whether you want the audio to play in one slide or across all your slides using 'play in background' option.

You can choose whether your audio plays automatically or if it starts when you click your mouse. You can adjust this using the 'start' setting on the audio options.

Screen Recording

Screen recording is useful if you are demonstrating something on your computer, or training someone to use a piece of software.

First, select a slide or insert a new one, then select your insert ribbon. From the insert ribbon click 'screen recording'.

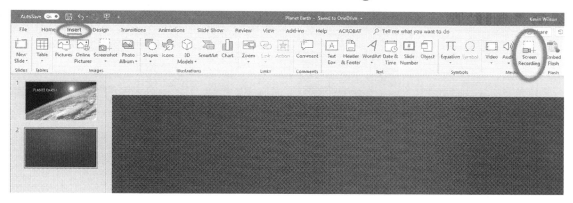

You will need to select the area of your screen you want to record. To do this, click and drag the selection box across the part of your screen to record, eg, click the top corner and drag your mouse across the screen, as shown below.

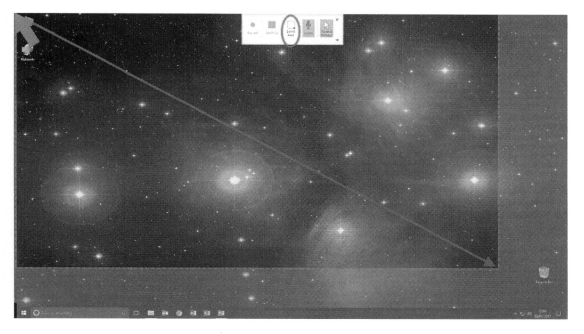

If you want the whole screen, click the top left corner and drag your mouse all the way to the bottom right corner.

When you have done that, click 'record' to start recording.

You'll get a 3 second countdown before you begin...

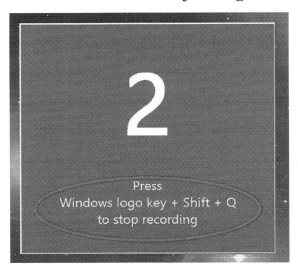

When the countdown hits zero, start the demonstration of what you're recording. PowerPoint will record your mouse clicks, applications opened and so on, within the area you selected in the previous step.

To stop recording, hold down Windows & Shift Key, then tap 'Q' - don't hold 'Q' down.

Your recorded screen video will appear in the selected slide. You may need to trim the screen recording because it's useful to remove the bits at the beginning where the control box is showing and at the end, so the screen recording just shows what you intended.

To do this, click on the screen recording video and from the playback ribbon click 'trim video'.

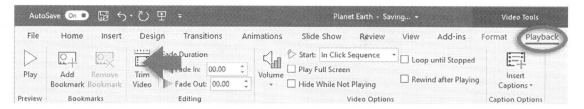

Now click and drag the beginning and end markers on the timeline to the points where you want the recording to start and where you want it to end.

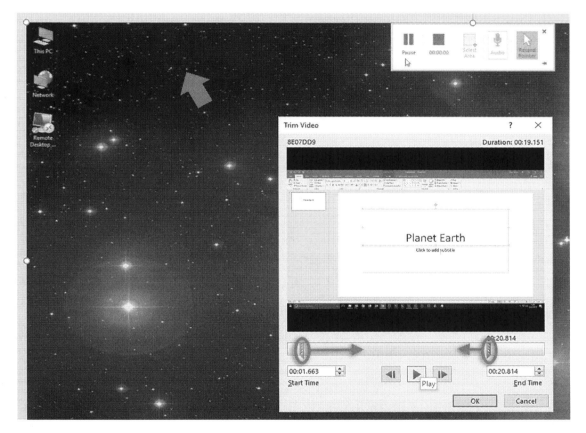

Click OK when you're done.

Recording Presentations

Record slide and animation timings, along with narrations, so the presentation will run through automatically.

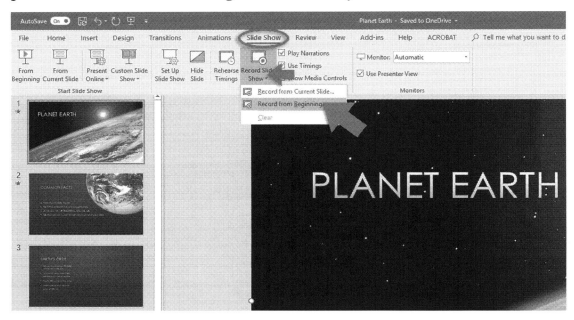

If you want to record narrations, click settings and make sure 'record audio' is checked and PowerPoint has found your microphone.

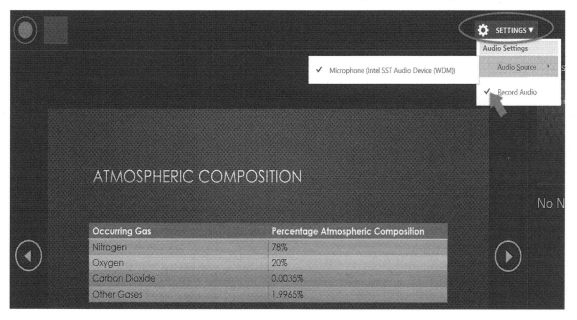

When you're ready, click the red button on the top left of the screen to start the recording.

Now give your presentation as if you were presenting to an audience, speaking into your microphone. It's best to be in a room where it is fairly quiet and with no echoes.

You can also use the screen annotation tools to draw on the slides, highlight points etc. PowerPoint will record your screen annotations, animations, bullets and transitions as you go through your presentation.

Once you are finished, click the stop button (large grey square on the top left).

Export your Presentation

You can export your presentation as a video file and upload it to YouTube or social media. This will include all your slide timings, transitions, animations, as well as your narrations.

Click File, then select export.

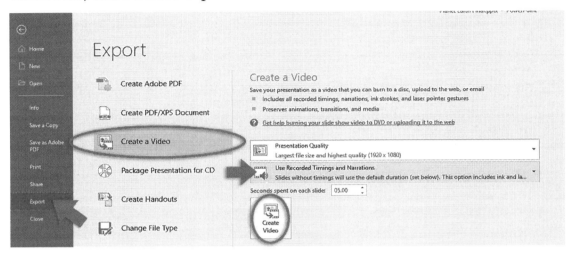

Set the presentation quality to the highest setting and select 'use recorded timings and narrations' to include your slide timings, annotations and narration recordings in the video.

Click 'create video', then select the folder you want to save it in. I'm saving my video in the 'videos' folder. Click 'save'.

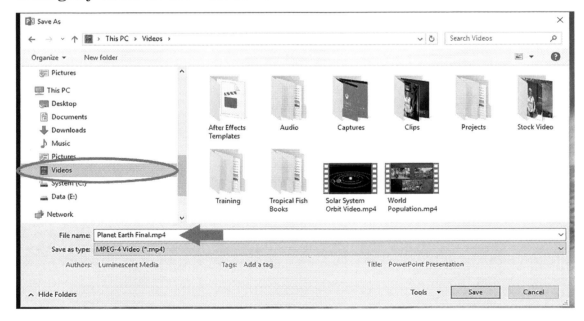

Photo Albums

There are two ways you can create photo albums. You can use the album generator on the insert ribbon, or you can use a photo album template from office.com.

First, lets have a look at some of the templates available on office.com. Go to FILE and click NEW.

Type 'Photo Album' into the search field. You'll see a list of templates appear in the search results.

Double click on one of the template thumbnails to open a new presentation with that template.

Now you can start adding your images to the photo place holders in the presentation.

If there is a sample image already on the slide, to change it, right click and from the popup menu select 'change image'. From the slide out, select 'from file'. This is for photos stored on your computer.

On the slides, you'll see image place holders already laid out on the slides. To add an image, click the image icon in the middle.

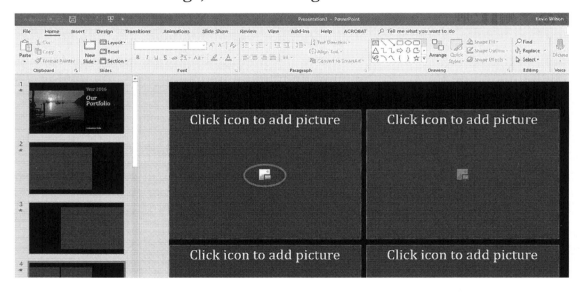

From the popup dialog box, select the image you want to insert. Do this with all the image place holders on all the slides.

You can also change the layouts of the photos. For example, on the second slide, say you wanted six small photos instead of one large photo.

To change the layout, click 'layout' from your home ribbon and select the layout from the drop down menu.

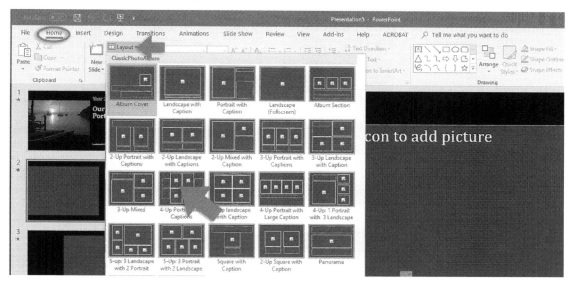

You can also add slide transitions as with ordinary slides, as well as animations for your photographs. To add animations, click your photo.

If you want to select more than one photo, hold down your control key while you select your photos.

From the animations ribbon, select an animation pre set. Do this with all the images you want effects on.

Chapter 5: Microsoft PowerPoint

You can also create a photo album using the album generator on the insert ribbon.

Go to your insert ribbon, and select 'photo album'.

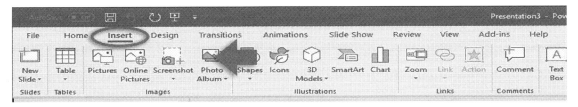

From the 'photo album' dialog box, click 'file/disk'.

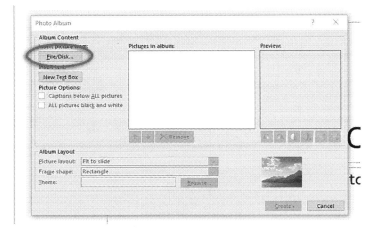

Then from the 'insert new pictures' dialog box, navigate to your pictures folder, or where your photos are stored, and click to select the ones you want. If you are selecting more than one photo, hold down the control key while you select your photos.

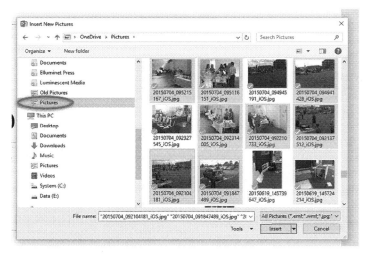

Click 'insert' when you're done.

You can also select a pre designed theme. To do this, click 'browse',

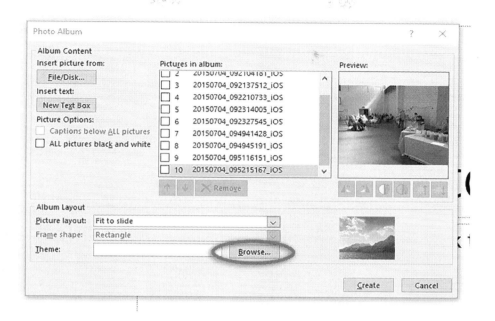

From the 'choose theme' dialog box, choose a theme from the list.

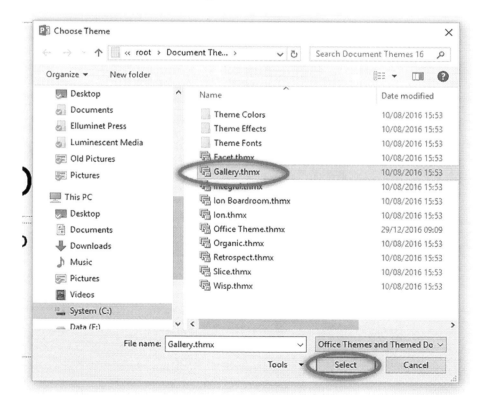

Click 'select' when you're done.

You can arrange the photos, one to a slide, more than one to a slide, or you can arrange to a slide with a title or caption.

To do this, click 'picture layout' and select an option. I'm going to select '1 picture with title'.

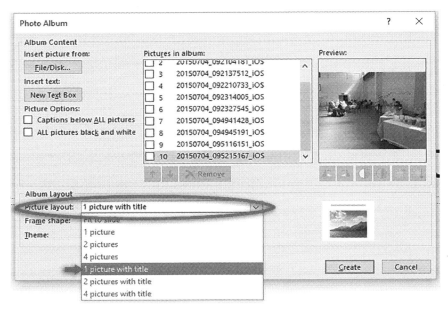

When you're done, click 'create'.

Now you can change the titles, add clipart and arrange the photos on your slides just like in any other PowerPoint presentation.

Edit your slides, add captions, headings and animations to your slides to make your album more exciting and interesting to watch.

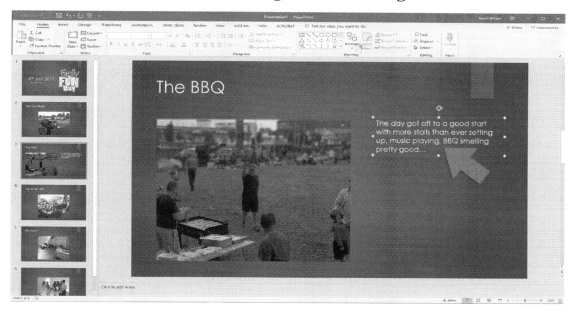

Run your photo album in the normal way. Press F5 on your keyboard.

Microsoft PowerPoint Pen Support

In Microsoft PowerPoint, you'll see an additional ribbon menu called 'draw'. This has all your drawing tools such as pens, highlighters and an eraser for you to annotate your presentations.

Select the 'draw' ribbon and select a pen colour from the selections in the centre of the ribbon. From here you can select the colour and thickness of your pen.

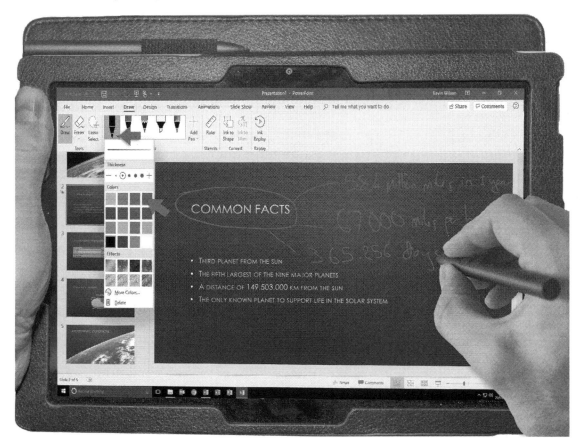

You can annotate and draw on your slides in preparation for your presentation and when you save your presentation, PowerPoint will save your drawings and annotations as well.

You can also use your pen tools while you are presenting.

All your annotations and illustrations will appear on your presentation for your audience to see.

PowerPoint will also give you an option to save your annotations added during your presentation.

You can then save the presentation with all the annotations and highlights as well as share these with colleagues or friends.

To share, click the share icon on the top right of your screen.

Enter the email address of the person to share the presentation with, then click 'share'.

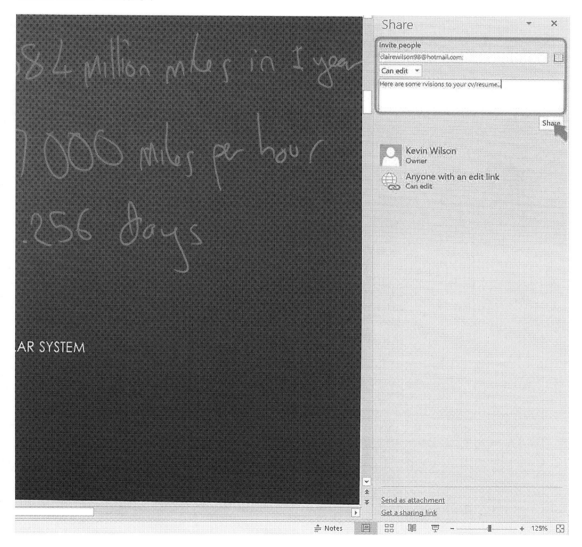

The other person will get a link in an email they can click on to view or edit the presentation.

Setting Up Projectors

Connect your laptop to your projector. Modern projectors either use a VGA or an HDMI cable to connect. The projector in the example uses a VGA, but the principle is the same regardless of what cable you're using.

Connect the other end to your laptop

Plug the power lead into the projector.

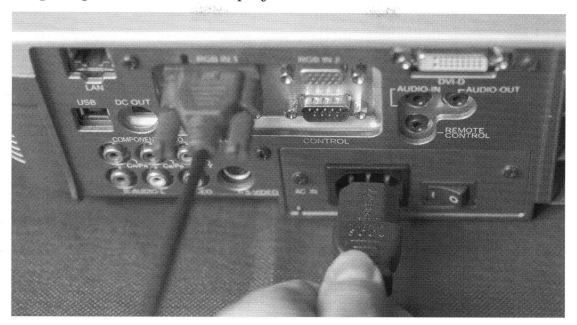

Now fire up the projector. Once the projector is running, start up your laptop.

On your laptop, the best way to use PowerPoint is to use an extended screen display. This means that the projector screen is an extension of your laptop screen, rather than a duplicate. This will allow you to have notes and to see the next slides coming up in your presentation - the presenter display.

In Windows 10, to do this, hold down the windows key then tap 'P'. From the side panel that opens up, click 'extend'.

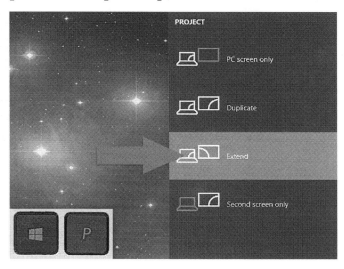

Running your Presentation

The controls for running your presentation can be found on the slide show ribbon.

On the right hand side of the ribbon, click the drop down box next to 'monitor' and select the name of your second screen or projector.

This tells PowerPoint, which screen to display your presentation on for your audience to see. Your laptop or tablet screen is your presenter view. This will show you any notes you have written as well as the next slide. If you want this feature, tick 'use presenter view'.

To run your presentation, click 'from beginning' icon on the left hand side (or press F5). This will run your presentation from the first slide.

You have a few useful tools available while you present (circled in the image above).

You can zoom into a specific part of the slide to highlight it, by clicking the magnifying glass icon and positioning the rectangle over the part of the slide you want to show.

You can annotate your slides with notes to help your audience understand your point. Click the pen tool, select the pen and draw on the slide with your finger, a stylus or a mouse.

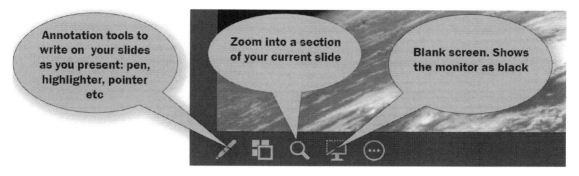

You can also present with a Windows 10 tablet running PowerPoint connected to a projector.

You may need a mini display port to VGA adapter, or a USB3 to VGA adapter to connect directly to the projector.

Wireless Presenting

If you're using Windows 10, there is a feature that allows you to project to another Windows 10 device. So you could have your Windows 10 laptop hooked up to the projector and use your Windows 10 tablet to wirelessly project to your laptop.

Both your laptop and tablet will need to be on the same wireless network for this to work. Some laptops wont support this, but most modern ones do. To connect, on your tablet open your action centre and tap 'connect'.

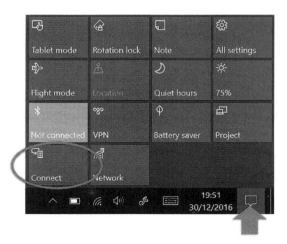

Your Windows 10 tablet will scan the network for your laptop... In this demo, the laptop's network name is 'Asus-Laptop' and the tablet's name is 'surfaceone'.

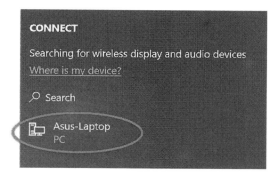

Once found, you'll see your laptop appear in the search results. Double tap on the name to connect.

On your laptop click 'yes' on the connection prompt that will appear on the bottom right of your screen.

Once you click 'yes', you'll see a blue screen on your laptop while your devices connect.

If you're having trouble, make sure your laptop is set up to receive. Go to your settings icon on the start menu, click system, then click 'projecting to this PC'.

Projecting to this PC

Projecting to this PC

Project your Windows phone or PC to this screen, and use its keyboard, mouse and other devices, too.

Windows PCs and phones can project to this PC when you say it's OK

| Available everywhere ⌄ |

Ask to project to this PC

| Every time a connection is requested ⌄ |

Require PIN for pairing

◉◯ Off

This PC can only be discovered for projection when it is plugged in

◯● On

PC name   Asus-Laptop

Rename your PC

Make sure your laptop supports wireless projection, and that the settings are set up as shown in the screen above. Also check your wifi settings on your laptop and tablet.

Now you can start PowerPoint on your tablet and you'll see the screen project to the laptop.

With the laptop connected to your projector, you're all set to present with a wireless tablet.

You can remote control the laptop from your surface tablet and present wirelessly, using the ink features of PowerPoint to highlight important points and concepts you want your audience to take note of.

You can now use PowerPoint on your tablet and run your presentation.

You can use the touch features on your tablet, such as a stylus and annotate your slides as you present.

Present Online

You can set up a presentation and present it online, so anyone with a link to your presentation can 'tune in' and watch.

To do this, open your presentation and from the slideshow ribbon, click 'present online'.

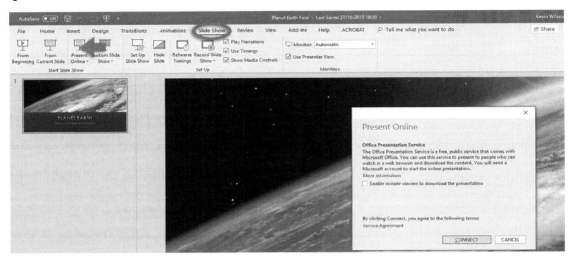

From the dialog box that appears, click 'connect'. *If you want your audience to be able to download a copy of your PowerPoint presentation, click the 'enable remove viewers to download the presentation'.*

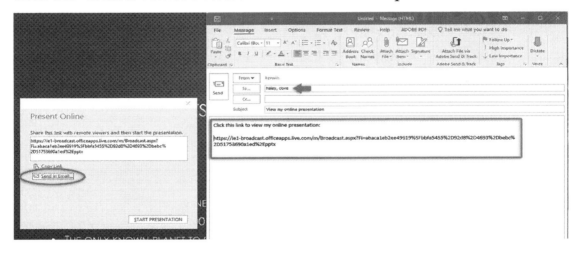

Next, invite the people you want to see your presentation. If you have Outlook installed on your machine, click 'send an email'. Add the email addresses to the email message that pops up. You can also click 'copy link' to copy to your clipboard and paste into sms/text message, imessage or skype.

When you are ready to begin, click 'start presentation' to begin your broadcast.

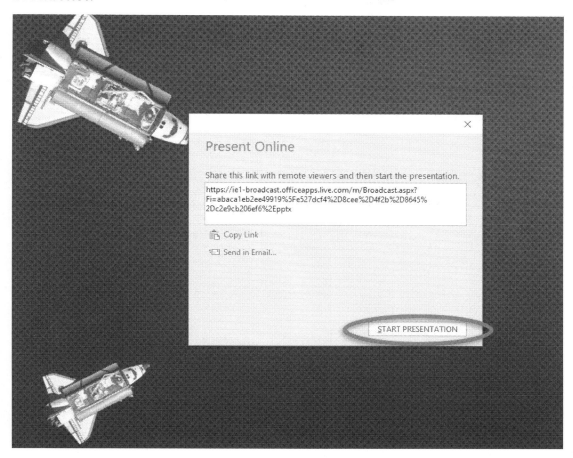

In the demonstration below, the laptop on the left is hosting the presentation.

The iPad and the Surface Tab are viewing the presentation in a web browser. These could be anywhere with an internet connection.

Opening a Saved Presentation

If PowerPoint is already open you can open previously saved presentations by clicking the FILE menu on the top left of your screen.

From the orange bar on the left hand side click 'open', then click 'OneDrive - Personal'.

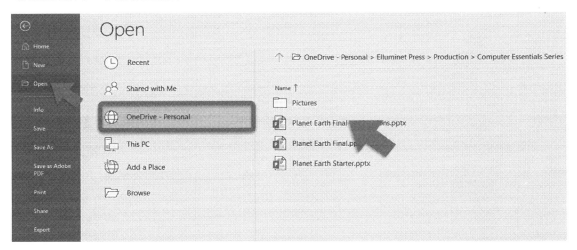

From the list, select the presentation you want to open. The presentation from the previous project was saved as 'planet earth.pptx', so this is the one I am going to open here.

For convenience, instead of searching through your OneDrive, PowerPoint lists all your most recently opened Presentations. You can view these by clicking 'Recent' instead of 'OneDrive - Personal'.

Your latest files will be listed first.

Double click the file name to open it.

Saving your Presentation

Click the small disk icon on the top left of the screen. If this is a new presentation that hasn't been saved before, PowerPoint will ask you where you want to save it. Save all your work onto your OneDrive.

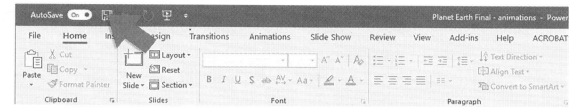

Click OneDrive Personal.

then enter a name for your presentation in the field indicated by the red arrow below.

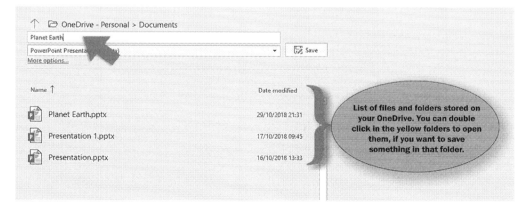

List of files and folders stored on your OneDrive. You can double click in the yellow folders to open them, if you want to save something in that folder.

When you have done that click save.

Save as a Different Format

To save your presentation in a different format, with your presentation open, click FILE.

From the backstage view, click 'Save As'.

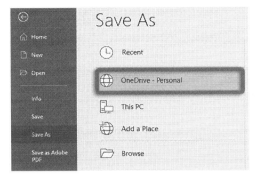

Select the folder you want to save your file in, eg, documents folder on your OneDrive.

Give your document a name, then underneath, click the down arrow and select a format. In this example, I am going to save the PowerPoint presentation as a PDF.

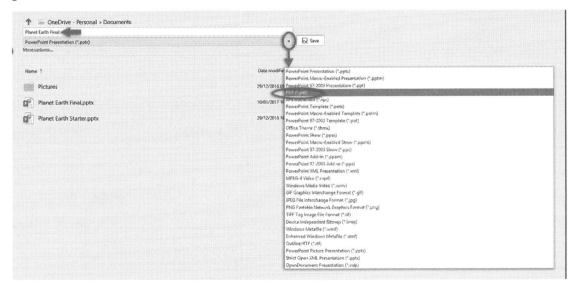

This is useful if you want to send a copy to someone that doesn't use Windows or have PowerPoint installed. Note with a PDF, you won't see all your animations or transitions in the file.

Click 'save' when you're done.

When you view the PDF version of your presentation, you'll see all the text and graphics.

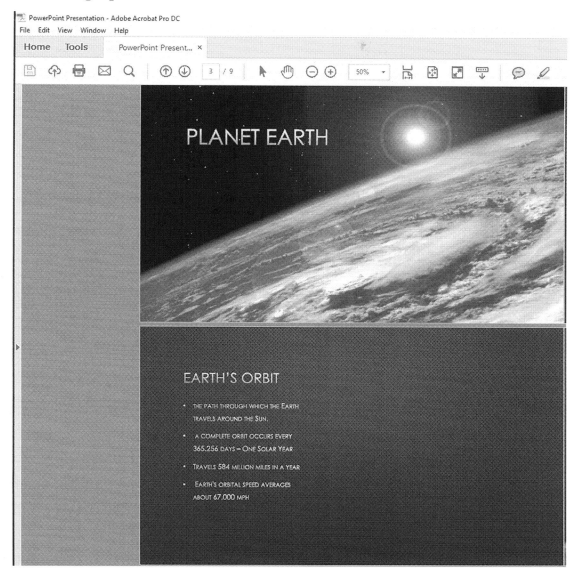

You can also save as a video. Use MPEG-4/MP4 video for Macs, Windows, Tablets, and Phones. Use Windows Media Video (WMV) if you're only using Windows based machines.

If you save your presentation as a video, you'll get all your transitions and animations saved along with any timings and voice recordings you have done. If you haven't, you'll get the default timings for each slide transition and animation. The video presentation will run automatically, you won't be able to click to advance any slides etc.

Print your Slides

To print your slides, click FILE on the top left hand corner of the screen, then select print.

In the screen below select the correct printer and number of copies you want.

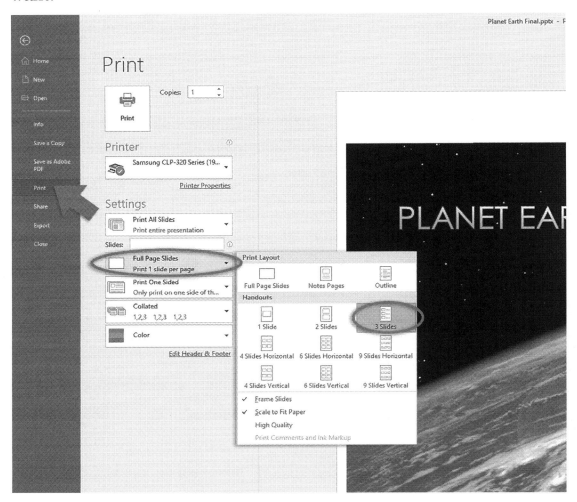

Then select how you want the slides to print out. Click where it says 'Full Page Slides'. 'Full Page Slides' prints out one slide per page and can be useful in some situations. If you are printing handouts, it makes sense to print more than one slide per page.

You'll see a pop up menu appear with some layout options for how to print out the slides on the page.

I usually select '3 slides', as it provides space for the audience to take notes on any particular slide.

You can then handout a copy of your slides to your audience so they can follow your presentation as you speak and take notes. I find this the most useful way to print slides.

If you just wanted the slides, you could also get six slides on a page. Just choose 'six horizontal slides' instead of '3 slides'.

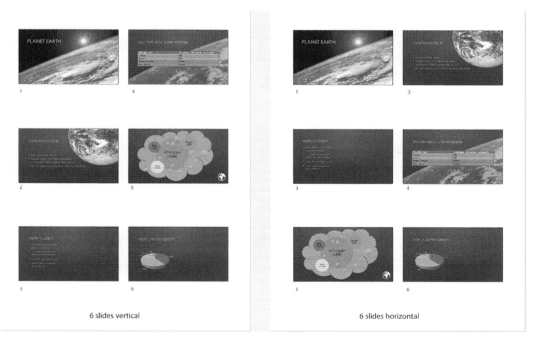

'Horizontal' means, the slides appear across the page rather than down the page. Notice how the slides are numbered above.

Sometimes it is useful to select 'black and white' or greyscale printing if you do not have a colour printer.

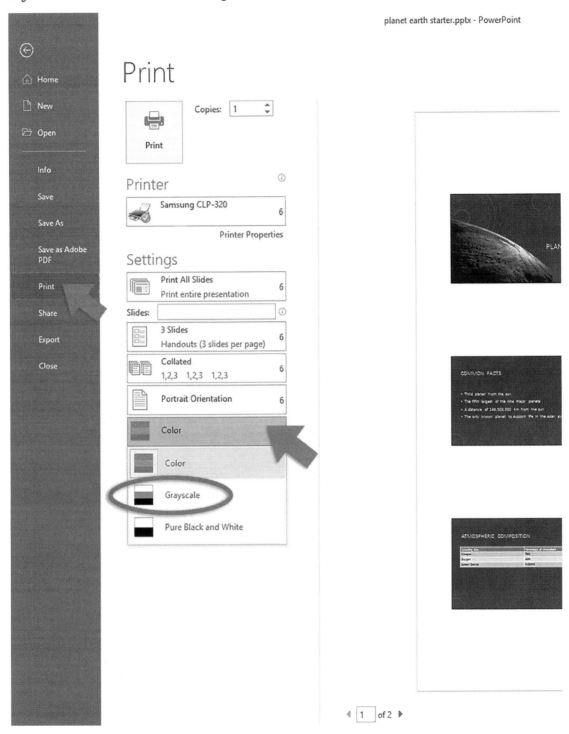

Click the print icon to print your presentation.

Online Collaboration

A new feature that allows users to share their work with others. In the demo below, the user on the laptop has shared the PowerPoint presentation with the user on the tablet.

In the top right of PowerPoint's main screen, there is a share button. You can share any document you are working on with friends and colleagues.

If you want to share the presentation you are working on, click on the share button and enter their email address. Click the contacts icon next to the address field to add names from your contacts. Double click on each name in the address book list to add.

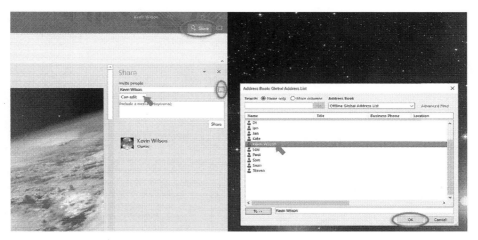

Select 'can edit' to allow people to make changes to your presentation. If you don't want people to make changes, change this option to 'can view'.

When the other person checks their email, on the tablet in this demonstration, they will receive a message inviting them to open the presentation you just shared.

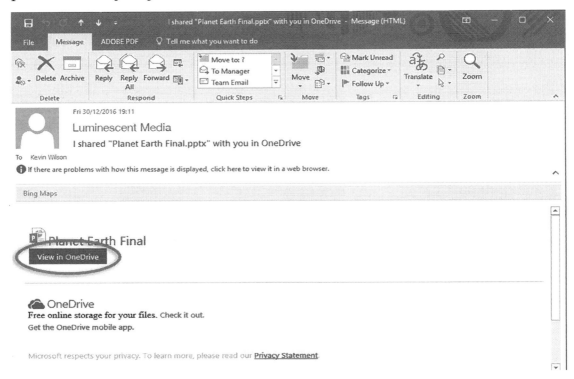

Click 'view in OneDrive', in the email message. The presentation will open in a web browser. Make sure you click 'sign in' on the top right of the screen and enter your Microsoft Account details when prompted.

Once you have signed in, click 'Edit Presentation', then click 'edit in PowerPoint'

This will download the document and open it up in PowerPoint installed on your computer (the tablet in this demo).

Here, the user on the tablet can start editing the presentation. As an example, they're going to add a bullet point to the list.

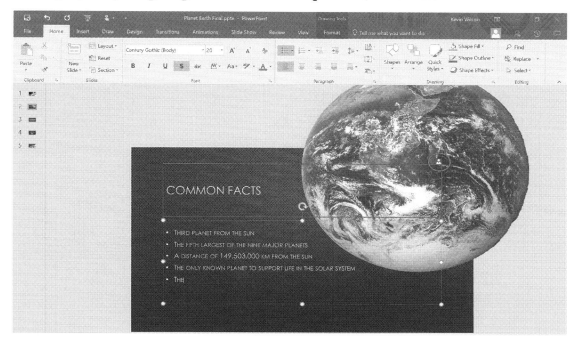

You'll be able to see who is editing what, indicated with a user icon on the top right of the text boxes, circled below.

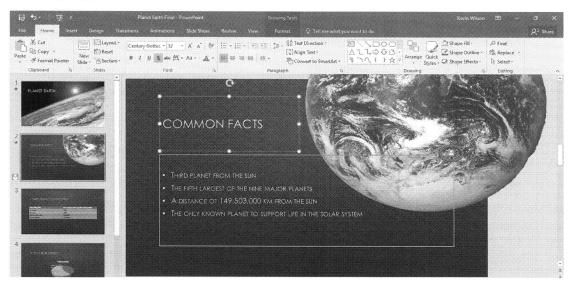

We can see here on the laptop screen, that the user on the tablet is editing the bottom text box.

Normal View

Normal view is the default view and the best way to design and develop your presentation. It lists all your slides down the left hand side, with the selected slide displayed in the centre of the screen for you to work on.

Outline View

The outline view, shows you a list of your slide's text, rather than a thumbnail view of the slide. You wont see any images or graphics inserted into any of your slides on the left hand side.

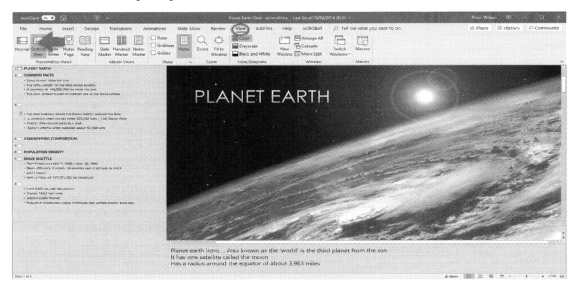

Slide Sorter View

The slide sorter view shows you a thumbnail list of all your slides in the presentation.

As the name suggests, it allows you to easily see all your slides and makes it easier for you to put them into the correct order.

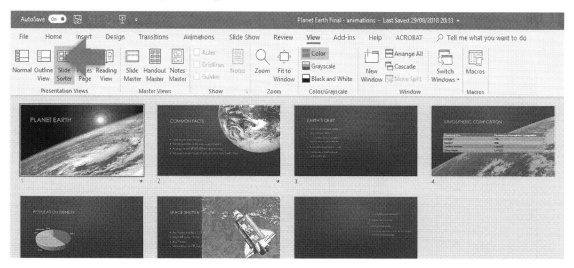

As well as hide certain slides you may not need in a particular session when presenting. To do this, right click the slide, then from the popup menu select 'hide slide'.

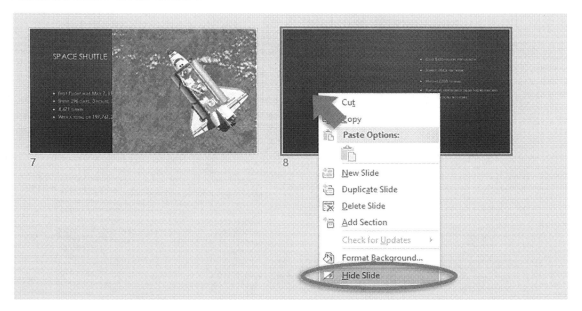

Hidden slides are greyed out with the slide number crossed out. To un-hide the slide, right click on the slide, and click 'hide slide' again.

Note Page View

Note page view, allows you to see the slide with the notes associated with that slide.

Select the view ribbon and click 'notes page'.

The notes view makes it easier to add notes to each slide, or to review notes already added.

Reading View

To switch to reading view, select the view ribbon and click 'reading view'.

This view allows you to play your PowerPoint presentation slideshow within the PowerPoint window.

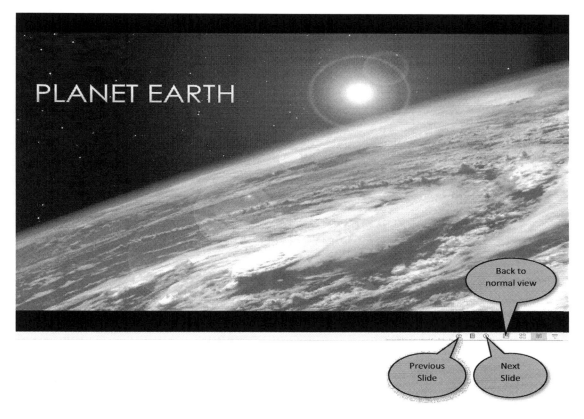

Chapter 6

Microsoft Access

Microsoft Access is a database management system (DBMS) that allows you to manage, store, and retrieve information.

You can store names and addresses of people you write to and quickly generate mail shots using mail merge.

If you run a business you can store all your suppliers, customers, orders, invoices and generate these as you service your customers or order new stock.

If you visit the doctor, your details are stored in a database.

These are just a few examples of databases.

To understand Access, you must first understand databases.

What is a Database

A database is a collection of records saved in a storage and retrieval system that allows users to enter, access, and analyse data in these records quickly and easily.

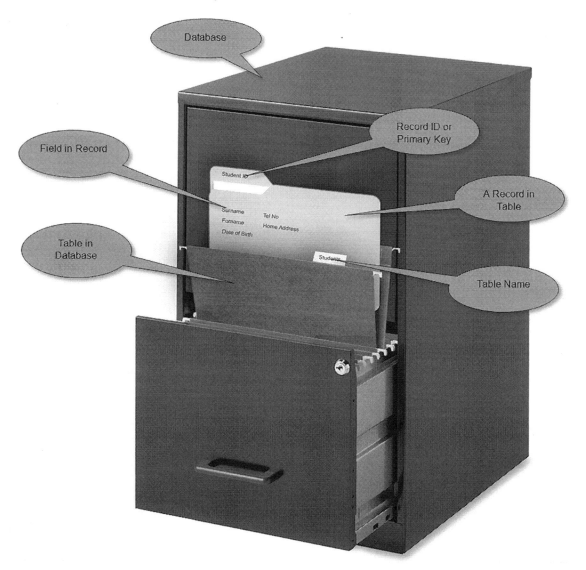

Databases can store information on almost anything, they're a bit like filing cabinets containing files with records stored inside them.

There are national databases that store driver and car registration details, patient records, criminal records, student records, employment records, financial records and so on.

Database Models

There are various database management systems available. Some common examples used on the web are MySQL and PostgreSQL. These types of databases form the basis of many modern websites. There is also Oracle, dBase and of course Microsoft Access that are commonly used in business applications.

There are many different types of database models, we'll take a look at the most common.

Relational Database

A large portion of databases today use the relational model. In this model, data stored in fields is organized into tables according to its function. Relationships between tables are made according to how the data in the tables is related.

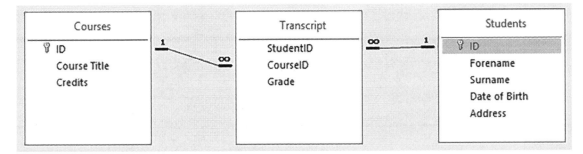

Hierarchical & Network

There are other database models such as the hierarchical model and the network model. In the hierarchical model, data is organized into a tree-like structure, with each record having one parent record and many child records. The network model is similar but allows each record to have multiple parent and child records. These two are somewhat obsolete now.

Object Oriented

With object oriented databases, data is organized into objects. Object oriented databases are designed to work with programming languages such as Python, Java, or C++ and are used in high performance, complex database systems.

Microsoft Access Databases

In Access, every database is stored in a single file that contains the database objects - tables, queries, forms, reports, macros and modules. Lets take a look at some of these objects. Microsoft Access is an example of a relational database.

Tables store information using individual fields. A field is just a piece of information such as name or date of birth. This is where you start to build your database, using tables to store your information.

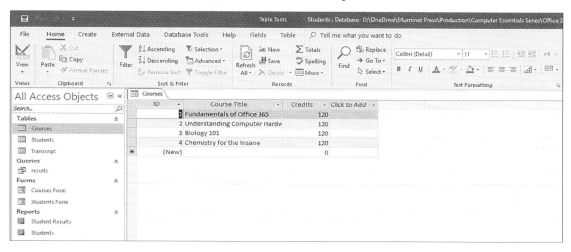

Queries let you retrieve information, or query the database. Depending on what your database stores, you can create queries to return a list of students in a particular year, or best selling items and so on.

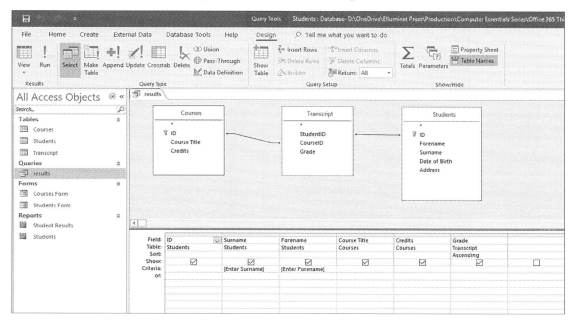

Chapter 6: Microsoft Access

Forms provide the user interface of the database and allow you to create arrange, and colourize the fields from your tables into an easy way for users to interact with the database.

Forms provide an easy way to view or change the information in a table in a more user friendly fashion.

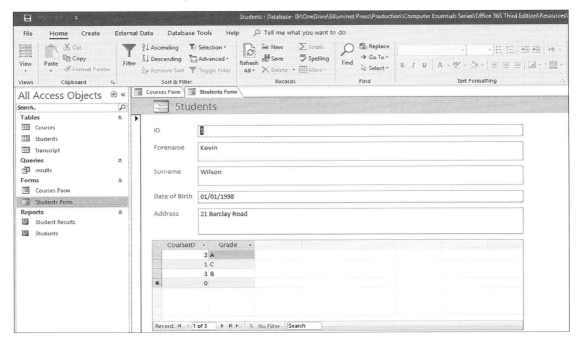

Reports allow you to print information from a table or query. You can format the information into easily readable reports direct from your tables or more commonly from a query. Eg a list of the students in a particular class or year.

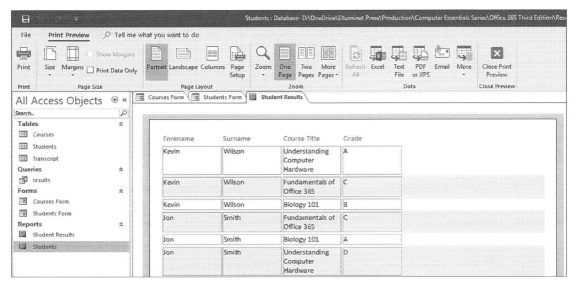

Starting Access

The quickest way to start Microsoft Access is to search for it using the Cortana search field on the bottom left of your task bar. Type "Access". From the search results, click 'Access'. You'll also find it on your start menu.

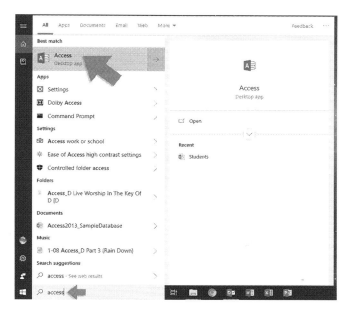

Once Access has started, you'll land on the home screen. On the home screen, you'll see some database templates in the main window, and your most recently saved documents listed down the left hand side.

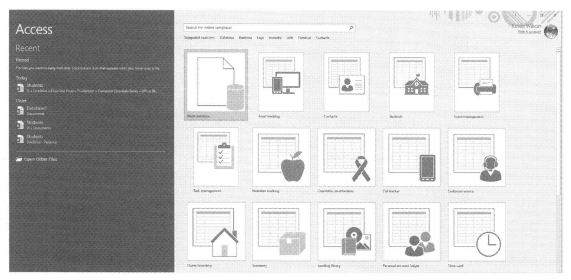

To begin, click 'blank database' to start. This will open up Access with a new database for you.

Creating a Database

To create a new database from scratch, click the "Blank desktop database" template.

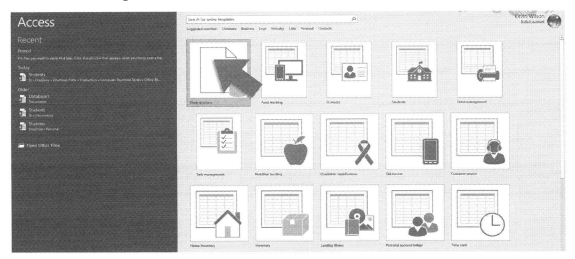

Type a file name for the database you're about to create. Click the yellow folder icon next to the file name if you want to save in a different directory. Click 'Create'.

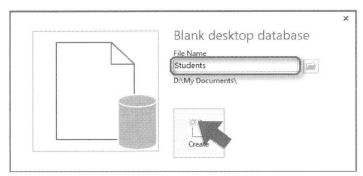

Once the new database has opened, you'll see the main screen. The first thing to take note of are the ribbons at the top of the screen. These contain your tools for working.

The Ribbon

All your tools for creating and manipulating databases are organised into a ribbon which is divided into ribbon tabs, each containing a specific set of tools.

The Home Ribbon

Clipboard, Sort & Filter, Records, Find, and Text Formatting

The Create Ribbon

Templates, New Tables, Queries, Forms, Reports, and Macros & Code

The External Data Ribbon

Import & Link to other databases, data sources or database servers

The Database Tools Ribbon

Macro, Entity Relationships, Analyse, Move Data, and Add-Ins

Creating Tables

For our student database, lets think about what information we need to store. This could be

Student ID, Forename, Surname, DOB, Address, Course ID, Course Title, Credits, and Grade.

Now, if we stored all this data in one table, we would have a lot of repeating data.

Students.ID	Forename	Surname	Date of Birth	Address	Courses.ID	Course Title	Credits	Grade
1	Kevin	Wilson	01/01/1998	21 Barclay Road	1	Fundamentals of Office 365	120	A
1	Kevin	Wilson	01/01/1998	21 Barclay Road	2	Understanding Computer Hardw	120	A
1	Kevin	Wilson	01/01/1998	21 Barclay Road	3	Biology 101	120	A
1	Kevin	Wilson	01/01/1998	21 Barclay Road	4	Chemistry for the Insane	120	A
2	Jon	Smith	05/09/1999	69 Lancaster Way	1	Fundamentals of Office 365	120	A
2	Jon	Smith	05/09/1999	69 Lancaster Way	2	Understanding Computer Hardw	120	A
2	Jon	Smith	05/09/1999	69 Lancaster Way	3	Biology 101	120	A
2	Jon	Smith	05/09/1999	69 Lancaster Way	4	Chemistry for the Insane	120	A
3	Claire	Wilson	06/12/1999	8 Janson Drive	1	Fundamentals of Office 365	120	A
3	Claire	Wilson	06/12/1999	8 Janson Drive	2	Understanding Computer Hardw	120	A
3	Claire	Wilson	06/12/1999	8 Janson Drive	3	Biology 101	120	A
3	Claire	Wilson	06/12/1999	8 Janson Drive	4	Chemistry for the Insane	120	A
4	Sophie	Johnston	09/01/1997	24 Ludsale Road	1	Fundamentals of Office 365	120	A
4	Sophie	Johnston	09/01/1997	24 Ludsale Road	2	Understanding Computer Hardw	120	A

Not very efficient. To do this we can normalise the tables. This database can be broken down into three tables: Students, Courses, Transcript.

First we can put all the fields describing students into a student table, and all the fields describing courses into the courses table.

Students (Student ID, Forename, Surname, DOB, Address)

Courses (Course ID, Course Title, Credits, Grade)

Now the courses table still has repeating data: Grade. We'd have to store multiple entries of each course to record the grade for each student.

ID	Course Title	Credits	Grade
3	Biology 101	120	A
2	Understanding Computer Hardware	120	A
3	Biology 101	120	B
1	Fundamentals of Office 365	120	C
1	Fundamentals of Office 365	120	C
1	Fundamentals of Office 365	120	C
2	Understanding Computer Hardware	120	D

We can move this field to a new table:

Transcript (Student ID, Course ID, Grade)

Remember each field in the table must describe the table (eg Student, Course or Transcript) and nothing else.

Now we have our three tables, we can create them in Microsoft Access.

Each table is made up of fields. Each field stores a bit of the data. For example you'd have a field for student name, one for address, one for date of birth and so on.

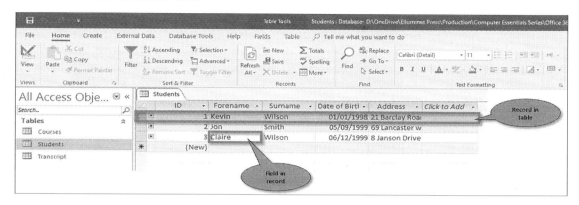

Each field can be assigned a data type. For example a students name is text, their date of birth is a date, their student ID could be a number, their tuition fee is currency, and so on.

To add your fields, click where it says 'click to add', from the drop down box select the data type. So the first field is going to be the student's Forename so the data type will be short text. Once selected enter 'forename'. Do the same for adding surname.

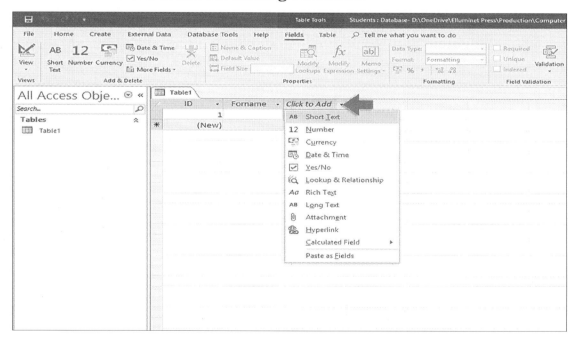

For Date of Birth, select the date & time data type.

For Address select long text as it will be more than one line of text.

Once you have created all your fields you can go into design view for the table to tweak or change any of the fields and data types you have created. To go into design view, right click on the table name on the left hand side of the screen and select 'design view'.

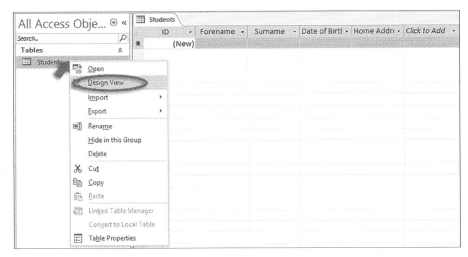

Now, each entry in the table needs a unique identifier. We can't use surname or forename as there might be more than one student with the same name. Each student is issued a student number when they enrol, this is unique and won't be duplicated with another student. So we can use this as StudentID.

To create a primary key, click the field you are using as the identifier, in this case StudentID.

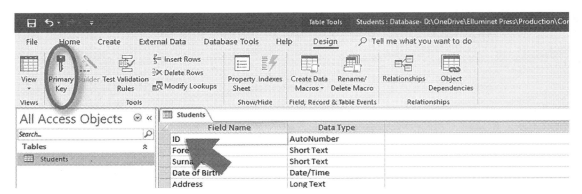

Then from the 'design' ribbon under, table tools, select 'primary key'. You'll notice a small yellow key symbol appear next to the field.

Do the same with the courses table, CourseID is the primary key.

For the transcript table, add StudentID, CourseID, and grade. You don't need to set a primary key for this one.

Relationships Between Tables

Each table in the database is related to the other tables. In our student database, the students table holds data on students. The courses table holds data on courses but nothing on students.

The transcript table holds the results obtained by the students. All this data needs to be related somehow. This is where entity relationships come in.

The relationships are linked using the ID called the primary key (indicated by the little key symbol next to the field).

Creating Relationships

Relationships can be one-to-one or one-to-many. For example a student takes more than one (or many) courses. So the relationship is one-to-many.

One course also has many students taking it at a time. Again one-to-many.

This results in a many-to-many relationship between the courses table and the students table. Microsoft Access doesn't support many-to-many relationships, so this is why we introduce a third table called transcripts to bridge the gap.

Now that we have our Entity Relationship Diagram, we can create the relationships in Microsoft Access.

First select your 'database tools' ribbon, and click 'relationships'.

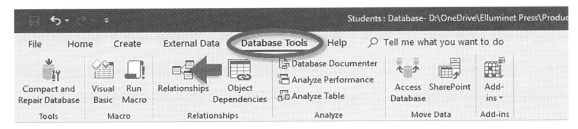

Drag the course, transcript and student tables onto the relationship tab.

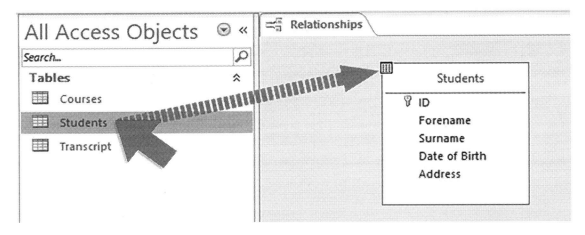

Now, create the relationships. To do this drag the 'ID' field from the students table to 'StudentID' on the transcript table. This is creating the 'one student takes many courses relationship'.

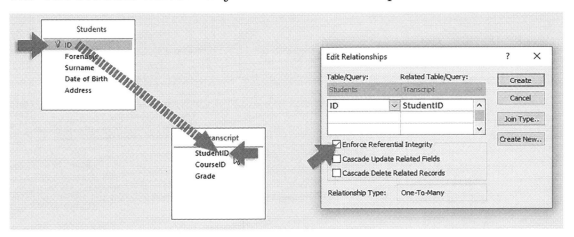

Click 'enforce referential integrity'. Notice the relationship is one to many.

Primary keys are unique so this leaves one StudentID per student.

Do the same for the courses table. Drag the 'ID' field from the courses table to the 'CourseID' field in the transcript table. Click 'enforce referential integrity'.

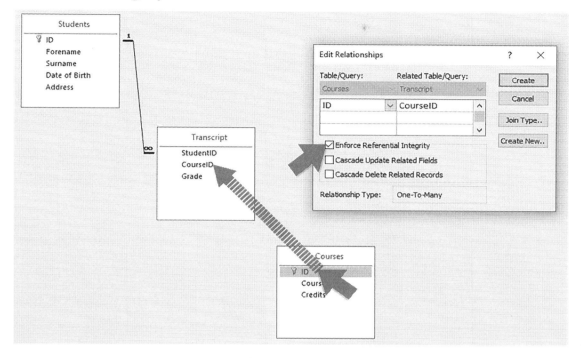

You'll end up with something like this. Click 'close' from the top right of the design ribbon.

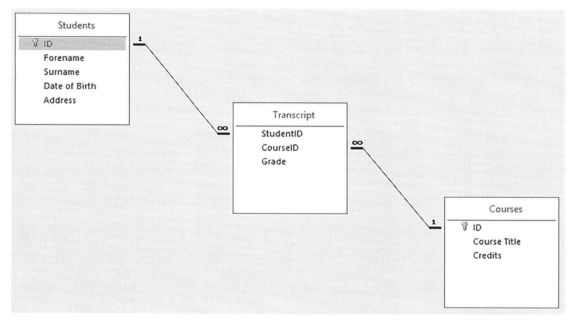

Click 'yes' to save the changes.

Entering Data

You can enter data directly into the tables as shown in this section, it's just a matter of adding the data to the fields to create the records.

You can also create a form to create a more user friendly interface to enter your data. We will take a look at that in the next section.

Lets take a quick look at adding simple records to a table.

Adding Records

To enter data, start typing it into the fields as shown below. Access will automatically add a new record each time you add a name.

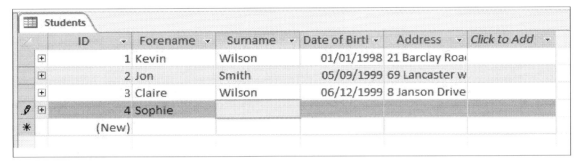

Deleting Records

Right click on the record by clicking the grey border on the left side of the record.

From the popup menu that appears select delete record.

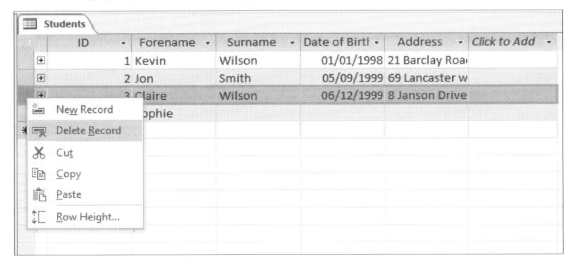

Creating Forms

Forms allow you to create a user interface and form the basis of the data entry for your database records.

This helps to simplify things and make them more user friendly as you may have seen from the previous section adding data directly to a table can be tricky. Forms provide a familiar looking interface where the user can enter data into the tables.

A form containing data from the tables created earlier might look like this:

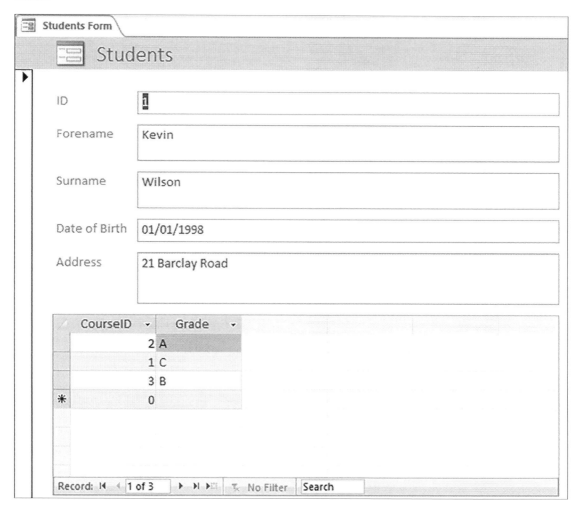

As you can see if you compare the form to the table on the opposite page the fields are the same but presented in a more user friendly way with one record at a time. This allows data to be entered and retrieved quickly.

Forms Wizard

The quickest way to create a form is to use the forms wizard. You can find this on the create ribbon

In this example I am going to create a form for entering course information into our database. Select the courses table on the left hand side.

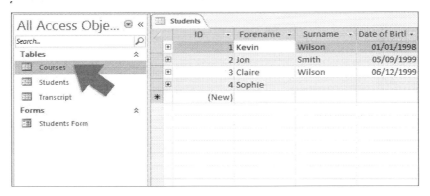

From the create ribbon, select 'form wizard'.

Next follow the instructions on the screen. Select the fields you want to include in the form. Select these from the 'available fields' box on the left hand side. Click the 'add arrow' in the middle to add the field.

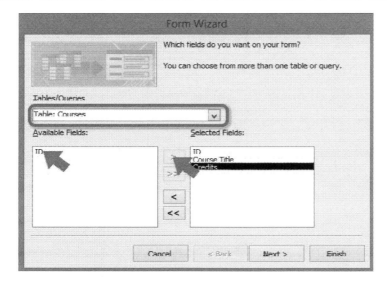

Click 'next'.

Select the layout of the form you want. 'Columnar' arranges the fields under one another (use this in example), 'tabular' arranges the fields next to one another, and 'datasheet' arranges the fields into a table.

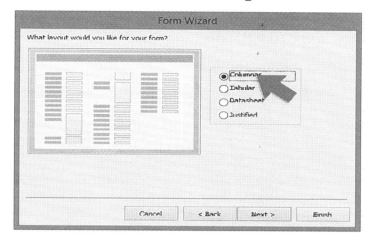

Give the form a meaningful name.

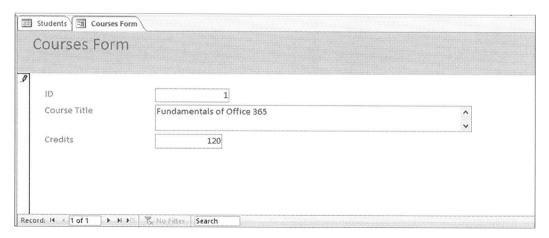

Click finish.

Creating Queries

Queries are a set of commands for retrieving data from one or more tables in the database.

When you build a query in Access, you are defining a specific search conditions to find exactly the data you want.

For this example, I want to create a query that will show me the results of all the students.

First select 'query design' from the create ribbon.

Then select the tables you require fields from.

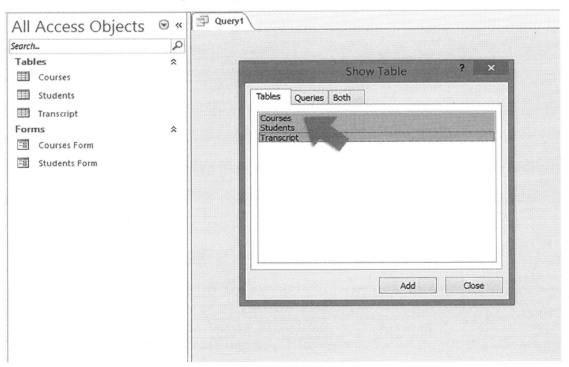

For this query to work I need students surname & forename from the students table, course name from the courses table, and result (or grade) from the transcript table.

Click & highlight all the tables in the dialog box. Click 'add'.

To build the query, double click the fields you need from the tables in the entity relationship diagram. For this query I need, surname, forename, course title, credits and grade.

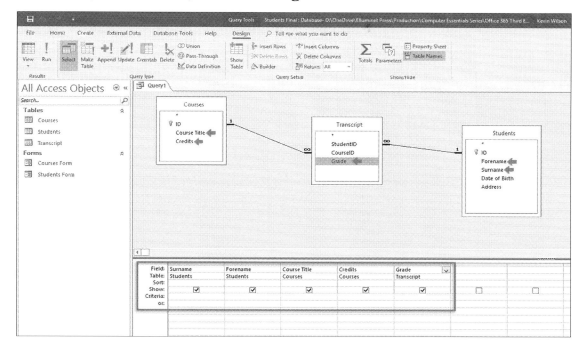

Click 'run' on the left hand side of the design ribbon.

You will see the results of your new query.

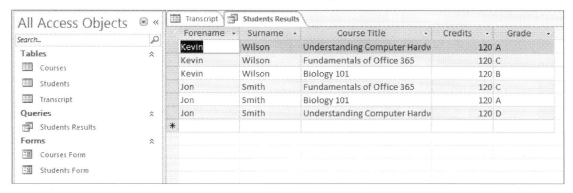

Notice however, that the query returns every student. This is fine, but what if we just wanted to check the progress of a particular student? We can do this using query parameters.

Query Parameters

In this example, I want to prompt the user for the student's surname and forename. To add a prompt, look at the criteria row under the surname and forename columns, circled below.

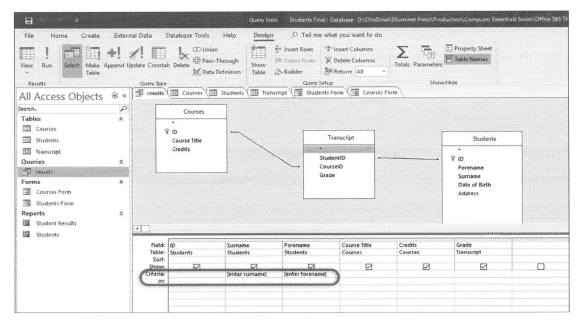

To prompt the user for data we enter the text we want to appear in the prompt in square brackets [ ].

When you run the query you'll get a popup box asking for the criteria for the fields.

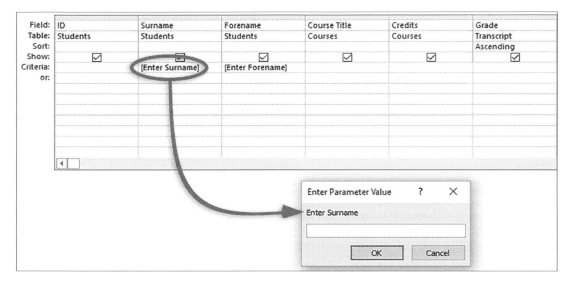

Any matching records will be returned in the query results

Creating Reports

Reports allow you to quickly display your data in printable form. This could be for income and expenses reports, names and addresses, student results, etc depending on what data your database stores. These can all be printed off or even emailed.

To create a report, click your data source from the Access Objects listed down the left hand side of your screen then click the Create ribbon.

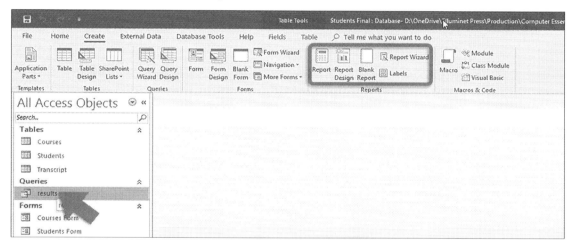

Report will automatically create report with all of the data from your table or query. This is the simplest report, Access will not structure or group any of the data.

Blank Report & Blank Design will create an empty canvas where you can manually add the fields you want and lay them out according to your own design.

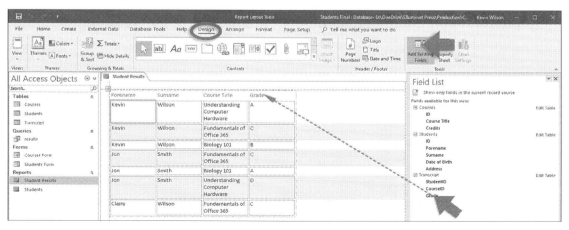

Click 'Add Existing Fields' and from the list drag the fields to your report as shown above.

Chapter 6: Microsoft Access

Report Wizard guides you through the report creation process, allowing to select the fields from your chosen source.

To create a report using the wizard, first select your data source from the 'Access Objects' listed down the left hand side. Reports are usually created from queries so in the student example, select the 'results' query.

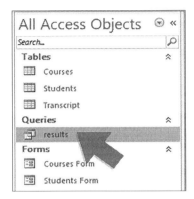

From the create ribbon select report wizard.

From the dialog box that appears, select the fields. For this particular report I want to show a list of students and the results they got for their classes. To do this I need the fields surname, forename, course title and grade.

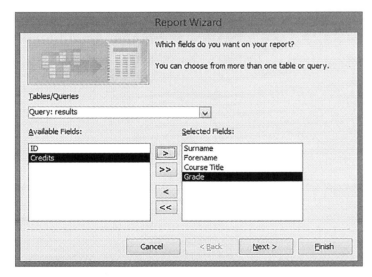

Show how you want to show your data. The results are presented per student so in this case I will show them by student

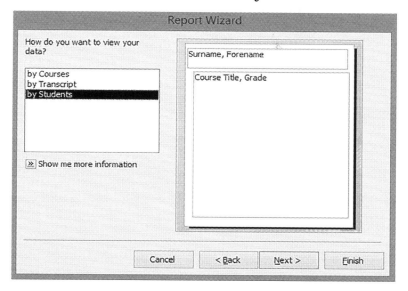

This means, the student's name is printed followed by a list of their results.

Click next, then finish when you get to the end of the wizard.

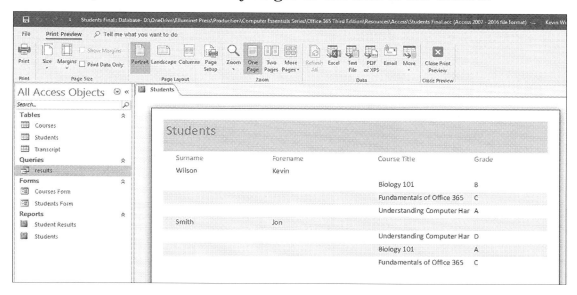

Microsoft Outlook

Microsoft Outlook is a personal information manager and email application available as a part of the Microsoft Office suite. It includes a calendar, contact list or address book as well as the ability to set reminders and make notes.

Outlook can be used as a stand-alone application for a personal email account, or can work with Microsoft Exchange for multiple users in an organization, such as shared mailboxes and calendars, public folders and meeting schedules.

Outlook organizes your email, calendars and contacts all in one place. It all starts with your email account.

From there you can start working with email, composing messages and replying to them. Storing the addresses of the people you interact with in your contacts, so you never have to remember an email address or phone number.

Also dealing with junk mail and clutter.

Let's start by taking a quick look at the basics.

Getting Started

The quickest way to start Microsoft Outlook is to search for it using the Cortana search field on the bottom left of your task bar. Type "Outlook".

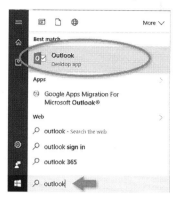

When you start Outlook you will see the main screen. By default, the screen is divided in to three panes: folder, message and reading page. With the ribbon menus across the top.

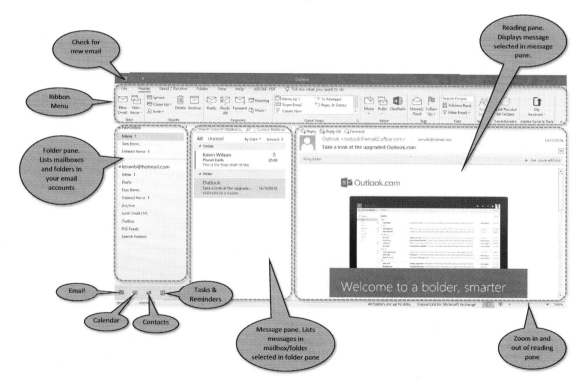

Unread messages are highlighted in bold in the messages pane. Selected messages are indicated with grey shading in the messages pane and the content is displayed in the reading pane.

Create a Shortcut

To make life easier, I find it useful to pin shortcuts to applications I use most often, and Outlook is one of them. Windows allows you to pin shortcuts to the taskbar at the bottom of your screen.

To do this, start the application as in the previous section, then right click the Outlook icon on the taskbar.

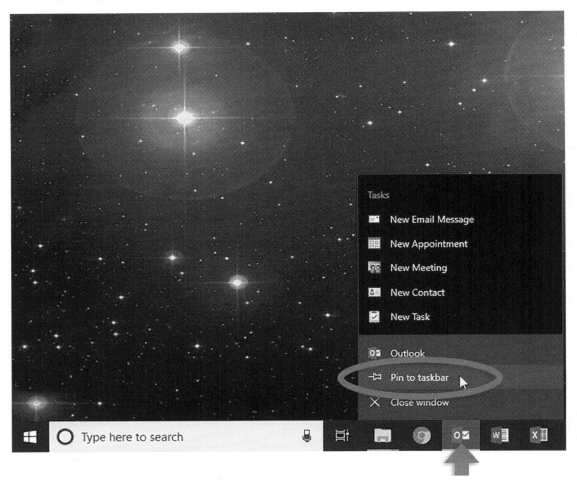

From the popup menu, select 'pin to taskbar'.

The Outlook icon will remain permanently on your taskbar. You can click and drag the icons across the taskbar to reorder them if you need to.

From now on you can just click the Outlook icon on your taskbar.

The Ribbon

All the main features and functions of Outlook are organised into a ribbon which is divided into ribbon tabs, each containing a specific set of tools.

The Home Ribbon

This is where you will find all your most used features such as composing new emails, reply and delete functions.

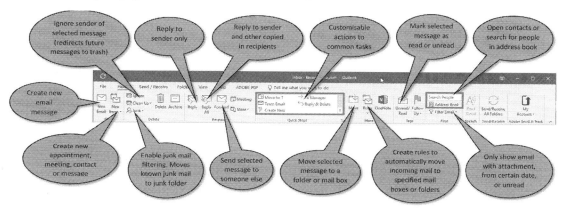

The Send/Receive Ribbon

This is where you will find all your functions for manual sending and receiving email.

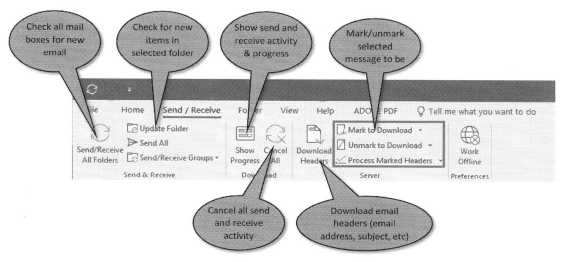

Most of the time you won't need to use these except when you want to manually check for new emails, etc.

The Folder Ribbon

The folder ribbon is where you will find functions to create folders for organizing your emails.

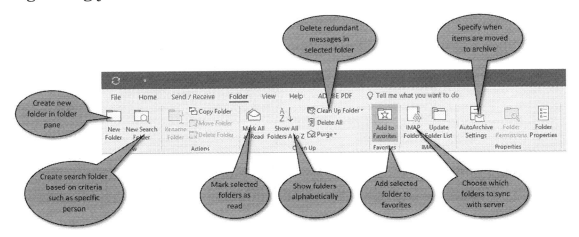

For example, perhaps a folder for "Vicki" for all email from Vicki, or folder for "Accounts" for all email from accounting/banking, etc.

Or all your in-boxes, if you have multiple email accounts, all listed under favourites.

To do this, click the 'show in favourites' icon.

The View Ribbon

The view ribbon allows you to sort your emails by name or date and allows you to turn on or off different sections, such as the reading pane.

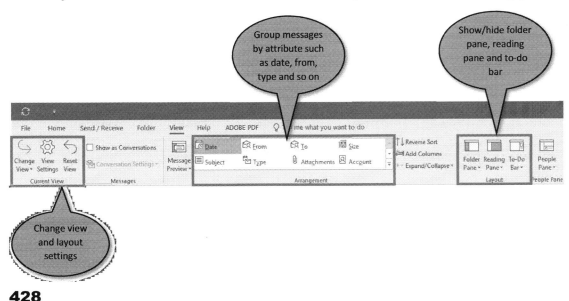

File BackStage

If you click 'File' on the top left of your screen, this will open up what Microsoft call the backstage.

This is where you can find all your printing, saving, import and account settings.

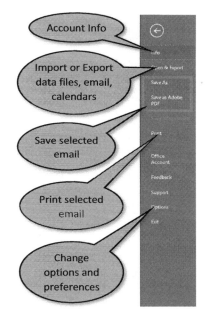

You can add email accounts and change the settings. You can also change your Outlook options and preferences.

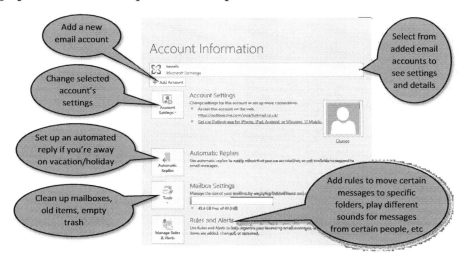

Email Message Ribbon

When you go to reply to an email message or compose a new one you will find that the message window has its own set of ribbon tabs.

The Message Ribbon

This ribbon shows up when you have opened an email message either to reply to one you have received or one you are composing.

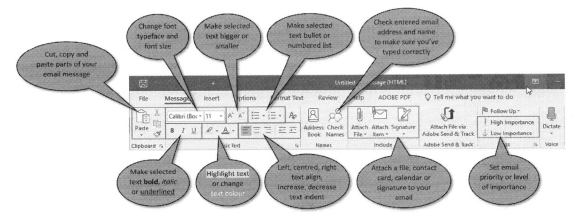

You can find all your common formatting tools here such as fonts, colours, text alignments etc. As well as address books and file attachments.

The Insert Ribbon

Use this ribbon if you want to insert shapes, charts, tables, calendar appointments, hyper-links or any kind of symbol.

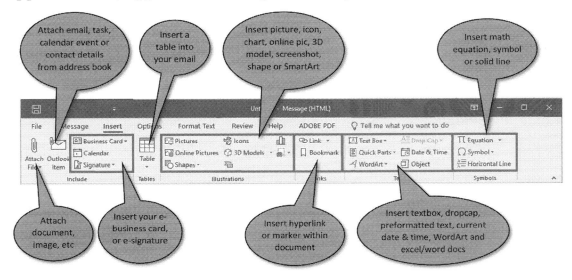

The Options Ribbon

Use this ribbon to enable the BCC field, set up delivery reports, page colours and effects.

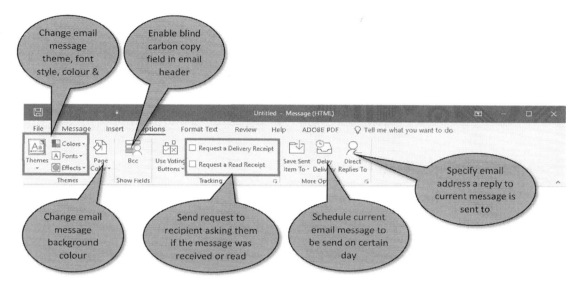

The Format Text Ribbon

Use this ribbon to format your text - change fonts, align text left or right, change font size, change line or paragraph indent, create bullet and numbered lists, and so on. This is very much like Microsoft Word.

The Review Ribbon

The review ribbon has features to check spelling and grammar. It also has statistical features such as word counts.

You can lookup certain words and find synonyms for words using a thesaurus or smart lookup and you can translate into different languages.

Sending Email

From the home ribbon click 'New E-mail' icon.

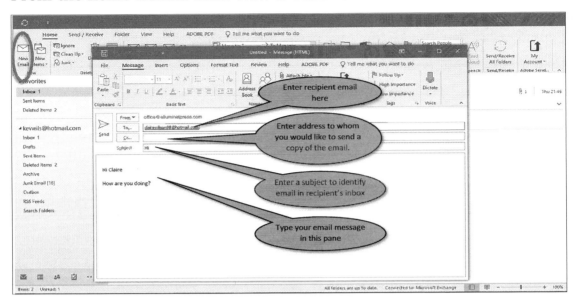

In the window that appears enter the email address of your recipient in the To field. You can do this by typing in the address and Outlook will search your contacts and display suggested addresses.

You can also add email addresses by clicking the 'To field' and selecting the recipients from your address book. Note you can select more than one if you want to send the same message to other people.

The Cc field is for carbon copies and is used to send a copy of the message to other people.

The Bcc field is for blind carbon copies - you can enable this on the options ribbon if it isn't there. This works like the Cc field, except the recipient can't see the addresses of the other people the message has been sent to.

Then type your message in at the bottom.

Adding Attachments

You can also send attachments, such as photos or documents. To do this click on the 'attach file' icon that looks like a paper clip.

When you click 'attach file', Outlook will list your most recently used documents.

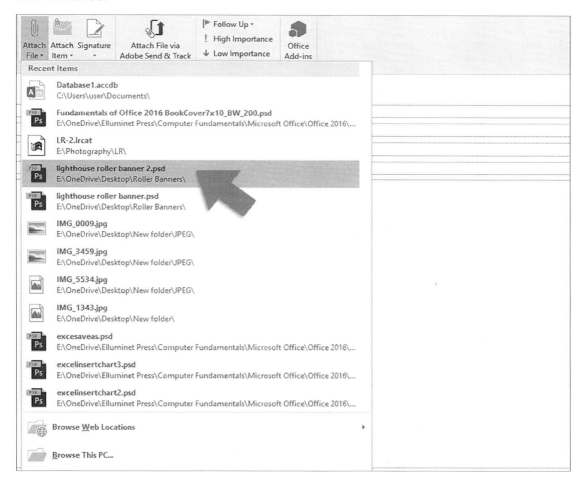

More often than not the file you want to attach is in this list. To attach it, just click on the file in the list.

If not click 'browse this PC' and navigate to the folder where you originally saved the file, eg, your documents folder.

Select your file from the insert file dialog box and click insert. You can select more than one file by holding down the control (ctrl) key on your keyboard, while you select your files.

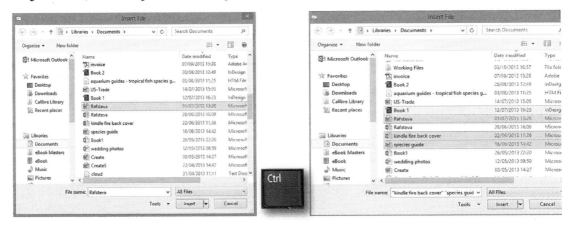

Click insert. You'll see a list of attachments appear under the subject field in your message window.

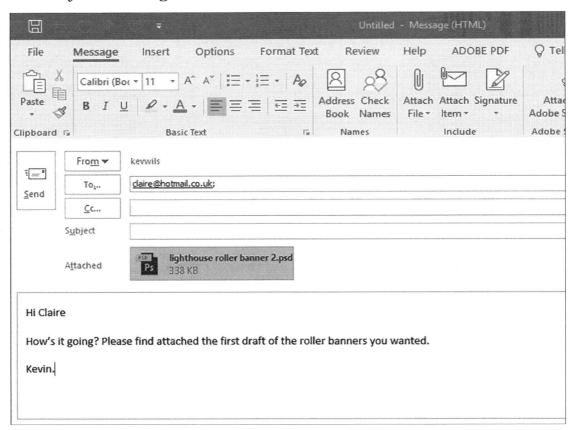

Once you're happy with your message, click 'Send'.

Saving Attachments

You can save attachments people send you through email to your OneDrive or a folder on your computer. Emails with attachments are indicated on the message in the message pane with a small paperclip, as shown below.

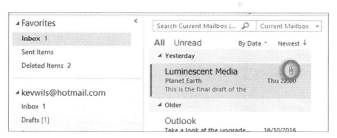

In the reading pane, attachments are listed along the top of your email message and usually appear as document icons.

To save the attachments to your PC, click the small arrow on the right of the attachment icon.

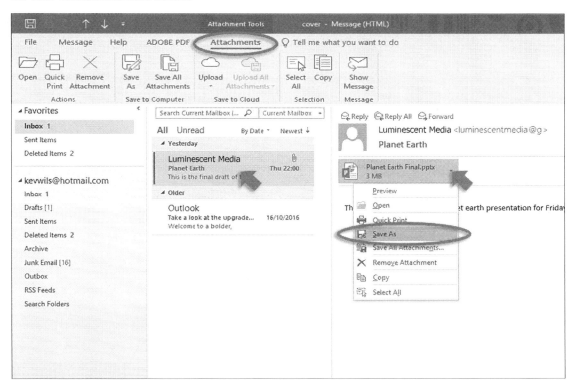

From the drop down menu, select 'save as'. If you have more than one attachment on the email, click 'save attachments' instead, this will save all of the files to your PC in one go.

From the dialog box that appears, select the folder you want to save your attachments in. In this example, I'm going to save the attachment in the documents folder on my PC.

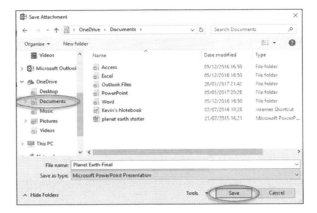

Previewing Attachments

With most documents and images, Outlook can show you a preview of the document. To see a preview of the document, click on the file icon in the reading pane.

If Outlook recognises the file, you'll see a preview of the file's contents. In this example, the PowerPoint presentation.

Scroll down the file if you need to. Click 'back to message' to close the preview.

Sending Email to Groups

Contact groups make it convenient for sending messages to groups, such as a specific team.

Creating Contact Groups

First switch to your contacts. Click the people icon on the bottom left of your screen.

To create a new group, from the home ribbon click 'new contact group'. Type in a name for your group. In this example, my group contains all the email addresses of people in my production team.

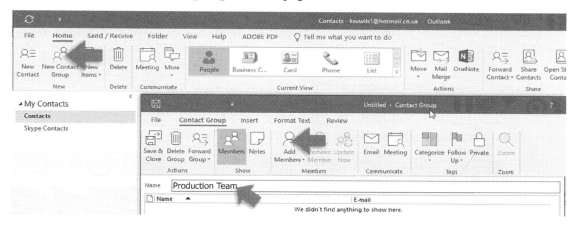

Click 'add members', then from the drop down click 'from outlook contacts', to add email addresses.

To add a member, double click on the name in the contact list to add the name to the 'members' field. Click OK when you're done.

On the 'contact group window' click 'save & close'.

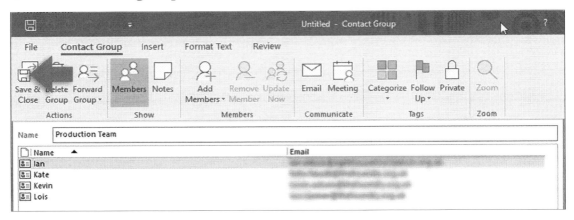

Now when you go to write a new email, you can select your group from the list of contacts.

In the 'to' field, start typing the name of your group. If outlook recognises the group name, it will list them in a drop down menu.

Click the name of the group in the drop down menu.

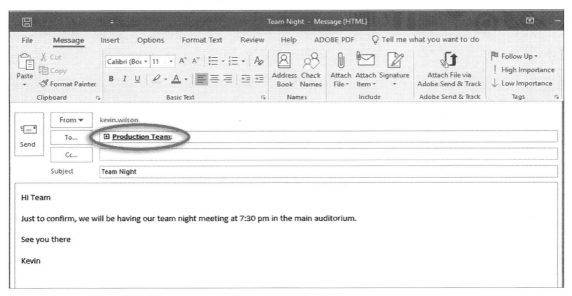

Now you can type your email as normal.

Click 'send' when you're done, and everyone in the team list will receive a copy of the email.

Managing Email Messages

Outlook allows you to create folders, rules and categories to manage your email messages.

Creating Folders

Folders keep your messages organised. In your mail account you'll see folders such as: Inbox, Drafts, Sent Items, Junk Email and Deleted Items. To create a folder, select your folder ribbon and click 'new folder'.

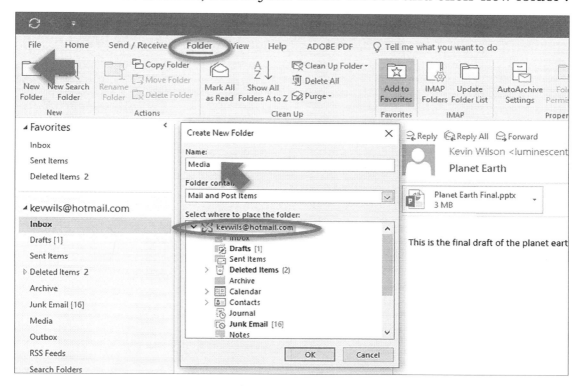

From the dialog box that appears, type the name of your folder. In this example I am creating a folder for all my messages to do with a media related projects. Set the field 'folder contains' to 'mail and post items' because we are storing email messages.

At the bottom under 'select where you want to place the folder', click on the folder where you want to add your new folder. I'm adding it to the same place all the others are so I'm going to click my email address.

Click OK when you're done.

You'll notice now, the folder will appear listed under your email account.

Organising Messages

You can click and drag messages from your inbox into your own folders.

In the example below, I'm putting all my emails from a media project, that arrive in my inbox, into the media folder, so they don't get lost.

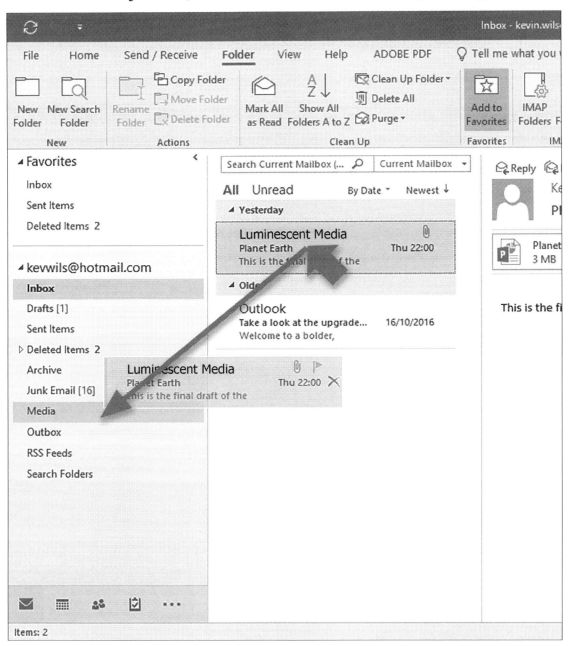

Just click and drag the message to the folder. To select multiple messages, hold down the control key on your keyboard as you select.

Creating Rules

You can create rules to perform tasks on messages that come into your email account.

To create a rule, go to your home ribbon and click 'rules'. From the drop down menu, select 'manage rules & alerts'.

In the 'rules and alerts' dialog box, click 'new rule'.

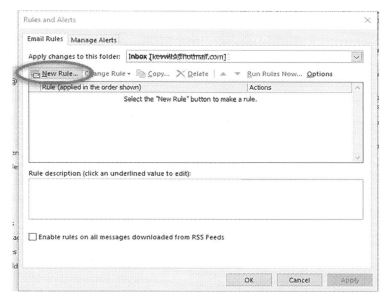

Now, in this example, I want to move all messages that come from people in my production team to the 'media' folder. So, from the 'rules wizard dialog box, under 'step 1', click 'move message from someone to a folder'.

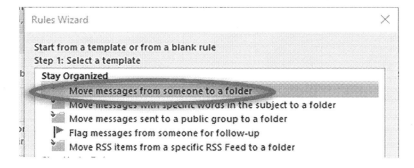

Under 'step 2', click 'people or public group' .

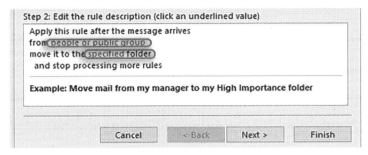

From the dialog box, double click the email addresses of the people or a contacts group you want to apply the rule to. Click OK.

Then under 'step 2' again, click 'specified folder'.

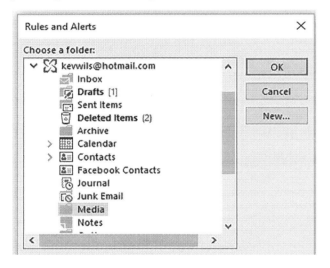

From the dialog box, select the folder in your email account to move the incoming messages into. In this example, I'm moving them into the 'media' folder.

Now all the messages that come from people involved in 'media' projects will go to the 'media' folder.

Click OK. Click Finish. Click OK.

Dealing with Junk Mail

If you have been using the internet you will no doubt have received junk mail in the past. Mail advertising products from unknown senders that you wonder how they got your email address.

Outlook has a junk mail filter. It is good practice to enable this filter as suspicious emails used for phishing personal details, etc.

To enable the filter click 'junk' from the home ribbon

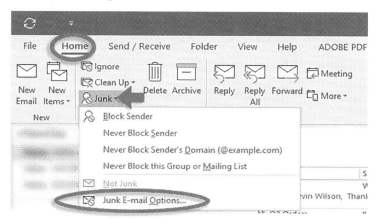

In the dialog box that pops up select 'low: move the most obvious junk email to the junk email folder'

Also select 'disable links...' and 'warn about suspicious domains...'.

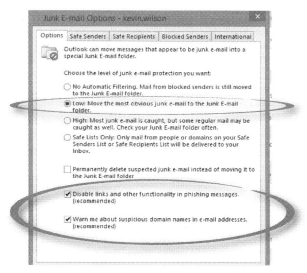

This helps to filter out emails sent from scammers etc. All these emails will be filtered into your junk mail box instead of your inbox.

Contacts

Contacts, people app or address book as it's sometimes called, is where all your contact details for your friends, family and colleagues are stored.

Adding new Contacts

Quickest way to add a new contact is to extract the email address from the email messages people have sent you. To do this, select the email message from your inbox and right click on the recipient's email address in the header of the reading pane of the message.

From the drop down menu, select 'add to outlook contacts'.

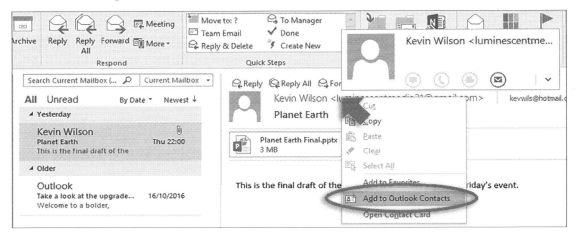

In the dialog box, check the email address and names to make sure they are correct, then click 'save'.

You can also create a new contact using the contacts page. First switch to your contacts. Click the people icon on the bottom left of your screen.

From the home ribbon, click 'new contact'.

Now fill out the details in the new contact form. Enter their full name, email address. You can also add other information such as job title, telephone numbers and website addresses if needed.

Click 'save and close' when you're done.

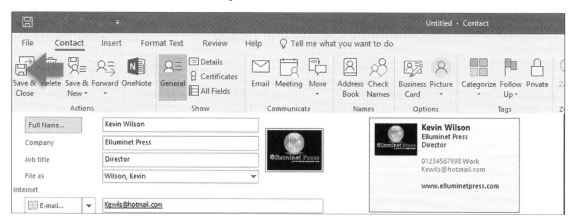

Calendar

To start your Calendar, click the calendar icon located at the bottom left of your screen.

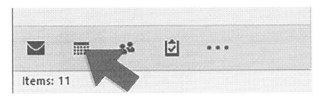

Once you are in your calendar you can see the calendar with months and dates. It is personal preference but I find it easier to work within month view.

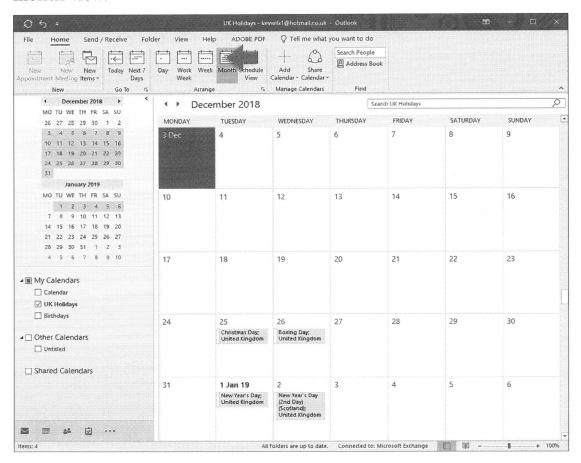

You can do this by clicking on the month icon on your home ribbon shown as shown above.

Add Appointment

The quickest way to add an event or appointment is to double click the day. So, for example, if you wanted to add an appointment on the 25th, double click 25.

From the dialog box that appears, remove the tick from "all day event". This will allow you to enter specific times such as start time and estimated finishing times.

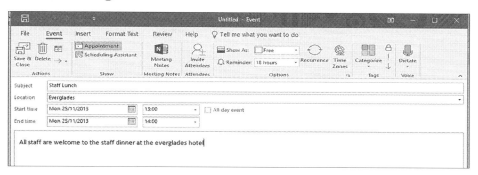

Click 'Save & Close' when you have finished.

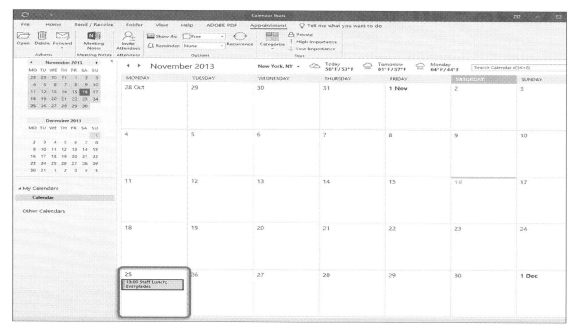

In the screen above you can see the appointment has been added.

Chapter 8

Microsoft OneNote

Microsoft OneNote is a digital note taking application and allows you to type notes, draw annotations on touch screen devices, add website clippings, photos, videos and images.

While you can use OneNote on your PC, laptop or notebook, OneNote really shines when you use it on a tablet. This is what we'll be doing in this chapter.

There are two versions of this program: OneNote that comes pre-installed in Windows 10, and OneNote that comes with Microsoft Office Suite.

Microsoft OneNote that comes pre installed in Windows 10 is a cut down touch screen oriented version of the App.

We'll be using Microsoft OneNote that comes with Microsoft Office Suite in this chapter. The full featured version.

Getting Started

Opening OneNote you'll see the home screen with the ribbon menus across the top.

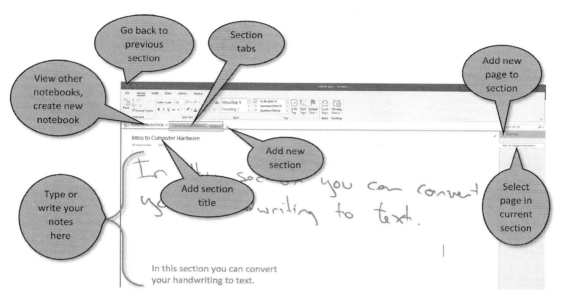

Along the top of your OneNote window, just under the ribbon menus, you'll see a list of tabs. These are your notebook section dividers, much like you'd have in a paper notebook. Within each section, you'd have pages where you would write your notes.

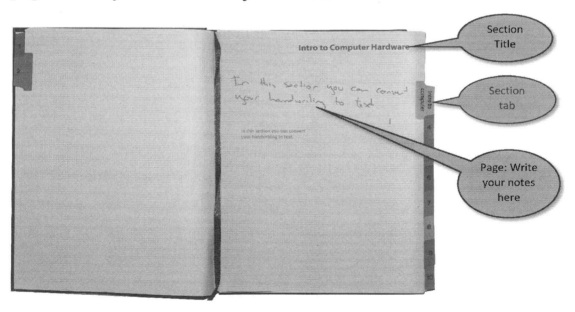

OneNote works in a very similar way. OneNote's tools and commands are organised into ribbons according to their use.

The Home Ribbon

On the home ribbon you'll find your most commonly used tools: **bold**, *italic,* underlined text, bullets and numbered lists, indentations for paragraphs and lines, to do list check marks, and paragraph alignment (left, right and centred).

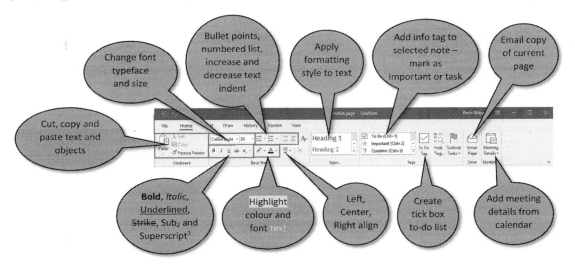

The Insert Ribbon

The insert ribbon will allow you to insert tables, attach a downloaded file, insert a picture or add a website link.

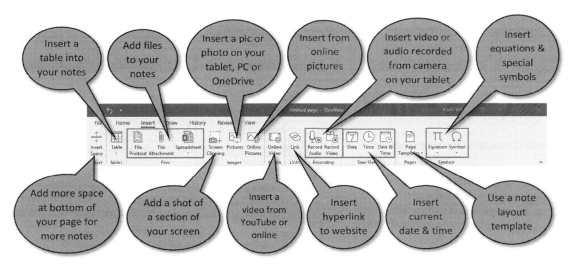

You can add symbols, video clips, audio, as well as use layout templates for lecture notes, meeting notes, agendas and so on.

The Draw Ribbon

From the draw ribbon you can select tools to make handwritten notes and annotations. You can select from coloured pens and highlighters as well as different colours.

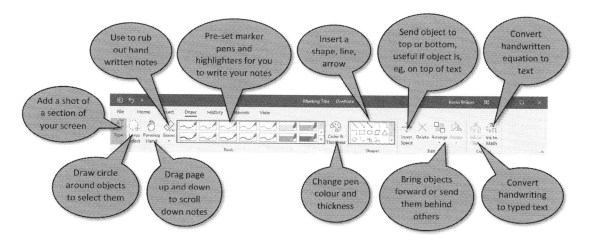

The Review Ribbon

Check spelling and grammar. You can find a thesaurus, translate text into another language and find research resources such as encyclopaedias.

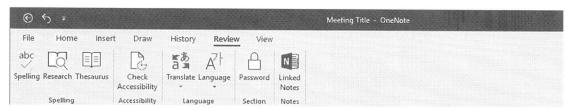

The View Ribbon

The view ribbon will allow you to zoom in and out of your notebook pages. You can also enable your ruled lines if you are hand writing notes these can be a helpful guide.

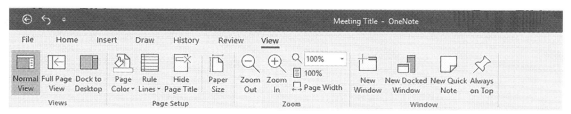

Taking Notes

You can take notes in a variety of ways, use annotated web pages, pictures, handwritten or typed notes.

Pictures

To insert pictures or photographs, make sure you tap the section, page or note you want the image to appear on, then from the insert ribbon tap 'pictures'.

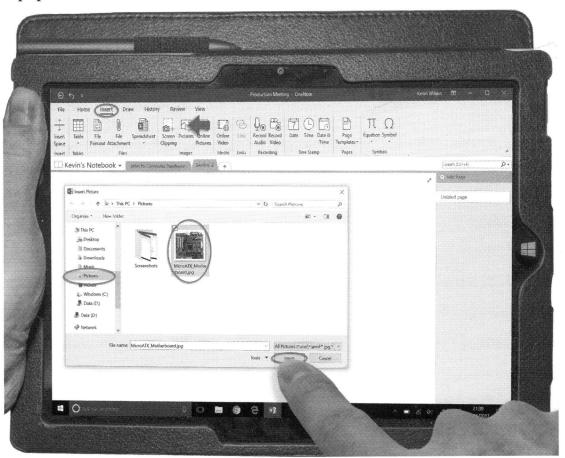

From the dialogue box that appears, choose the image you want and tap 'insert'.

I'm going to insert a photo of a PC motherboard for my lecture on computer hardware.

You can move your image on your notes. You might also need to resize your image.

Tables

To insert tables, make sure you tap on the note you want the table to appear, then from the insert ribbon tap 'table'.

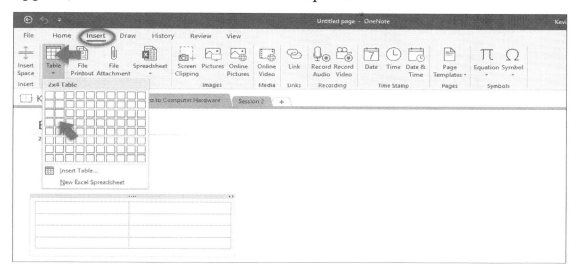

Use the grid that appears to select the number of rows and columns you want in your table. In the example above, I want to add a table that has two columns and four rows - so select a 2x4 table on the grid.

Your table will appear in your note. You can drag the table to the position you want it. Tap in the cells to enter your data.

To add insert a row, tap on the cell where you want to insert a row. From the layout ribbon, tap 'insert below'. This adds a row after the selected cell. You can also tap the tab key to add rows to the end of the table.

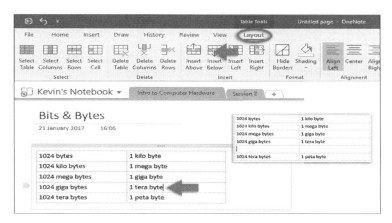

Similarly to add columns, tap 'insert right' instead, to add a column to the right of the selected cell.

Type Notes

You can type notes by tapping on the screen where you want your note to appear and on the keyboard that appears type your information

Tap on your screen, where you want to add some notes, you'll see a flashing cursor bar appear and an on screen keyboard will appear.

If the keyboard doesn't appear, tap the small keyboard icon located on the very bottom right of your screen. You can also use the external keyboard on your laptop or if you have one on your tablet.

Type your notes. Your typed notes will appear in a text box which you can move around your screen using your finger or mouse.

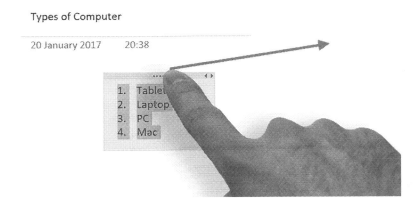

Write Notes

You can handwrite notes and annotations using either your finger or a stylus. Tap on the draw ribbon along the top of your screen.

From this ribbon you'll see a number of tools.

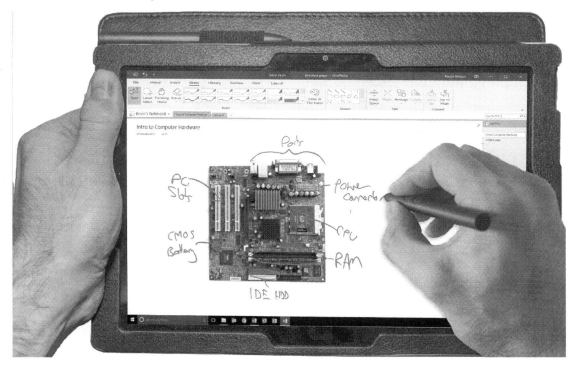

The first two icons are to select objects. You can use these to select and move your text boxes, photos, annotations etc. You also have an eraser, thin marker, highlighter, draw with finger and your colour pallet to change the colour of your pen.

You can change the colour and size of your pen. To do this, from your draw ribbon, tap 'colour & thickness'. From the dialog box that appears, select your pen type - highlighter or marker pen. On the next row, select your pen thickness. On the bottom section, select the colour.

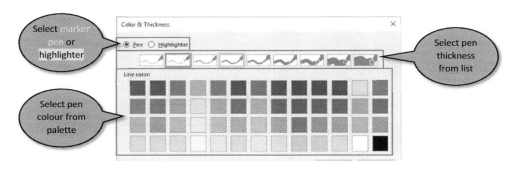

Screen Clippings

First open up the application you want to create a clipping of. For example, I'm going to add a recommended website for a book to use in my lectures.

Next open up OneNote, turn to a page in your notebook and from the insert ribbon, tap 'screen clipping'. At this point, OneNote will minimise and you'll see a greyed out screen. Tap and drag the box around the bit of the screen you want to clip.

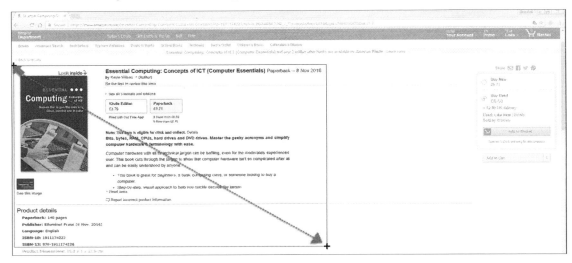

Once you've done that, OneNote will open up again and you'll see the clipped part of your screen is inserted onto your note page.

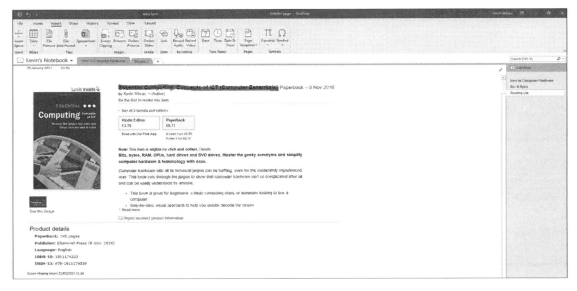

You can annotate your clipping and add notes.

Audio & Video

You can record audio and video using the built in camera and microphone on your tablet.

To record video, from your insert ribbon, tap 'record video'. OneNote will start recording from your built in camera.

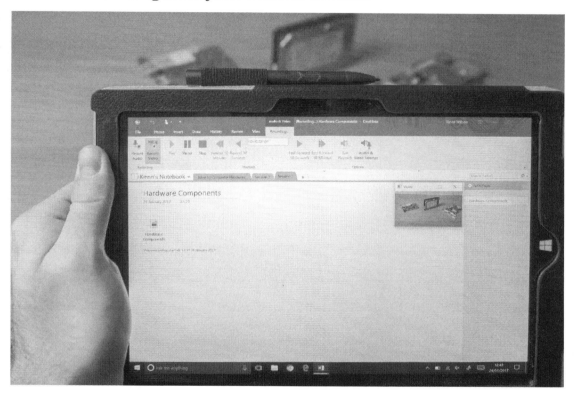

While you're recording, you'll see a new ribbon appear. Tap pause to temporary halt recording or hit stop to stop recording and save video file.

Your video file will be saved to your selected note. Double click on the video file icon in your notes to play the video. You can start, stop, rewind and fast forward your video using the playback ribbon.

Recording audio is the same except from the insert ribbon tap 'record audio' instead.

Using Tags

You can tag parts of your notes. This helps you to organise and prioritise notes and to do lists. You can tag things as important (illustrated with a star) or as critical so you can mark things you need to do right away or to highlight.

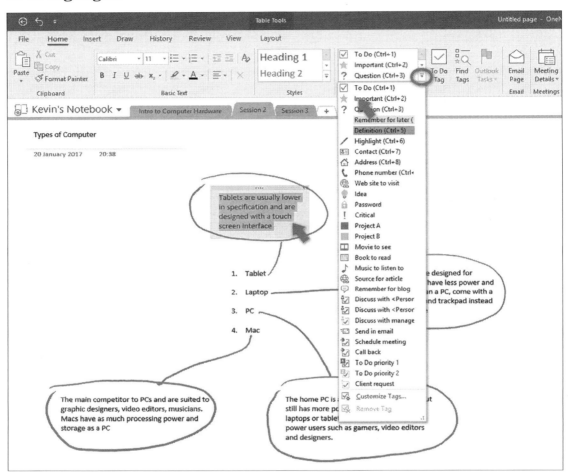

OneNote will add a small icon to your object, circled below. This tag indicates that the object is tagged. In this case tagged as important.

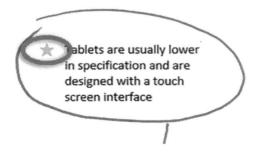

To-do List

You can create to-do lists in your notes. To do this, tap or select your text - drag your finger over the text in the text box to highlight it, if it's typed. If you have hand written your notes, you'll need to select the object with the lasso. Tap your finger on the top left of your written text block, you'll see a small circle appear. Tap and drag this circle around the text block as shown below. You'll see a dotted line appear as you move your finger. Go all the way around the written text, then release your finger.

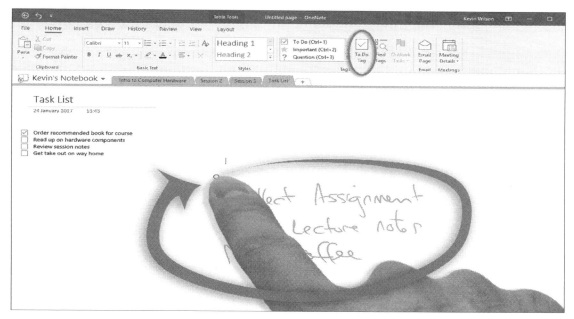

Your written text block will now be selected. This is indicated with a box with a dotted line around the object. To turn the object into a 'todo' list, from your home ribbon, tap the 'to-do tag' icon.

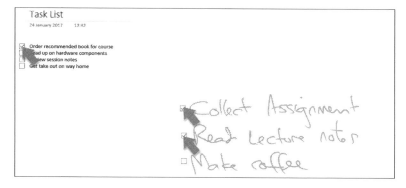

This will add a square check box next to the note. Tap on the check box to mark item as done. This will add a small tick.

Note Templates

OneNote has a selection of layout templates to help you take notes. You'll find templates for lecture notes, meeting agendas, planners and to do lists.

To find your templates, go to the insert ribbon and select 'page templates'.

In the drop down menu, you'll see a list of your most recently used templates. To see all available templates, select 'page templates'.

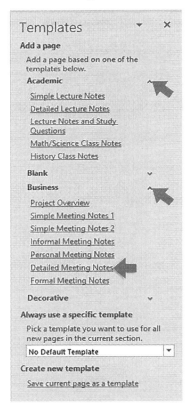

You'll see some sections: academic, business, decorative. Click the small down arrows next to the sections to open them up. Click on a template to apply it to your page.

You can type in your notes, use video and photos as you have done in previous sections. You can also draw directly onto the notes page with your pen, using the tools on the draw ribbon.

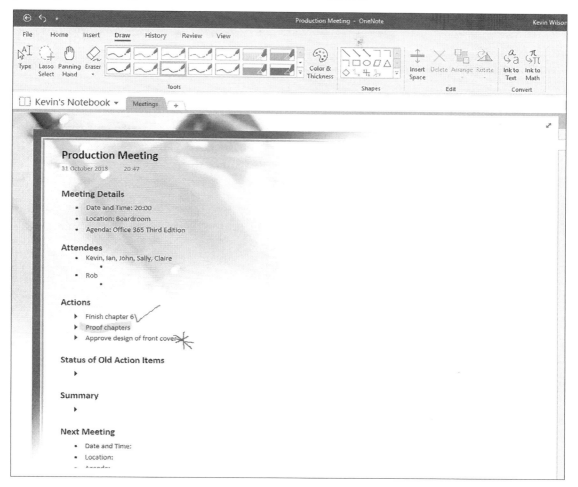

Index

Index

Index

Index

Printed in Great Britain
by Amazon